Collecting RAILWAYANA

John Mander

MPC

British Library Cataloguing in Publication Data

Mander, J.
    Collecting railwayana.
    1. Railways. Items associated with
    railways - Collectors' guides
    I. Title
    625.1

ISBN 0 86190 164 9

The author wishes to thank the following who
generously provided photographs for this work:

Ron Cross
Ivor Edmonds
Roger & Martin Fuller
Bob Grant
David Hall
John Jenkins of Onslow's Auctions
David Jones of Premier Auctions
Ken Jones
John Kilburn
David Love
Ian Lyman
Mike Henney
Andrew Mc'Craig'
Peter Rogers
David Scudamore (colour slides)
Paul Tilley
Geoff & Sue Woodward

Published by;
Moorland Publishing Co Ltd,
Moor Farm Road, Ashbourne,
Derbyshire, DE6 1HD, England

Printed in the UK by:
Butler and Tanner Ltd,
Frome, Somerset

Contents

Introduction   7
1 Station Railwayana   9
2 Goods Transportation   23
3 Railway Tableware   46
4 Locomotive, Wagon and Carriage Railwayana   68
5 Signalling Equipment   87
6 Railway Lamps   99
7 Along the Tracks   117
8 Railwayana of Railway Workers   131
9 Railway Documents & Publicity   147
10 How and Where to Collect Railwayana   181
   Railwayana Museums   183
   Glossary   184
   Acknowledgements   188
   Bibliography   189
   Index   190

Introduction

Railwayana has been collected for over sixty years, initially by a handful of enthusiasts. I have spoken to people now in the seventy to eighty age range who remember kicking dusty works-plates lying on the floor as they went round Swindon in the 1920 era, and saw nameplates piled up which no-one wanted, and which were eventually melted down!

Another group were the railway employees, some of whom were in the habit of bringing home items which they knew would otherwise have been smashed; in the late 1940s and 1950s GWR Black Leaf china used to come up from Swansea via GWR employees who would exchange it with LMS employees at Shrewsbury and Wellington.

There were examples of far-seeing individuals like Mr Cattell of Sutton Coldfield who amassed legendary collections as early as the 1950s, and of course there was Clapham Transport Museum, to which many antiquities found their way.

These examples were the exception, not the rule, until the end of steam on British Railways in 1968. It seems that this thunderclap diverted the energies of many railway lovers into new channels. They were disinterested in spending their leisure time watching diesels and yet there were, at that time, almost limitless quantities of railway items lying around, in and on the stations, warehouses and lines closed for ever by the Beeching Axe. Significantly, 1968 was also the foundation year of *The Railway Collectors' Newsletter* and around this year British Railways opened their Collector's Corner by Euston station for the sale of redundant items. These two names have been written large in the story of railwayana collecting from then until the present.

Another strand in the story was the early BR railwayana auctions at Stoke, Derby, Manchester and elsewhere, when pre-grouping pewter inkwells, umbrella stands and the like were going for the proverbial song. The 1970s saw steady but unspectacular growth in railwayana collecting but without a doubt it has been the 1980s which have seen the pastime 'take off'. In the years 1986-8 in particular, values of many areas of railwayana have escalated by several hundred per cent and whole areas which were once neglected have become frantically competitive.

We have recently seen the birth of auctions run on a professional basis by some of the well known collectors and this looks like the pattern of the future with Sheffield Auctions and Premier Auctions being the market leaders. 1985 saw the birth of *On the Line (The Railwayana Journal)* which quickly established itself as an essential forum for the railwayana world. *OTL* has pioneered attempts to describe and classify the hundreds of lamp, china and silver patterns and to establish relative rarities.

Until the present book, there has been no major attempt to write a book of reference extending across the whole vast range of our railwayana inheritance, although in this book the emphasis is on those areas where little has appeared in print before, so subjects such as locomotive nemeplates, tickets and railway postcards, which already have books devoted to them are given less prominence than the vast range of other items which were used on the railway systems of Britain. Invariably it is those items, no matter how humble, which have been marked in some way with a railway company's name or initials, which are now so eagerly collected, so it is on these collectables that this book concentrates.

John Mander
October 1988

1
Station Railwayana

Station Forecourts and Approaches
The property owned by railway companies often included long approach drives, which were often legally demarcated by private rights of way notices. This was almost standard on Great Western Railway stations (**Fig 1**) which often had a further 'To GWR Station' cast-iron sign mounted at the base. The GWR & LMS Joint Lines had a similar GWR style notice; the last ones to survive were on Ludlow, Llandidloes and Shrewsbury stations, being bolted onto the station brickwork. At the latter the sign was a familiar sight until sold by British Rail to a collector. Usually these signs were at the start of the drive to the station. There are quite a few GWR ones still on posts in the West Midlands and are greatly sought after. Other lines had a similar practice (**Fig 2**). Often, 'road' was distinguished from 'footpath', while the LNER was meticulous in its distinction, having different castings for company subways, footbridges, footpaths and causeways.

Both the London Chatham and Dover Railway and the South Eastern Railway protected their property against becoming a public right of way by signs reserving their right to close their private access routes on one day per year (**Fig 3**) (both these signs are believed to be unique survivors). The LMS seem to have been content with a simple small black and white enamel rectangle referring to an LMS private footpath or road.

Often small company plaques marking the start of railway property were buried in asphalt or concrete. Brass examples were used by the Metropolitan Railway and its subsidiaries. The prop-

1 Cast iron private road sign

2 L & SWR property notice

9

erty of the GWR and Metropolitan Joint Committee was at one time festooned with signs made of brass, cast-iron and enamel; similar ones were to be found embedded in pavements by the Metropolitan and Great Central lines through the Chilterns, and one or two at Watford Joint Station (Metropolitan & LNER Joint).

Many railway artefacts were less conspicuous and were largely unseen by most travellers. Examples of these are firepoints and water and gas stop valves. There were at least a dozen GWR types of these ranging from the huge GWR storm water and sewer covers to fire hydrants and circular gas or oil manholes. Companies marking their services points include TVR, LSWR, SDJ, SECD (several types) SR, SECR, LYR, CLC, MSLR, GCR, Birkenhead Joint, Midland Railway and LMS.

Probably the strangest and rarest fire hydrant plate is the 'practice' sign, which once adorned the wall of Stalybridge Joint Station (**Colour Plate 1**).

Guarding the station entrance were

some of the most priceless items of railwayana, often bearing the name of the station. For instance, there are pictures of cast-iron entrance trespass signs labelled 'Carlisle Citadel Station Committee' and 'Carlisle Goods Traffic Committee'.

Probably the most extraordinary cast-iron notice ever produced were the two of which guarded the precincts of Aylesbury Joint Station where the GW & GC Joint Railway rubbed shoulders with the Metropolitan & GC Joint Railway. Alas, this historic piece now resides in a pile of half forgotten unrestored cast-iron in a barn.

3 *(above)* Private property notice from the London, Chatham and Dover Railway

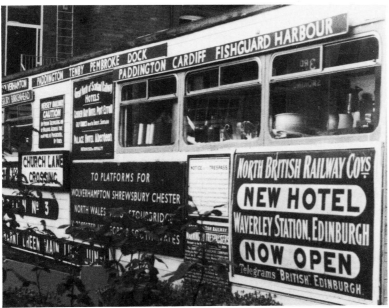

4 *(left)* Various railway hotel enamel advert signs, carriage boards and signal box nameboards.

The Station Hotel

A large number of railway employees were involved in the day-to-day running of a large company hotel. The following were employed by the North British Railway at their Edinburgh and Glasgow Hotels and fell in World War I, as recorded on the NBR war memorial on Waverley Station: cloakroom attendant, head hotel cellarman, cellarman, stoker, coal porter, hotel porter, lad porter, night porter, summer porter, baker, table foreman, waiter, hotel clerk, liftboy, liftman, and even this is a small fraction of the number of employees required in a large establishment.

We know that for other companies, for instance the North Eastern Railway, employees had full company uniform with lapel and arm badges, one grade of which was marked 'Out-Porter'. It was natural for passengers at the start and end of a long journey to put up in company hotels, often built integrally with the station.

Examples were the GWR at Paddington, the Midland & LNWR at New Street, Birmingham, the Midland at Manchester, the NBR at Waverley. Access was often direct from the station platform. Large prominent company advertising signs greeted travellers, such as the ones in **Fig 4**.

Station Furniture

Passengers needed to sit down and the railway companies took the chance to produce their monogram and initials on a great range of furniture divided into prosaic waiting room chairs, grander dining room and refreshment room chairs and station benches. A great many of these have been preserved, partly because they are functional, sturdy and were mostly under cover.

5 Seat with the cast monogram of the Caledonian Railway

6 Wooden chair frm the South Devon Railway

Named or initialled furniture is known from the following companies: GCR (several types), GN & GC Joint, Midland, LMS, Taff Vale Railway, GWR, MSLR, GER, LTSR, Sheffield & Midland Committee, Caledonian Railway, South Devon Railway, Bristol & Exeter, Bristol Joint Station, S & WJR. Large numbers of other railway companies made dis-

7 Seat from Yarmouth South Town station at the National Railway Museum

8 Plain station bench, probably from the London, Brighton and South Coast Railway

tinctive patterns, for instance the famous squirrel-ended Furness Railway benches, while others, such as the Bristol and Exeter Railway and S & MJL, had upholstered interior benches.

Seatbacks are now a major collectors' item. These had the station names pre-cast and either screwed whole, or as separate letters into the seatback. They were made mainly in cast-iron for the GNR and LNER, and by several other companies in enamel. The LNWR and some others used separate letters, but these are not much sought after.

Wheelbarrows were a feature of most stations, large and small, and were made in very large numbers. H.N. Twells in *LMS Miscellany* Vol 1 shows pictures of apprentice joiners making these for the LMS at Crewe in 1936 at a rate of thirty-one a day. The types were often not standardised and a company may have had several different patterns. One that was 'revised' for use was seen at Dumfries in 1986 with a modern GSWR transfer stuck on. Some ornamental 'first day sod barrows' together with the spades used (sometimes of silver) are preserved (**Fig 9**).

Sack trucks and four-wheel platform trolleys are quickly becoming extinct on most BR stations and the marked ones

will become eagerly sought after. There are not many pre-1923 examples preserved due to the fact that they have worn out and been replaced by post-grouping trucks, many of which are still around, especially LMS. They were often stencilled in paint or branded at Wolverton or Crewe. Some had tiny cast station names like Euston, King's Cross and York. These little plates are rather more common and are becoming much sought after.

Many railways had their own fireplace fenders, although they are usually marked with initials only. Ones known are NER, LYR, LNWR, MGWR, RR, CLC, TVR, SECR, MSLR, GNR, Cambrian Railway, LNER, GER. Fenders are quite common at present as most waiting rooms, hotels and refreshment rooms had them, and they are a durable item.

More significant were company fireplaces, although few companies marked these. Among those that did were the M & GNJR who cast their initials above the cowl in small letters. Unfortunately, almost all have been destroyed, partly due to the small letters and only two are known to have survived, one having been auctioned at Sheffield, in January 1987. Far more significant are the inspired GER creations in three sizes and

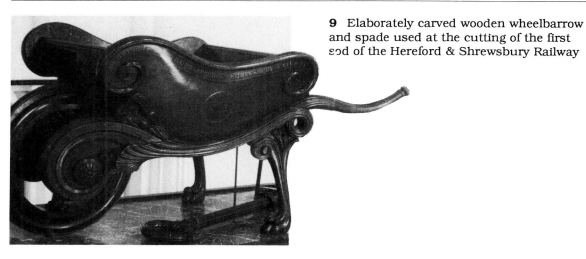

9 Elaborately carved wooden wheelbarrow and spade used at the cutting of the first sod of the Hereford & Shrewsbury Railway

types. **Fig 10** shows an example in Moseley Railwayana Museum. Inside the full name is the GER crest (unrestored here). There were also matching fenders in three sizes. Quite a few of these fireplaces are preserved and one was seen in a closed off station in 1986, so there may be others.

Fireside furniture is a class in itself and can still be collected cheaply. Good collections can be seen at Winchcombe Railway Museum and Moseley Railwayana Museum, though very few pregrouping items seem to have survived. Most common are coal buckets or scuttles (LNER, LMS, GWR are still common). Small marked coal shovels are found occasionally, as are pokers and tongs. The Winchcombe Railway Museum has a GNSR marked poker and LNWR tongs, while GER and TVR marked pokers exist, and Midland Railway examples were sold in 1986. Fireside hobs exist and railway kettles are becoming collectable, with any except BR examples being rarities. Large and small versions of those used by the 'Big Four' are more common. Winchcombe Railway Museum has an LMS No 4 kettle.

Inside some waiting rooms (and more often in signalboxes, mess rooms and gangers' huts) glowed the warming sight of company marked stoves. **Fig 11** shows a delightful LMS example at Warwick Railway Museum. Most common were the GWR ones of which there were many varieties. The marked fronts of GNR and LNER stoves exist, but few others are known.

Few of the great variety of railway brushes would have been noticed by most travellers as their uses were rather prosaic. Post-grouping ones are still plentiful and cheaply available. The LMS catalogued over thirty separate types of official brushes including those for whitewash, poster mounting, bitumen, painting, platform, toilet, waiting room, hearth and shoes. Certainly the LNER and the GWR and probably the SR required as large a range. Almost all have letters branded into the wood, although some had the initials highlighted with different coloured bristles.

Booking Offices and Waiting Rooms
The passenger booking office, together with the goods offices were arguably the two most critical points on every railway system as they were the financial interface between the railway company and

10 *(left)* GER fireplace with fender, coal buckets, shovel, kettle and bricks, all marked with railway company initials

11 *(below)* LMS heating stove

receipts, without which the company would go bankrupt. The lavishness of many of the large city offices bears testimony to this.

The area needed large circulation space for queues and plenty of seating. Order was essential so the GWR had guide rails to marshal people in a defile past the window, with 'IN' and 'OUT' cast-iron notices affixed as a standard feature. A narrow 'tickets' sign was used, while the GNR and M & GNJR lines had standard blue enamel warning notices regarding the opening of booking offices so many minutes before trains departed **(Colour Plate 2)** to prevent last minute stampedes through the barriers. The SR and SDJC also had

similar signs. Older readers may remember the first class and third class insets often in carved wood, and also 'Season Tickets Only'.

The atmosphere of the booking office area had to impress customers, hence the tall cavernous booking halls, as distinct from the booking offices, found at large stations. Present day Marylebone Station (onetime headquarters of the Great Central Railway) still has this atmosphere.

Many company poster board headings, handbill containers and letter racks have survived. The long and short SECR poster board headings are quite common, together with the block and shaded GWR chocolate and red, and the

SR 'sunshine' script ones, while a very few GNR and GCR ones in blue have appeared recently.

Company timetables were enclosed under company titles, some in wood, others metal. Few have survived as they were quickly superseded by BR, or have just decayed. An SDJC board survives at Moseley Railway Museum. This was rescued from a Bath garden over 10 years ago, rotting away in the open, together with others which could not be saved. The great prize was the original cast-iron letters. It is one of only a handful of survivors from all the stations of this railway. The strange arrangement of the letters suggests that it may have been originally from the Dorset Central Railway, one of the constituent companies of the SDJC.

Railway Clocks and Watches
For most of the great railway era almost every station, apart from very small ones and halts, had a clock on public display. Indeed, the railway introduced standard time in Britain very early on, led by the LNWR in 1847 who standardised Greenwich time all over their system, and in 1852 daily time was telegraphed centrally to all signal boxes. Prior to this, passengers from London to Bristol would arrive to find, say, a 10-minute time difference although the train was on schedule. Hence the sanctity of 'railway time'.

The railway clock industry was extensive with many private firms involved, as well as companies such as the Great Western which had its own clock manufactory. Some of the private firms include: John Walker of South Molton Street, London (and Princes Street, Soho) who made for the LSWR and SR; S. Ball & Co, of Leicester (**Fig 13**) who made *inter alia* the delightful example

shown here with turned side spindles; Thos Armstrong Bros of Manchester (**Fig 12**); Joyce's of Whitchurch, Shropshire, one of the main makers. They always put 'Whitchurch' below the company name and maker's name.

Fig 14 shows a Joyce 12in diameter dial No 1313 and **Fig 15** a Joyce long case 14in diameter ex-Penmaenmawr booking office clock No 2470, sold by BR in 1988. LNWR does not appear on the face, but is marked elsewhere. The signal box at that station also had a Joyce 12in clock, No 2434. An 8in Joyce dropdial No 2682 was allocated to the Shrewsbury area.

Fig 16 shows a typical wall mounted two-face Joyce clock still in use at Northwich in 1986. These two-faced ones were very early and were platform mounted to allow both train crews as well as passengers to check the time. Another well known maker was John Smith, Midland Clock Works, Queen Street, Derby who made extensively for the Midland Railway. Most of their clocks are marked as above and they continued to make for the LMS; G. Eccles & Son of Liverpool made long case clocks for the GLC and some of these in a derelict state are still extant: Edwards & Son of Glasgow made long case clocks for Scottish lines including the Caledonian Railway.

Other railway clock makers include Thwaite & Read, Kay's of Paris, well known for brass travelling clocks; Stockall Marples of Clerkenwell for the GNR, and Winterholder & Hofmeyer of Newstadt, Germany for the Caledonian. Besides those pictured here, there were many other types, including office mantelpiece clocks, some set in marble; various notable turret clocks used by each company as the central time source for the whole system.

12 *(left)* A North Staffordshire Railway wall clock by Thomas Armstrong

13 *(right)* A Midland Railway wall clock by Ball of Leicester

14 *(left)* A Joyce clock for the LNWR

15 *(right)* An LNWR clock by Joyce of Whitchurch

As virtually every station had at least one, and often several clocks, the possible number of survivors is quite large, especially as they have tended to be preserved more readily than other types of railwayana. Value, on the whole, is related to condition and type, not to the company concerned.

17 A GER clock with fusee movement from the booking hall at Newport (Cambridgeshire)

16 A Joyce clock at Northwich Station

Railway watches were standard official issue to all guards (passenger and freight) and to key station staff. Many other grades procured unofficial watches from several companies by mail order. One of the main producers was J.W. Benson of Ludgate Hill for the NBR, SER, etc. These had the maker's name engraved on the face. Another was the Lancashire Watch Company of Prescot, Lancashire, which existed during 1889-1910, selling watches at three guineas each, but they went out of business owing to cheaper mass producing firms such as Seth Thomas of Connecticut and Waltham (USA) who produced for the LBSCR. Swiss firms like Cyma and Omega made for the LSWR and GNR(I) and as early as 1865 Thornton of Paris was making for the Edinburgh & Glasgow Railway.

18 Cast iron spandrels from the former Eastern & Midlands Railway at Cromer Station

Spandrels and Heraldic Devices

On Britain's railways in the nineteenth century there was a wealth of initialled ironwork. Marked company benches have already been described under station furniture, but there was also much initialled iron, stone, copper, tiles and wood. **Fig 18** shows six Eastern & Midlands Railway spandrels still extant in 1986 at Cromer Station. There used to be a platform full of M & GNJR ones at that company's Yarmouth terminus,

19 GSWR spandrels at Kilmarnock Station

20 LBSC initials at Hove Station

latterly a coach station. Another company whose initials are still to be seen is the GSWR, whose spandrels survive at Kilmarnock Station (**Fig 19**). The coat of arms of the GSWR, cut into sandstone, survives on the original Ayr Station Hotel.

The LBSCR, known for its lavish ornamentation in many fields, can still be seen proudly advertising its presence above the *porte-cochère* adjoining Hove Station — one is in green tile (**Fig 20**), the other in a cast shield. For some unknown reason, on this one station, both

motifs are different.

Spandrels do become available with station demolition and in some cases may be the only marked item to be preserved for a whole railway. An example of this is the famous MTR spandrel now in Moseley Railwayana Museum, the subject of some correspondence in the letters column of *The Railway Magazine* some years ago as to whether it is Mersey Railway Tunnel Company, or Mersey Tunnel Railway, as it was on an ex-Mersey Railway Station. Other known spandrels show Taff Vale Railway and Cardiff Railway, but on the whole, major lines did not use them, while minor lines did.

It is still possible to see pre-grouping heraldry in position. **Fig 21** shows the Midland Railway's famous wyvern surmounting the clock some 200yd north of the new Derby Station entrance. Incidentally, the newly cast MR coat of arms adorns this new entrance.

21 The Midland Railway's wyvern from the old station entrance at Derby, now adorning the car park

Station Name Signs

It was the policy for railway companies

to display station names boldly and frequently so passengers in different carriages could look out and see quickly where they were, especially at night. The practice then grew up of having very large 'running-in' boards near the ends of the platforms, sometimes with names in huge letters.

Smaller names would be suspended from lamp posts — as on the GCR — or stuck on gummed labels of different colours inside lamp glasses as on the LBSCR, LMS, LNER and many other lines. In the BR era, names known as 'totems', were placed on lamp posts, walls and in all manner of strange places using either a wood backing or pairs of interlocking metal grips tightened by screws at the base. Often the large nameboards were mounted on wooden legs and enclosed inside specially made frames. Good examples of these were the well-known LMS 'Hawkseye targets'. These were of a special reflective alloy to show up at night and made by 'Hawkseye', they were painted maroon on yellow and were the standard LMS sign. **Fig 22** shows one of the originals from Berkeley Road Station.

Other types of special Hawkseyes were made for individual locations where a very large name was needed. The example shown in **Fig 23** for Great Bridge in the Black Country was to distinguish it from the same name on the GWR, hence its great size.

Smaller rectangles were also used by the LMS, painted yellow and black as the Deepfields and Coseley sign shown in **Fig 24**. The number of survivors of signs even as common and as recent as these is very low indeed. Each station of the size of the latter would have had around ten or more, multiply that by the number of LMS stations and it is clear

22-5 Station name signs

there were tens of thousands of such names at one time, just on one of the 'Big Four' railways. We would surmise that the survival rate is under 1 per cent, judged by the number of such signs known in collections.

Well known, and in a few cases surviving to this day, were the great GWR wooden nameboards with cast or wooden letters supported by massive round stanchions either end and always white on a black background, with a white surround. **Fig 25** shows one at the Warwick Railway Museum recovered from one of the two Birmingham

GWR stations.

In the pre-grouping days, most railway companies had wooden nameboards, sometimes with screwed on letters, others just painted on wood. Some had attractive dark blue enamel names with letters in white. Many examples of these survive at Winchcombe Railway Museum.

The Southern Railway had 'targets' which consisted of a green enamel plate with a white circle, with the name across the middle. These survive in quantity. In BR days regional colours were chosen for the new totems which swiftly replaced those of the 'Big Four'. Orange for the North-Eastern Region, deep blue for the Eastern Region, light blue for the Scottish Region, maroon for the London-Midland Region, green for the Southern Region and chocolate for the Western Region. These survive in large numbers and is a case where nostalgia for the personally-remembered past has elevated a very modern item of railwayana into a enthusiastically collected class, for most of today's collectors were train spotting when they were erected and remember them with great affection. As the last ones came down in the early 1980s, they are readily available. A further colour used for a short trial period at a very limited number of Western Region stations was black with white letters. **Colour Plate 3** shows some examples of totems. The first totem was reputed to have been put up at West Ealing around 1950. Early ones were single flanged but these were later replaced, because vandals bent the ends.

Rare types are blue lettered in yellow Pen-y-Chain — colours unique to Butlin's Holiday Camp; Besses o' the' Barn which had script writing rather than capitals; over-sized totems at Broad Street; roundel totems at Birmingham Snow Hill, Paddington and Bristol Temple Meads in chocolate and cream. The top five in value terms up to 1987 are: Shap, Dent, Kyle of Lochalsh, Bassenthwaite Lake and Ilfracombe. Other valued totems are: Settle & Carlisle; West Country green especially Cornwall; South Lincs blue; Rare Scottish; North Wales maroon; Great Central maroon; tangerine.

Anomalies existed in that certain large terminal stations like Inverness had no totems, while remote, almost unused halts like Borrobol Platform had them. Apparently these were put up because of a disintegrating running-in board when the rest of the line was being signed. It was intended to re-sign the whole system in black and white totems but the first and only four were at Bourne End, Hayes & Harlington, Langley (Bucks) and Devonport.

Longtown was the only station in England to have Scottish coloured totems. Originally, tangerine totems were orange and white unlined, but these could not easily be seen, especially on sunny days and were replaced by tangerine coloured totems which were black lined. Some tangerines were flangeless, eg Beverley, Eaglescliffe, Morley Top and Leeds Central.

Fawkham for Longfield & Hartley is an SR green totem with the most number of standard letters. The shortest names are Wye (SR), Ayr (ScR) and Rye (SR). The most unusual names are Bat & Ball (SR), Heddon-on-the-Wall (NER), Denham Golf Club (WR) and Colnbrook Estate Halt (WR). The highest altitude totem was at Corrour.

Some totems were re-painted over older ones, eg Dent was painted over Bolton-le-Sands, Buxted was painted over Wraysbury (about three examples

26 GWR stationmaster sign

survive). The latter was different in that it had no white lines. Bere Ferrers was painted over Bingham Road. Totems on the GWR & GCR Joint Committee lines were all painted black and white over the original chocolate and cream enamel, eg Seer Green & Jordans, Beaconsfield.

Some stations had home-produced totems, usually of wood made by proud station staff, such as at Horton-in-Ribblesdale.

A number of interesting totems have been discovered in recent years. Although Leeds City had twenty-one platforms, only four totems are known to survive. Two of these were found in an East Anglian scrap merchant's yard still *in situ* on the original cast-iron columns from the station and was a rare find. One avid Settle & Carlisle fan followed a tip-off to the remotest Fens to capture a beloved Appleby totem, and was puzzled as to why it was dark blue; he was then disappointed to find that it was Appleby (Scunthorpe)! Another interesting find was a Garve totem on a hen house in Scotland. When Pontefract was reduced to one station, new totems were made, but they were never put up. A number of totems have the same name, for instance Wellington (Salop) WR, Wellington (Somerset) WR; Newport (IWR) SR, Newport (Essex) ER, Newport, (South Wales) WR.

27 LSWR war memorial at Waterloo Station

Many signs directing passengers to station services survive, eg gentlemen, waiting room, booking office, stationmaster etc, and are still available. **Fig 26** shows a GWR stationmaster sign. Many such signs were double-sided so as to be visible up and down the platform. Examples of these were on the LMS and GCR and such signs were usually cast-iron. GCR ones had fretted edges. Large stations had grandiose frontages often with elaborate pieces of art. **Fig 27** shows the LSWR emblem above the steps of Waterloo Station, built as a war memorial to the company's employees, while the window inside the station has the crest and the company name with the counties served by the railway in the stones around.

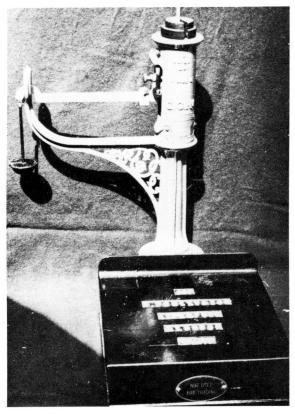

28   A Great Central Railway weighing machine

Other Station Railwayana

Any work on railwayana of stations must not omit to mention the wealth of fittings which were once an everyday part of railway life in addition to those already itemised under station approaches, booking offices and waiting rooms etc.

Platforms and circulating areas had many examples. Weighing machines were commonly found. The Great Central Railway marked theirs with a plate bearing the initials 'G.C.R.' and under this the familiar Pooley's maker's plate (**Fig 28**). Very few complete machines have survived with integral railway company names as distinct from

Pooley's plates. Another is known from the GWR & GCR Joint Committee. Another item sometimes marked were the cast-iron weights. There were small parcels machines usually in parcels and goods offices, as well as platform-based items for weighing trolleys. It is just possible to see the few last examples of these, one was recently extant at Hellifield in Yorkshire. The maker's plates on these machines are quite common and include the railway company's initials; BR continued their issue.

Platform ticket machines often bore company markings. They are now extremely rare and almost all have gravitated towards working steam railways, and a few more to railwayana museums. Relative to the large numbers which existed, very few have survived. Their original numbers can be equated roughly with the number of stations which have ever issued platform tickets, although it is likely that a few stations issued them at booking offices only.

Company urinals were at one time almost universal until British Railways decided to close or charge for their use. A well-known GWR sign, urging the adjustment of dress before leaving was always placed either on the toilet wall above people's heads, or on the way out. The GWR, of course, always had screens at the entrance to urinals and many of these are still in existence. Some remarkable notices in cast-iron survive regarding the proper and improper use of company toilets, often with company initials. Especially fierce were imprecations against the placing of waste shavings down basins! There has been a report of a complete NBR marked wrought-iron urinal in recent use on a farm.

2
Goods Transportation

It is significant that some of the most prominent railway landmarks in Britain's towns and cities constitute the blocks of old goods warehouses on which can still be read GWR, LMS and even pre-group names like CLC, Midland and Great Northern. This is because they were competing companies in the same towns and the tall brickwork served as huge advertisements for their services. As towns expanded, initially due to canals and later railways, it is not surprising that warehouses were built near the stations, and near the town centres. It is difficult only for us in a largely motorised age, with extreme congestion in such areas, to imagine how different these locations were 150 years ago when there were no motors and the railway had a virtual monopoly.

Railways arose initially to transport goods, and in many cases freight revenue remained paramount for companies like the NER and the Midland Railway. So a plethora of railwayana has been left to us from the goods departments.

It should be realised that as this book is about railwayana, we concentrate on collectable objects and not on buildings as such; also although very few horse drays have survived, we shall not go into much detail as this is available in other books.

Goods Depots and Signs

Almost always, the depot entrance had a height gauge, and usually at the large depots, a wooden notice above the roller doors reading 'No Company Locos allowed in this Shed' or similar, as movement inside was by rope capstans or

29 (*above*) Railway fire buckets and signs

30 (*right*) Restored M & GNJR fire buckets and sign at Sheringham Station.

31 LNWR fire hydrant sign

horse shunting. As most pre-group sheds were of wood, the walls usually had marked fire buckets, bucket brackets and often fire bucket notices. **Fig 29** shows an SDJC notice and a Midland Railway Engineer's Department notice. Others were provided by the NSJC, M & GNR and the Rhymney Railway.

Fire buckets are a whole field in themselves and examples exist of the famous deep pattern GWR (letters hand painted), LNER, LMS, GNR and Midland Railway and the rare LNWR type with two lots of very small impressed letters. Other companies which produced marked buckets include SR, GNR and NER, but other than this, few or even none have survived; perhaps they wore out and were quickly replaced. On the other hand, a wider range of marked support brackets are known including LDECR, GNR, Midland Railway, and TVR. **Fig 30** shows a restored M & GNJR fire bucket rail at Sheringham station.

Fixed to the walls were often a whole series of cast-iron notices marked 'F.P.' so many feet/inches, to denote fire hydrants. The MSLR, GCR, CLC and LNWR had large numbers of these, with the LNWR often naming the location as shown in **Fig 31**. Some of these were still visible from the platform at Crewe North

in 1986, on the periphery of the Crewe Arms Hotel. One of the most rare of all SDJR signs, of which only two are known, is the sign 'Water Stop Valve 3' marked SDJR.

There were multitudes of other signs for gas, oil and water points. Two very rare ones still *in situ* outside Swindon Works in 1985 were marked 'GWR Sewer and Storm Water'. Marked hydrant and stop valve covers were also used by a number of railways.

In front of many goods yards, save for the very small ones, were weighbridges, with small control offices which could also be used by the public for a fee. They were guarded by weight warnings, of which the LNER had the widest range. **Fig 32** shows such a notice warning all mechanical vehicles using the weighbridge, of a 5 ton limit. Another strict limit was against the approach of heavy goods vehicles near enough to loading edges to risk crushing them or over-balancing out onto the line. This was prohibited as in the LNER 4' limit sign.

A very well known goods warehouse sign warned against the 'dangerous practice of propping up wagon doors whilst loading' (**Fig 33**). This was produced by the GWR, with revised

32 LNER weighbridge sign

signings by J. Inglis, Frank Potter and J. Milne, while the SR had just one version. The GWR sign was replicated by the LNWR & GWR Joint Lines. Cranes themselves usually had cast-iron company notices. Cranes on the LNW and the LNWR & GWR Joint Line (**Fig 33**) all had numbers and virtually every goods yard often had one outside at country depots. The GCR had an attractive rectangular sign in several versions, as did the GWR & GCR Joint Committee and the Midland Railway. Cranes often adjoined depots, eg along quays as shown in the GWR sign (which is perhaps unique) in Warwick Railway Museum, marked GWR and laying down tonnages moveable by cranes along the quays.

Many of the separate rooms such as weigh office, goods office, stores, parcels office, storeroom, number takers, had door plates in cast-iron (**Fig 34**). Number takers, recorded wagon numbers of home and 'foreign' companies, and they were employed in considerable numbers by the LNWR.

Fig 35 shows two of the best designed inspection cover tops, used by the SEC and its SR successor. These were located inside Ashford Works only,

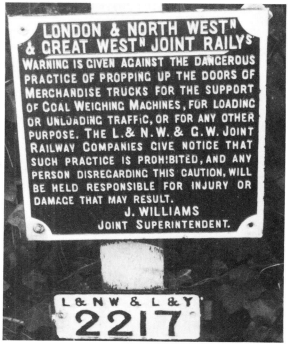

33 LNWR & GWR warehouse notice with a LNWR & LYR crane number below

though various other SE&CDR designs exist, some of them very rare. This is a collecting field which has so far been neglected.

Some depots had wagon traversers, others used shunting poles, others mechanical or hydraulic capstans, oth-

34 A wide variety of cast iron door signs

35 Two clearly marked inspection covers

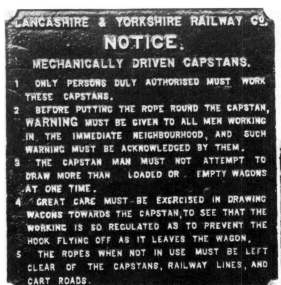

37 LYR capstan warning notice

36 Southern Railway warning notice

ers had wagon lifts down to lower level vaults as at Birmingham Moor Street and at St Pancras. The need for extensive warnings and precaution is seen in the number of different goods depot notices surviving. GWR depots had various 'No Smoking' notices in cast-iron screwed on the outside.

The Southern Railway was almost obsessive regarding keeping people from walking on their asbestos roofs. (**Fig 36**). There are three varieties of this notice, one in 'sunshine' script. The Cardiff Railway had a welter of enamel

signs marked 'No Smoking' inside its Bute Road warehouse. Undoubtedly, the most accident conscious line was the LYR which had a multitude of cast-iron notices referring to mechanical capstans, hydraulic jiggers, hydraulic capstans and hydraulic cranes (**Fig 37**). **Fig 38** shows a transitional LNWR & LYR sign, as the latter was taken over by the former in 1921, before the LMS was formed in 1923. The LYR was burnt off and a LNW cast name inserted! The LNWR & LYR Joint Lines had equivalent signs. **Fig 39** shows the only sign known which includes a mention of horse shunting; it also includes the various risks from cranes, jibs, overhead chutes, closing buffers and coupling hazards. Notice the reference to 'fatal accidents'.

Staff walking through LMS warehouses were warned in the sign shown in **Fig 40** to ensure that capstan control levers were off, while the LNER had well known cast-iron notices protecting its petroleum store, as did the LSWR and SR, and its fragile roofs, similar to the

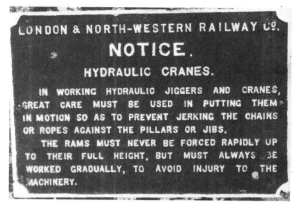

38 LNWR crane notice

39 LNWR & LYR Joint Railway warning notice

40 LMS warehouse warning notice

Southern Railway. Other companies did not seem so concerned.

Horses

We would refer readers to the excellent set of pictures of GWR working horses in J.K.L. Russell's *GWR Company Servants*, Figs 269-82, showing the relation of horses to the movement of goods.

In 1926 the LNER owned 5,000 horse and 7,100 road vehicles at its 2,500 stations and depots. The company had 7,500 steam locomotives, so there were two horses for every three locomotives and averaged two for every station, although of course they were not distributed thus.

The railwayana of railway horses may be summarised as follows:

a Drays, tilt trucks, parcels vans, horse omnibuses, brakes, gigs (traps).

b Horse brasses. See the recent book *Railway Horse Brasses*, Ran Hawthorne, National Horse Brass Society, 1987.

c Marked dray hub caps, horse shoes, farriers' tools, dray lamps, saddles, bridles and other leather items.

d Paper history.

A surprising amount of horse traffic was run jointly, eg LMS & LNER; LNWR & NER; LNWR & GWR; LMS & GWR, as well as by most of the pre-grouping companies. Excellent pictures exist of LNWR horse conveyances in *LNWR Miscellany*, Vol 2, by E. Talbot (OPC, 1980) plates 213-25, showing one-, two- and three-horse vehicles. Four horses were used on very heavy carting.

Of category **a** very few have survived for us to see. There is a resplendent LYR parcels van at the National Railway Museum complete with tarpaulin sheet, an LMS & GWR one at Winchcombe Railway Museum (plus LMS and GWR ones awaiting restoration) the Severn Valley Railway have a restored GWR

41 A collection of railway horse brasses

42 LMS saddle and reins

van, as does Didcot GWR Centre and an LMS one is being restored at Warwick Railway Museum. Some horse and omnibus ownership plates were fixed to the sides in the same way as by modern bus companies.

Marked horse brasses have survived from at least the following companies: Cal R, CLC, FR, GCR, GER, GNR, GSWR, GWR, LBSCR, LCDR, LMS, LNER, LNWR, LSWR, LYR, Metropolitan Railway, Midland Railway, N & GNR, NER, NSR, SDJC, SMR, SR, SECR, THJR, TVR, GC & LNWJ, LNWR & GWR, GW & LNEJ, GW & MidJ, GWR & LMS, LNWR & LYJ, Mid & LNWR, LNWR & GWR.

The frontispiece of *Railway Horse Brasses*, by Ran Hawthorne, shows the main types, of which rosettes and name plates are the most sought after. The main shapes can be seen from the line drawings in *Railway Horse Brasses*. **Fig 41** is a selection of horse brasses in the Gordon Blears Collection.

As with so much railwayana, grouping produced a multitude of transitional patterns, as with the NER rosette passing into LNER, GSWR and Caledonian Railway into LMS, Midland Railway into LMS and LBSCR into Southern Railway. Almost all, save the Metropolitan and Caledonian Railways, carried initials only. The degree of survival is indicated by the belief that there are only two or three of the LYR hame plates generally known at present, with only one known LMS noseband brass. While a good rosette is probably worth three figures, on the whole values remain moderate as there are a relatively low number of serious collectors.

A little known area for collectors is that of horse bridle buckles, made by the Caledonian Railway, GSWR, LMS, LNWR, GWR, NER and LNER. There are several known saddlers' tools marked LNWR and LMS. Several companies including the NER, LYR, GNR, Midland Railway, LNER and LMS made hub caps, the LYR in bronze, the others in brass; LMS ones were both brass and iron. **Fig 42** shows an LMS saddle with several brasses plus the reins, also brassed. There are very few railway saddles extant, with LMS, GWR and LNWR known.

Local records of large railway horse stables are known, though mostly they are now mere sites. Examples are Aston and Camden. During the re-opening of the Snow Hill tunnel in Birmingham a complete railway saddle and harness was discovered, while an LNWR one turned up in 1986 in a farm barn in North Yorkshire. The largest stables had railway farriers and blacksmiths with horse shoes made *in situ.* LNER ones are known to exist. The LNWR had a very large horse department and even had official animal inspectors and assistant inspectors, and below this, a whole range of grades down to horse boy. A very few associated items have been found. For instance in November 1986 a 10 x 6in stoneware jar was discovered marked 'Veterinary Dept. Derby'.

A very limited amount of paper and label history survives regarding railway cartage. Invoices for horse provender from the LNWR horse department, Birmingham exist, as does a GNR wagon label regarding the carriage of horses. If a company stable like GWR Hockley or LNWR Aston housed say 100 horses, then large stores would certainly be needed. The number of horses can be seen from the pictures in Russell (*op cit*, p180) of Hockley in 1927 where forty carts and drays can be seen.

Parcel Stamps

Many of the four-wheel carts were actually parcels vans as distinct from general merchandise vehicles and two specific grades on the NBR were parcels porters' vans and parcel deliverers' vans. Parcels were stamped with official railway company parcels stamps which have survived in great numbers and from extremely small companies. Indeed, in the cases of some of the smallest, the stamps represent the few pieces of history of any sort surviving from those companies.

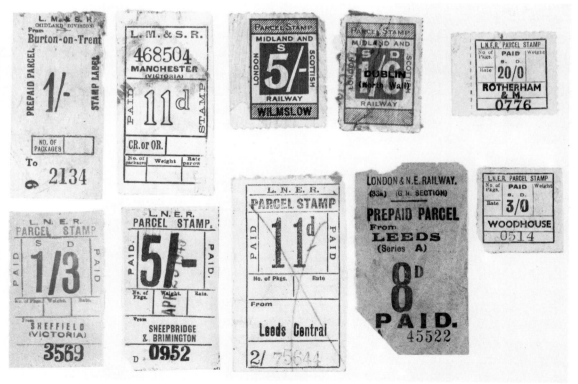

43 LMS and LNER parcels stamps

Colour Plate 4 and **Fig 43** show examples of pre- and post-grouping parcel stamps from NBR, LYR, LNWR, GWR, GER, Midland Railway, NER, GNR, LMSR and LNER. The GER ones show designs intended to counteract counterfeit; the 1/- of 16-3-1923 was a very late issue, although, of course, usage of old stock continued after the 'Big Four' railway companies were formed. As with tickets, these include examples from many stations long since closed and unrecognisable, eg LNWR Spon Lane, LYR Stubbins, LNER Sheffield (Victoria) LNER Sheepbridge & Brimington, LNER Woodhouse and LMS Dublin North Wall. They were often overstamped with station and date, but larger depots had pre-printed stamps; others like Spon Lane and Dublin had overprinted names.

One recurrent theme in railwayana is transitional issues, as has been seen above with horse brasses. Here we see the LNW red square turn into the LMS orange version, and the Midland Railway black on white into LMS Midland Division. The LMS Manchester Victoria looks like a combined LNWR and Midland! The GNR 2/- turns into LNER (GN Section) and maintains the print code 33a.

Companies with examples in collections of railway letter, parcel and newspaper stamps include: Caledonian Railway, CLC, City of Glasgow Union, CWJR CK & PR, CVR, D & AJR, EWJR, EMR, ELR, Furness Railway, Garstang & Knott End, GSWR, GB & KJR, GCR, GER, GNR, GN & GC, GNSR, GWR, HBR, I WR, IWCR, LYR, LDECR, LBSCR, LNWR, LSWR, LTSR, Macclesfield Committee, MSLR, MMR, MSJAR, MCR, Metropolitan Railway, Metropolitan & GCJC, Midland Railway, M & GNJR, M & SWJR, N & Banbury J, NBR, NCR,

NSR, OAGBR, PWR, PTRDCo, S & Midland, SDJR, Southern & LMS, SR, Southwold Railway, TVR, West Lancashire Railway.

Railway Sacks and Sheets

Whole departments existed on the larger lines to deal with areas of rail working which were essential at the time, but in today's commerce have been almost entirely superseded. Sack provision is one of these. Forms have survived showing empty/full sack hire from the HBWRJRD (grain or seed), together with demurrage charge (**Fig 44**). One exists from the Caledonian Railway dated 1923, and also a letter from the LNER sack department headquarters at Lincoln. It should be noted that very few companies marked their sacks. The Midland Railway, GCR, GER and LNER did, although examples are very rare. Most companies transmitted customers' sacks and hired them out. LMS had $1\frac{1}{2}$ million grain sacks in 1947, with a repair depot at Trent Junction.

Fig 45 shows the connection between sack contractors and railways in 1888 at Northampton. Most interesting is the small print allowing 12 days for a company transit, after which $\frac{1}{2}$d per part of a week per sack was payable.

Fig 46 gives insight into wagon stock checks on the GNR, showing the count of MSLR and GER wagons in 1896 at GNR stations. Before the recent overall computer control of wagon locations (TOPS), these depot reports were one of the few checks on what was where at a time when twelve days were allowed for consignment!

Tarpaulin sheets are a type of railwayana of which little seems to have been preserved, although hundreds of thousands of marked sheets must have been made and can be seen on photo-

Hull, Barnsley and West-Riding Junction Railway and Dock Company.

G. B. 48.

No.

D

No. **8**   **E**   RETURN OF THE SACKS.   Full Sacks

_____ July 1 188 _   The Clerk in Charge must see that the Sacks are in good order
and that the Bundles contain the number stated to be in them.

ETWALL G. N. R. _____ *Station,*

Date of Return	Number Returned Empty	Number Returned Full	Demurrage.				Reference to " Full or Empty Sack Receipt	Reference to Warehouse or Special Debit Book
			No. of weeks	Amount.				
				£	s.	d.		

Received _____ 50 _____

Sacks filled with Grain or Seed, per Invoice _____ 1 ____

Date _____ June 30 _____

From _____ Neptune St. _____ *Station,*

| | Date of Invoice | Number of | Number |
| | | | |

subject to the conditions on back hereof, of which I have received

Signature of

THE GREAT NORTHERN RAILWAY. (401)

Station. Oct 23 1896

No. 347 **CARRIAGE AND TRUCK REPORT.**

PASSENGER DEPARTMENT.	On Hand.	Wanted addition- al.	To Spare.	M.S.&L. on Hand.	G.E.R. on Hand.	REMARKS.
Covered Carriage Trucks						
Open ,, ,,	1					
Horse Boxes ,,						
Cattle ,,						

GOODS DEPARTMENT.	Loaded.	Empty.	Wanted addition- al.	To Spare.
Box Wagons ...	4			
Flat ,,				
Engine ,,				
Long Rail Wagons				
Colwick Wagons	8			
Cattle ,,				
High Sided Wagons				
Single Bolstered Timber				
Double ,,	7	2		
Goods or Fruit Vans ...				
Sheets ...				
Travelling Crane	2			
G.N. Wagons on hand with Coal				
M.S.&L. Co.'s Goods Wagons				
,, ,, Cattle				
,, ,, Timber ,,				
,, ,, Sheets ,,				
G.E.R. Goods Wagons ...				
,, ,, Cattle ,,				
,, ,, Timber ,,				
,, ,, Sheets ...				

(C. 1027.) **WILLIAM OULTON, Sack Contractor.**

RECEIPT BOOK FOR FULL SACKS.

No. _____ _____ *Railway.*

Received from *Park Lane* Oct. 8

Sacks marked *W. O.* 188 _ _____ _____ *Station.*

_____ filled with Grain.

Also the terms upon which the above-mentioned Sacks are hired by me, the undersigned, of WILLIAM OULTON, viz. :—

The charge for Sack Hire is one half-penny per sack per week, parts of a week
charged as a whole week, commencing on the twelfth day after the date of the
Company's forwarding Invoice (_____). That being the time
allowed for the transit and delivery.

For *J.C. Greensmith*

Signature _____ *Hilton* mills

N.B.—The Merchants, &c., &c., are required to furnish proof of the return of the Sacks
to the same Station from which they have been taken. It is, therefore, necessary for their
protection that the signature be obtained from the Clerk in charge upon return of the em
Sacks, and that they be duly addressed to the depot.

Sack Depot, London and North Western Railway Station, NORTHAMPTON.

44-6 Documents for sacks and wagon stock

graphs in specialist company histories. The LMS had sheet works at St Helens Junction, Trent Junction (founded there at the centre of the Midland Railway system), at Manchester Osbourne Street and Glasgow, the department employing 500. Details of manufacture are given in Twell's *LMS Miscellany*, Vol 1. Readers should not forget the famous sheet stores at Trent Junction.

Goods Departments Paper History

Happily, there are quite large numbers of preserved historic railway wagons, though these lie outside the scope of this book. There are also multitudes of wagon plates and labels (of which more later) and there are also plenty of small country goods sheds left (though a declining number of big town and city warehouses) as well as very large quantities of paper invoices and the like.

What has gone, never to return, apart from short simulated shunts on preserved lines are the sights, the smells and the sounds of a slow clanking Midland coal train straining its way southwards to Brent, the twice daily LNWR pick-up goods from Carnforth to Kendal and Windermere, beating its way up the North West main line, usually tender first; gone forever is the insistent beat of a Woofy 4F slogging through Oxenholme with a train of South Durham coke empties from Barrow via Hincaster and Stainmore Summit.

No more to be seen is the long frame of an ex-LNWR 0-8-0 blasting its way backwards from Preston Docks up the precipitous incline...into silence perpetual goes the frenzied rattle of the regular milk tanker strung on the end of the Glasgow to Birmingham Express dashing down Shap at 80...no more is the engine changed at Broom on a Bristol to St Pancras Banana Special to take on two SMJC locos en route to Ravenstone Wood JC. The bosses decided they could not bother with eggs, with fish, with cattle, nor horses, nor sheep, or hay or bananas, so we must rely on our memories and on our precious relics.

The vision of a 'real' goods train can be evoked as much by a collection of wagon invoices or labels as by musing over the cast-iron trespass signs which used to nod at level crossings as the succession of freight wagons plodded by.

To help appreciate the following examples of goods department paperwork the reader should have a pre-grouping rail atlas close at hand to visualise some of the routes shown on the goods invoices. **Figs 47-50** shows four invoices, the lower three are 17 x 4in, the LDECR is 17 x 5in. They were made out at the start and handed in sheafs to the

goods guard and checked at the end, having been stamped, often during transhipment points. On the LDECR invoice there were over twenty main columns of possible data including the truck/wagon numbers, weights, goods descriptions, payment/under/over charge, possible porter and postage on charges. The G44 at top right was the company's print code. Early invoices were often in purple as they had to be hand-copied via a laborious pressing process (hence reference in the LDECR one to copyable ink, top left). The LYR invoice was LYR Newton Heath to Doldowlod on the Central Wales Line in Radnor and appears routed via Chester, Whitchurch, Wem and Shrewsbury. It took one day only. There were wide differences in company invoices. An LNWR one of 1867 from Monument Lane Birmingham to Audlem has a nice LNWR stamp on the top right, and early spelling of 'waggon'. A Wirral example of 1919 gave free cartage to consignee on arrival at Keswick. In this case, the CK & PR at Keswick (or carter) would have charged the consignee at Birkenhead, who would reclaim from the Wirral Railway.

A Neath & Brecon green coal invoice of 1912 took two days from Seven Sisters to Doldowlod via Brecon and the Central Wales Railway! Two very rare Glyn Valley Tramway advice notes show a common practice of advising the arrival of goods to be collected. The Kington & Eardisley Railway referred to payment to carman, and an extra charge if beyond its normal delivery area.

Fig 51 shows waybills (strictly speaking, not issued at goods depots but from stations) for horses, parcels, carriages and dogs. These were very common items used on most lines. They covered traffic entrusted to passenger guards.

"DUKERIES ROUTE." (G 44)

LANCASHIRE, DERBYSHIRE & EAST COAST RAILWAY.

Progressive No.

Invoice No. Date 190 From To Station Ry., via

Owner and Nos. of Trucks Invoice arrived 190 M. Goods arrived 190 M. Goods unloaded 190 M.

Invoice No. Date 18 From HULL, ALEXANDRA DOCK

HULL, BARNSLEY AND WEST-RIDING JUNCTION RAILWAY AND DOCK COMPANY, to Station

Owner and No. of Wagon No. of Sheet Invoice Arrived 18 h. m. Goods Arrived 18 h. m.

(CARE OF MIDLAND RAILWAY COMPANY.)

MIDLAND RAILWAY. G. F. 31.

Goods Invoice Date Sep 24 1900 No. From BURTON, To Skipton Station Ry., via

Owners and Nos. of Wagons Invoice arrived 190 M Goods arrived 190 M. Goods unloaded 190 M.

Invoice No.

LANCASHIRE AND YORKSHIRE RAILWAY. (G.T. 58)

Pro. No.

Date June 25 1912 From to Dolddowlod Station

Invoice Arrived 26 6 12 Goods Arrived

Received the above in good order by Carter's Signature Date

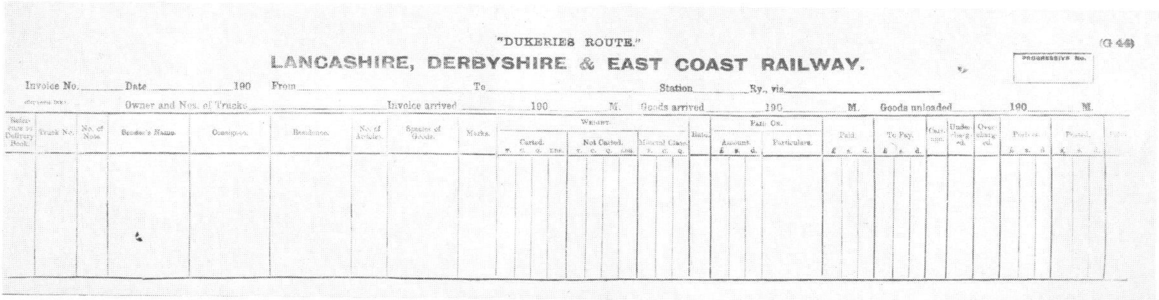

47-50 Four goods invoices

All four are examples where there are virtually no other historical remains of the railway concerned except paper history. **Fig 52** shows four goods memos; very rare ones include the examples from the St Helens Canal & Railway, 1863, giving warning about the contents of a truck received; a Mid Wales Railway memo from Kerry of 1890 and an 1884 Bourn & Lynn Joint Lines memo regarding an incorrect invoice. The LYR & LNWR Joint memo refers to the onetime Fleetwood Steamer Service.

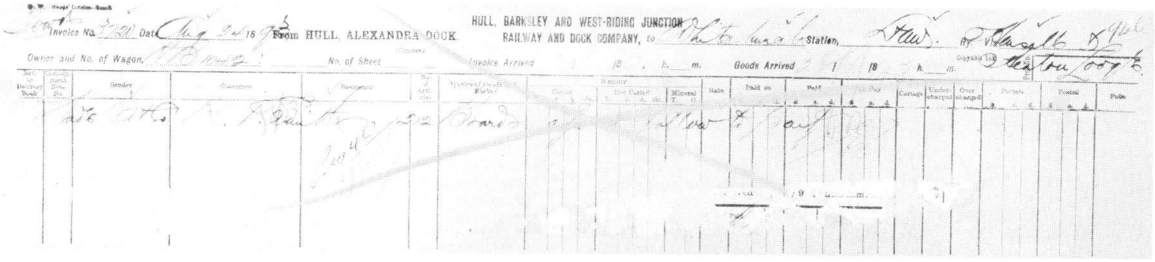

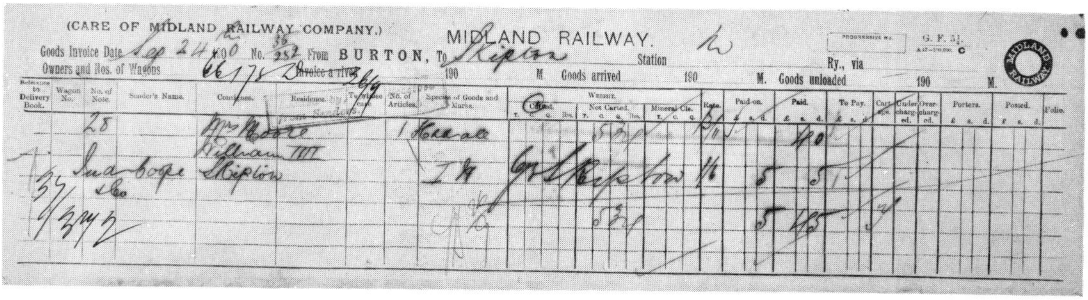

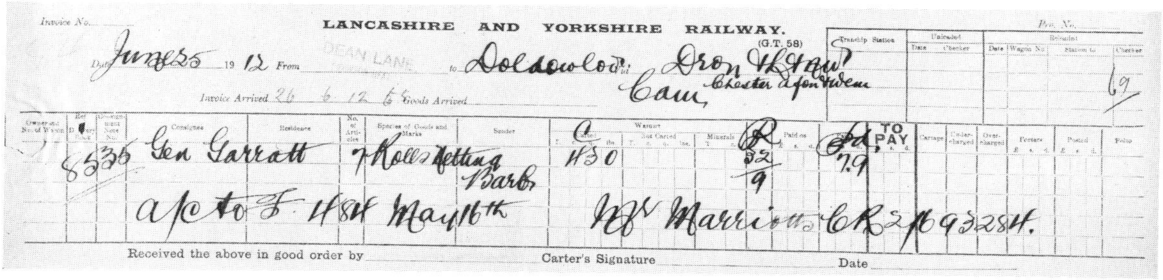

Mistakes and omissions seem to have

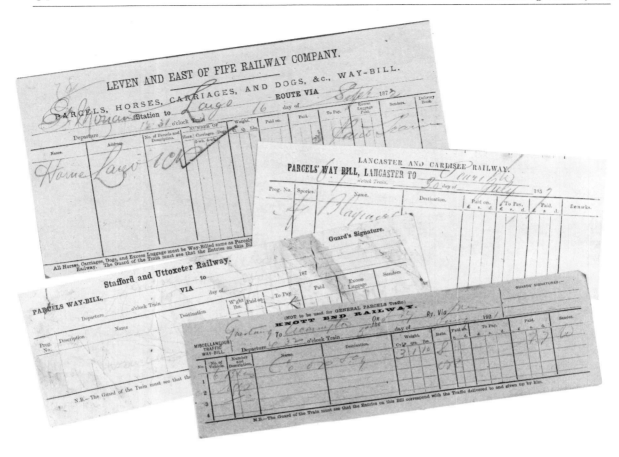

51 A collection of early railway waybills

happened frequently and written provision was available on printed forms. The LDECR had a range of forms numbered G35-8 covering 'Goods not Received', 'Goods in Bad Order', 'Goods Received Different to Invoice', 'Goods not Invoiced or Waybilled'. These had to be signed by the station master, showing how, on smaller lines, overall charge of many areas fell to the station master, although on larger lines and stations there would be separate goods agents. Even tiny lines needed such forms and we can suggest that almost all railways must have printed this type of form. Moseley Railwayana Museum has an example from the East & West Yorkshire Union Railway.

A notable point about paper history is that only a small percentage emanated from goods depots, probably due to much of the administration being worked from stations. The LMS, for example, derived £35.9 million receipts from goods and £19.5 million from passengers in 1935, and although there are a considerable number of different goods invoices, many related to mineral traffic which did not pass through goods warehouses. Even a small line such as the Seacombe, Hoylake & Deeside Railway had a plethora of forms and we can take this line as a possible exemplar. It seems likely that there were forms 1 to 100, and although there is one numbered 313 the existence of forms in

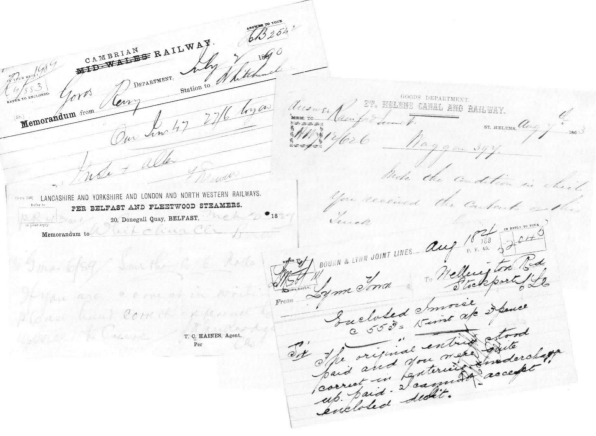

52 A group of nineteenth-century goods memos

between is unknown. Study of the un-numbered forms turns up several questions. Was the numbering system introduced later, or were only some forms ever numbered? It is worth noting that the company of that name only existed between 1881 and July 1891! Previously it was the Hoylake & Birkenhead Railway and Tramway and it became the Wirral Railway in 1891. Hence, some of the paperwork is overstamped by the latter. Details provided on one form include two rates of carriage, with and without liability; warning of 3s per day per truck demurrage charge. Some of the numbered forms include:

1	miscellaneous waybill
2	small memo
3	large memo
12	parcels waybill
16	general parcels waybill (small)
21	abstract of all traffic other than passengers
22A	abstract of all traffic other than passengers (received)
42	consignment note
45	porters' waybill
46	goods advice note, red/black print
64	horse & dog ticket
69	delivery note
91	left luggage ticket
98	stationery requisition
313	telegraph message

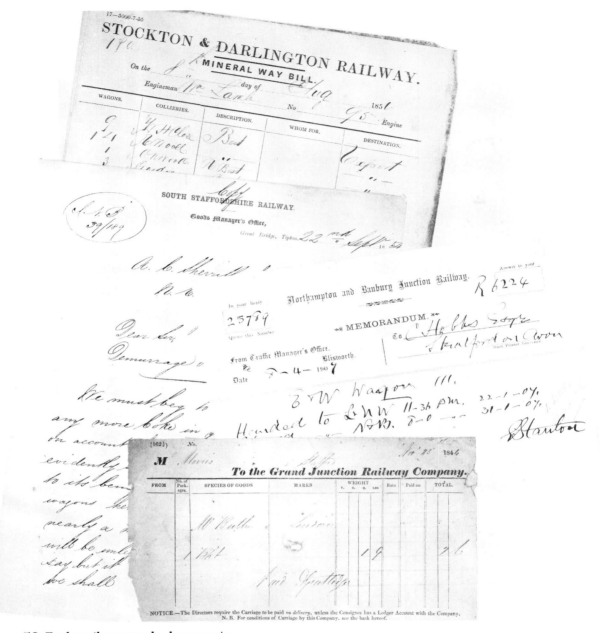

53 Early railway goods documents

There were also apparently unnumbered forms dealing with goods consigned at owner's risk (yellow form); daily goods cash summary; season ticket notes (two sizes); requisitions for season tickets; audit office letters; general letters; station return regarding overcharges; invoice of goods arrived; daily summary of remittances; general manager memo; return not to hand; excess luggage; contract ticket; requisition; stores requisition.

Fig 53 is included to show some of the earliest railway goods documents. The

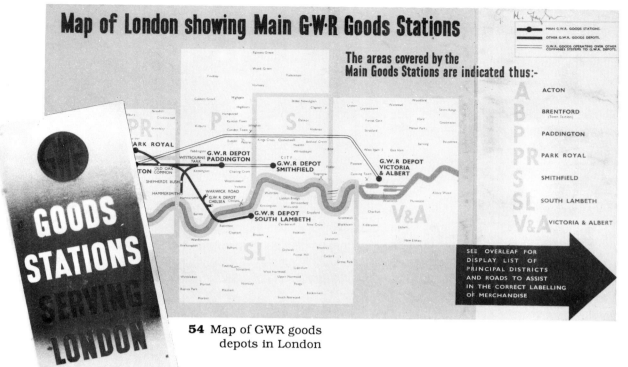

54 Map of GWR goods depots in London

SDR form is a mineral waybill of 1856 where the locoman's name is given and the number of the locomotive; the GJR bill of 1846 lists the company's agents. The N & BJR memo of 1907 is a wagon report referring to the EWJR and the LNWR, and the letter from the South Staffordshire Railway in 1854 is another demurrage complaint to the NER at York for the latter having allowed NER coke trucks to reside for a month at Tipton as the private sender had not secured a buyer at the South Staffordshire end!

Fig 54 shows part of the publicity material for goods services. It is a folded label map of the GWR goods depots in London, with the addresses on the other side.

Wagon Labels

While the public would rarely see invoices, and only see waybills when signing the latter, wagon labels were and are readily visible. Very little has ever been published in book form on this subject, which is lamentable as the labels convey a wealth of atmosphere about the scale and routes of Victorian and early twentieth-century railways.

Labels were issued referring to the following types of freight or special freight conditions: bags, cattle, castings, coal, dangerous goods, due off, empty, explosives, express, eggs, from general store, grain, green peas, heavy traffic, home empty, home removal, horses, horsebox, important goods, large urgent, livestock, loco coal, loco & carriage department, market goods, mineral load, passenger rated traffic, passenger train traffic, perishables, potatoes, road transhipment, road wagon, road side wagon, sack bundles, shunt with great care, special vehicle required, station trunk, sugar beet, tariff van, to be weighed, two/three sheet truck, under sheet, urgent.

It is very likely that this list will be added to in the future.

Most of the medium size companies and all the major lines printed wagon labels for ease of identity of make up of each wagon. The main companies known to have used them are as follows:

Barry Dock & Railways	KER
Bishop's Castle Railway	Knott End
	LBSCR
	LMSR
Bristol & Exeter Railway	LNER
	LNWR
Caledonian Railway	LSWR
Cam R	LTSR
CLC	LYR
CK&PR	MSCR
DVR	MSJAR
D&AJR	MCR
Easingwold Railway	Mid R
EMR	MSLR
EWJR	MWR
EWYUR	MRC Co
Felixstowe Docks and Railway Co	N&BR
	NBR
Festiniog Railway (FR)	NLR
	NSR
Furness Railway (FR)	P&WJR
	RSBR
GCR	Rhymney Railway (RR)
GER	
GB&KJR	Sirhowy Railway
GNR	S&M Comm
GNSR	S&MR
GWR	SER
GSWR	SR
Highland Railway (HR)	TVR
	WLR
HBR	WCP
HBWRJRDCo	WRJC
KESR	WMCQR

Other Lines Including Joint:

GN&GEJ	Macclesfield Committee
GWR&LMS (Severn & Wye)	M&SWJR
LNWR and NER	Met & GCJC
	SDJC

There was little conformity in size and layout even within the same company. For example, there were four very different ones in use on the Caledonian Railway, the common factor being station of origin and destination and date. Sizes were 4 x 3in, 6 x 4in and 5 x 4in.

On Cambrian Railway wagon labels consignee and any charge was printed on, and the company had at least six types in No 39 series as well as a huge 'Road Side Wagon' label measuring 6 x 6½in.

On the CLC, some of the routes given seem very roundabout. **Fig 55** shows label No 187 Huskisson Station, Liverpool to Etwall on the GNR via Godley Junction, Beighton & Annesley, all across the Pennines down the east and round the south. (The shortest line route via Crewe and Uttoxeter would have been only a third of the distance.) Does this imply that the CLC had no running powers over the LNWR? Another No 187 on a blue label claims Birkenhead to Skipton via Chinley! Did this really happen?

Furness labels are fairly rare and the illustration also shows a Furness & Midland Joint Line label of 1894. There were, however, 5,000 printed in 1894 alone.

Some labels were left blank, as the No 3672 GCR buff type. Others had the route on as in the red and buff GCR label, Nottingham to Bristol via Banbury.

Some of the most dramatically marked labels are the GER series shown in **Fig 55** where the blue circle marked

55 Wagon labels

the GN & GE Joint Line via Spalding and Doncaster for grain goods and red circle with oblong in red for perishables. A blue cross marked traffic via Peterborough and the LNWR route to Rugby. There were other plain buff labels for cattle, perishable goods, grain etc with no serial numbers. All GER labels seem to be buff.

Fig 68 also shows an extremely rare label from the Glasgow, Barrhead and Kilmarnock Joint Railway. The GNR had a wide range of labels which are almost all about 3 x 4in. All have a white or buff background. The two with stripes are route codes.

The GWR's labels are usually 3 x 4$\frac{1}{2}$ in, although some were smaller, and one was large, an orange station truck label (No 3141). All are numbered in standard GWR stationery code. An unusual one is marked 'Empty Wagon Homeward' No 3005; No 999 is yellow; No 2829 is 'Market Goods'; No 900-2 has both large and small versions. In later times the familiar upright pattern replaced the early horizontal style as in the case of the LMS, LNER and SR.

The Hull & Barnsley Railway wagon labels show the change in name from full to short title in both label types G177 and G92, between 1899 and 1900. The undersheet wagon label is a rare type.

The LNWR showed unusual colours and a great variety in the size of its wagon labels. Burton to Barmouth via Salop of 1875, is yellow with blue and red broad crossed stripes; 1896 Liverpool to Etwall via Egginton Junction has two double red bands as route code, while another, No 793 is orange. No 764 in blue is of interest: it enjoins being nailed onto wagon sides as a 'foreign' label and 'to be due off' LNWR before 0600hrs 20/4/1895. Very common

LNWR labels are the small buff 3$\frac{1}{2}$ x 2in No 790/791, while No 2433, a package label is a much later label from 1917.

LYR labels were varied, with many stripes as shown in **Colour Plate 5**. Routes from Liverpool North and South Docks carried two or one blue, or red stripes as on M238/9 and M132/217. M129 was a striking 'potatoes' label. Some traffic from Hull by 1912 carried a blue green label (M271) with two red diagonal stripes. Potato labels had official Nos and would have been on potato sacks. The Maryport and Carlisle Railway label is a rare example, coloured buff. M & GNJR continued the GN pattern (No 476) and in post-grouping times used LMS label No ERO 61638 for sugar beet. The Manchester, Sheffield and Lincolnshire Railway is another rarity with a buff label No 291h marked MSLR.

Midland Railway labels were a mass of route data rather than being striking. They are almost all green/red/black on buff and numbered mostly in a GF sequence, although a few colliery ones were in MF sequence. MF 80/81 give routes via the F & MJR and via Bordesley Junction and the GWR. 'Heavy Traffic' had at least three types, No GF804, and together with 'Express' and 'Tariff Van Goods' are quite rare denominations. At 3$\frac{3}{4}$ x 4$\frac{3}{4}$in, some are large.

The North British Railway seem to have used large labels 4 x 5in, mostly numbered in the 444 series. Other Scottish companies are named on their labels, eg Alford, the terminus of the Great North of Scotland branch, via the Forth and Tay Bridges. The NER had small labels 4 x 2$\frac{1}{4}$in, some orange, others white. Early ones had no serial numbers. They had a horse box label from Scarborough. There were other large labels 6 x 5in for livestock and

56 Wagon labels

collieries, Nos H54 and 58.

It is arguable that the North Staffordshire Railway had one of the most attractive and varied range. Most were marked NSR but there were 'North Staff Ry' and full worded examples. WL18 was red with black diamond route tag, WL23 was orange. There were also orange labels in the C2118-40 range with black diamonds of different sizes, a white label giving Burton Station St Station as its name, a white with red diamond, and a full title orange. A notable feature is the uniformity of size, 4 x $2^3/_4$ in.

A very rare one sheet label is that from

the Portpatrick and Wigtownshire Joint Railway. The South Eastern and Chatham Railway produced one buff label from Chatham Dockyard. The Sheffield and Midland Committee produced small white labels. The Wrexham, Mold and Connah's Quay Railway had labels in its 345-7 series with the full company name. Some had the addition of Wirral Railway and were overstamped Great Central. The Southern Railway produced some pleasant colour contrasts and styles as the illustrations show. The 1930 style 746AA had a green diagonal on buff for traffic to LMS (Midland) while 1937 746BB still refers to LNWR and even the 1946 746C green on pink refers to LNER GC section. The Great Western and Midland (Severn & Wye) pre-group label (SW 170A) of 1915 is for grain and shows the full name, while the post-group label for waste wood is LMS pattern. The Somerset and Dorset Joint Railway latterly used LMS-style labels, eg ERO 59044.

The early LNER transitional types (444B) of 1923 were replaced by serial Nos in the 6000 range, such as the horizontal blanks 6013/4/36 and then the vertical pattern. It appears strange that the earlier print date on 0.6036 of 1924 carries a later serial number than 0.6013/4 of 1932/4. Probably the two latter had the earlier style (hence the earlier serial number) and were then reprinted in later styles. This is true also of horizontal 0.6049 'butter'. On the whole however it is clear that in the early 1930s LNER style changed to upright, with 0.6025 'grain', 0.6029 'potatoes', 0.6036 'urgent' (Rosyth Dockyard 1944) and the interesting 1943 three-sheet 'wagon' from LNER Victoria Docks to West Hartlepool via Doncaster with green registered LNER arrow and blue circle route. 0.6015 was 'returned

empties'. 0.6070/82 was two types of 'road wagon', and one of the latest issues 0.6412 of 1947 'urgent household removal'. The existence of 0.6086 'fish by goods train' in 1924 suggest again that many of the vertical names were present in the earlier horizontal pattern. 0.6323 of 1937 'dangerous shunt with care' was used for acids, but not inflammable liquids or explosives. It will be noted that the LNER used large upright buff labels, $3\frac{3}{4}$ x 5in.

The LMS had numerous wagon labels and the following have been identified:

GF 21	Perishable 09a	
GF 29	Not to go 09a	
GF 155a	Blank	
GF 155D	Blank Midland Railway type	
GF 525	Home empty	
GF 536	To be weighed. GF 536A To be Weighed.	
46 151	Caledonian section livestock	
46 168	Caledonian section (horizontal) 1923	
46 175	Caledonian section blank	
190A	Portpatrick & Wigtown section. Livestock. Almost identical with P & WJR pattern	
349	GSWR section	
358	GSWR section blank	
398	To be weighed at	
790	Blank	
791 1926	Empty. Plant cleansed & disinfected	
792b	LNWR transition. Port Dinorwic.	
825	Green & red on buff. Livestock. Highland? 1920s.	
P1172	Highland section blank	
P1172	Highland section perishable goods	
ERO 5401-3/1		Home empty
7639		Empty
10187		For repairs
19362		Special vehicle urgently required
19612		Passenger train traffic
20473		Brakevan deficiency. Report.

57 Wagon labels

21545	Livestock M96
23437	Empty for LMS loco coal
32739	Bundles of LMS sacks (tie on)
34005	Blank
34007/1	1932 blank. Red over stamp S3.
34012/65	Empty. Not to be intercepted.
34014/1	Empty cattle wagon. Cleansed & disinfected.
34032	Perishables
34044	Urgent
34065/2	Red/green on buff. Livestock. 1932. Same as Highland 825.
34065/2	Black on buff. Milking. Numbers of cattle, horses, sheep, pigs.
34076/1	Shunt with great care. Load and unload outside goods sheds.
34200	Sender
34203	three-sheet blank
34203/576s	Sheet. Printed Inverness.
34204	2 Sheet blank
34205	Red 'urgent'
34207	Livestock. Watered (fed) milking.
34209	Empties
34210	Tariff van
34219	Shunt with care
34230	Empty wagons
34232	Sugar beet
34247	Passenger related livestock
34248	Household removal
48751	Green pea traffic. Knottingley.
48881	Accompanied traffic
49632	Inspection for leakage. Carriage & Wagon Department.
59020	Home Empty SDJ section

Study of this LMS list of wagon labels yields a valuable insight into the sheer enormity of the traffic of what was, at the time, the largest joint stock company in the world. It must be realised that the ERO numbers were part of the entire LMS ERO series for all printed matter.

Very early ex-Caledonian Railway sections have a transitional number, eg 09a; later ones have a 46xxx prefix. Ex-Midland lines have GF prefix. Ex-GSWR lines have numbers in the 300s. One ex-LNWR label is in the 700 sequence and one ex-Highland in the 800s, although P1172 is also ex-Highland, and one Portpatrick & Wigtown Section has number 190A. It is of interest that ex-Furness Railway labels seem not to have transitional numbers and we do not have an ex-NSR one to judge. We should also note how early styles continued, hardly changed, but with later numbers, eg 48751 green pea traffic are dated in the late 1930s and 1940s.

The rest speak for themselves. There are some sixty types listed, and there is no doubt at all that more, perhaps many more, remain to be unearthed.

Railway Pencils, Pens and Pen Nibs
Essential utensils of goods, booking and luggage offices before the age of ball-point pens and printers were pencils and ink pens. **Fig 58** shows some railway pencils; the LMS ones include a 3H (ERO 90252) marked 6in by Venus Pencil Co, though its actual length is 7in; an LMS ERO 90269 with no maker or hardness marked and a dark black LMS ERO 90256. The two Southern Railway ones are by George Rowney, one marked for 'copying'. The two LNER ones are grade H and 4H, the latter made in Bavaria, both also hexagonal. The LNER look to be the same pattern. GWR 1785 'Sun' pattern is a thick blue marker made by the Eagle Pencil Company of London.

Other pencils are known from the CLC, GNR , GER and GCR, and other railways, but pre-grouping ones are rare. It is almost certain that most of the larger companies would have had their own marked pencils and we may confidently expect others to emerge. There were also company-marked pencil holders — one is known marked 'Great Northern Railway Hotels, London Peterborough Leeds & Bradford'.

Surprise is sometimes expressed at the obvious scale and variety of railway pen nibs, but this shows insufficient thought about the subject. Bearing in mind what was said in the section on North British grades where clerks occupy a high percentage of all employees, we must remember that even 80 years ago virtually all invoices and many many letters and memos were all hand-written (and earlier on, hand copied) so the fact that large companies, eg the GWR, had at least fifteen grades of nibs, is not surprising.

Unusual rarities survive from the LSWR, the Highland Railway and the Taff Vale Railway. Very few people have taken the trouble to collect or save them

58 Pencils marked with railway names and initials

and that is the reason for their rarity. We would expect, as with pencils, many others to turn up in time.

There are occasionally seen marked writing pens, sometimes silver cased, which would have been used in hotels and probably by high ranking officials, but these are extremely rare. It is worth pointing out that this area of railwayana is directly linked to that of inkwells and paperweights dealt with elsewhere.

3
Railway Tableware

Extrapolating data from H.N. Twell's two books on the LMS (OPC 1982-4), it is easy to work out how many tableware articles — at an absolute minimum — were owned by one company alone. It is as follows:

Post-group dining car inventory 56 places (including 36 in the dining car and 20 in adjacent carriages). Glass 136 pieces, china 687 pieces, plates 687 pieces, totalling 1,510 pieces per dining car. With over 175 dining car services per day and allowing two journeys per car and only one fully kitted dining car per train (an underestimate), with say 87 cars this results in 131,000 pieces of tableware.

There were 40 hotels in 1923 and 28 in 1939. The larger ones are believed to have served up to 2,000 meals a day. Assuming a medium size hotel dining room seated 60 at one sitting, at least 2,000 pieces would be needed, assuming some 20 to 30 pieces per person. With place settings for soup, starter, fish/meat, dessert, cheese, coffee, water/wine plus all the vegetables, gravy, sauces, condiments, flower holders, menu holders and the like it is easy to account for over 20 pieces per person. If 30 hotels only had 2,000 pieces each, there would be 60,000 pieces, but many hotels would have had a lot more so we can say 100,000 pieces very easily and probably a lot more.

On LMS ships, of which there were 65 in the mid-1930s (not counting dredgers etc) assuming only 30 prepared meals, catering for say the equal of two dining cars at a sitting, this would give some 90,000 pieces.

On dry land again, there were 134 refreshment rooms, dining rooms and tea rooms — see the picture of Rugby refreshment room in Twell's *LMS Miscellany*, Vol 2. If they averaged out at twice the complement for a dining car, giving say 3,000 items, there would have been 100,000 items, giving surely a conservative total, at a mid-point estimate of some 420,000 items!

China, glass, pottery and silver plate is one of the major 'growth' areas in railwayana collecting at present. This has happened since about 1984. Prior to this, few people collected it enthusiastically, but all this has changed. It is especially exciting as many unknown items keep appearing and each sends tremors through the market with prices rocketing and then falling back as more examples appear.

Apart from share certificates, heraldry and locomotives probably some of the finest designs to be seen on the railways were in the form of tableware as we shall show. We have items marked 'hotels', 'dining and refreshment cars', 'refreshment rooms', 'steamships' and a limited amount used by railway dining clubs and lastly, rougher ware used in hotels and staff canteens. With the

59 Tureen, lid and stand from the Great North of Scotland Railway

smaller lines, these department sub-divisions did not exist. Very little has been written or photographed on this subject, save for Rex Blaker's excellent contribution in *Railway Relics and Regalia* (Country Life 1975) where pictures of forty-one items can be found.

Companies presently known to have marked any of their tableware are as follows:

Caledonian, Cambrian, Carlisle Citadel Station Committee, Furness, Great Central, Great Eastern, Great Northern, Great Northern & Great Eastern Joint, Great North of Scotland, Great Western, Glasgow & South Western, Highland, London Brighton & South Coast, London Chatham & Dover, Lancashire & Yorkshire, Lancashire & Yorkshire & London North Western Joint, London & North Western, London & South Western, Midland, Midland & Great Northern Joint, Manchester, Sheffield & Lincolnshire, North British, North Eastern, North Stafford, South Eastern & Chatham. Also East Coast Joint Stock, West Coast Joint Stock and the post-grouping companies.

Most of the pre-grouping companies did not have any marked items. Some of the others seem to have done very little. For example, the total number of North Staffordshire Railway items so far known is less than five; the Furness Railway is known so far only for cutlery and one crested plate as is the GN & GE Joint. The Cambrian Railway so far has cups and saucers only, while the M & GNJR has little so far save teapots and a cup and saucer.

There are several obvious reasons for such scarcity: some lines had no dining cars of their own, no company hotels or steamships so items could only be used in refreshment and dining rooms. Such a case was the M & GNJR whose possibilities for refreshment were very limited as it went through largely rural areas. Indeed, its wares were directly produced in the same pattern as one of its owners, the GNR. The Furness Railway and the NSR were both small local lines without dining cars of their own and each owning only one or two hotels. On the other hand, the Great North of Scotland, another strictly regional line, made some masterpieces, many of which survive against enormous odds. Most have come from the efforts of one celebrated GNSR collector whose efforts

60 *(left)* Three types of LNER cups

61 *(below)* Cake dish from an LNER blue and gold service

62 *(bottom)* Plate from an LNER Steamships service

were auctioned by Phillips in Glasgow in 1985. Prior to that several wonderful pieces found their way into English hands. **Fig 59** shows a Great North of Scotland tureen with three separate GNSR crests, complete with lid and stand; one of the finest surviving are marked GNSR forks from Aberdeen Hotel, a metal egg cup and a kidney shaped dessert dish. As to the value, the latter in an auction would almost certainly go into three figures and the tureen much higher.

Consider now a company with a very large output — the LNER. We are still at the stage of classifying basic types of chinaware. The most beautiful is surely the blue and gold rimmed hotel pattern with interlaced scroll letters (**Fig 61**). There is a similar design of GN & GE plate. There also exists an LNER semi-circular cheese/dessert dish and soup bowl and a chamber pot. It is hoped that sideplates, cups and saucers, will also turn up.

Other presumed services in various patterns exist. One has interlaced scroll letters in blue with narrow and wider blue rim lines. At present only a coffee cup and a tea cup are known. Another type has 'LNER Refreshment Department' in a blue lozenge pattern. (**Fig 60**). There are also the common straight black, and black scroll lettered examples seen on cups, saucers, plates, soup plates, teapots, pint pots and egg cups. Another type, looking like steam-

ship or hotel ware has a double rim, with LNER in a garter. This is so far extremely rare. A further type is found in a cup

Plate 1 Cast-iron fire hydrant practice sign, formerly at Stalybridge Joint Station (GCR & LNWR Joint). *(MRM)*

Plate 2 Blue enamel booking office notice from the Great Northern Railway. *(Paul Tilley Collection)*

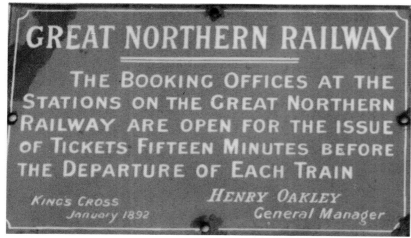

Plate 3 Coloured station totems, with examples from most of the British Railways regions. Bourne End is one of the four stations that had black totems before the regional colours were adopted. *(Paul Tilley Collection)*

Plate 4 Parcels stamps from the North British Railway, GER, Midland Railway, NER, Lancashire & Yorkshire Railway, LNWR, GWR and Great Northern Railway. *(MRM)*

with low sides and scroll letters. There also exist several items from the GCR & LNER transitional period marked LNER.GC; a later service is marked LNER Steamships (see **Fig 62**) in blue (GCR pattern) and various GC patterns marked Marylebone. Yet another is a blue Minton design with interlaced letters, with a prominent 'E'. An LNER Grimsby Social & Athletic Department sideplate exists as does a type with 'Marine Department' on the base. There are also Kesick and Keswick services. Therefore at least twelve different types are in existence!

The GWR seems to have had a much more restricted range although it had variations marked 'Hotels', 'Dining Cars' and 'Refreshment Department' as well as for stations. It had script letters and roundel patterns with black letters. Cream jugs, cups, saucers, egg cups, side, dinner and soup plates and teapots exist but are not very common so far. There are also cups and saucers with the words 'return to Paddington' in brown or black in a curve (**Fig 63**). Other stations marked are Oxford and Reading, these having coats of arms as well. Pint mugs exist in various scripts. Another service is blue-rimmed with base marking. Yet another pattern has 'GWR' in a diamond at the top of the item (an example is in Didcot Small Relics Museum). There is also a pattern consisting of two brown and one blue circle inside the rim of soup bowls, plates and on a teapot, the latter having full crest and title both on the lid and on the side. An ornate service existed, base marked, with blue rim and a complex serrated pattern in gold.

The Southern Railway by comparison had far more variety, colour and interest due to its steamer fleet and its various divisions. There are also several transi-

63 GWR cups

64 A Southern Railway Central Division plate

tionals from its constituents. A common type shows the house flag of the shipping service. Cream jugs, meat dishes, soup bowls, cups and saucers, sugar bowls and side plates are already known and this service is notable for the variety of colours used. A third sort has the company name in block black letters, marked 'Central Division'. A dinner plate is known of this type, and the common block lettered tea cup probably goes with this (see **Fig 64**). There are also items marked SE Division and various articles ex-SR hotels, eg water

65 *(left)* GCR dinner plate from Grimsby

66 *(right)* LNWR refreshment room milk jug

67 *(below)* LNWR refreshment room plate

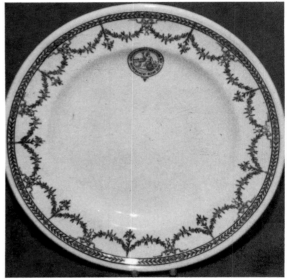

jugs (Charing Cross Hotel) and various types of crested china ashtrays.

Only limited amounts of GNR china are known so far. There are extremely common brown milk jugs, fairly common brown teapots (marked both 'Refreshment Department' and 'Dining Cars'), a cup, saucer and side plate with 'GNR Refreshment Department' in blue and a coffee cup and saucer. Half and 1-pint milk jugs marked 'GNR Station Hotel Lincoln' exist. Divided white condiment trays marked GNR are also known as well as some marked GN & GC, which are the same as those produced for the NER. There was also a GNR Temperance Society and a side-plate is known from this service.

Far more survives from the GCR which produced some of the most desirable of all china. Most famed is the blue rimmed service of which the full size dinner plates, plus a smaller version, and the side plates and saucers are not uncommon (**Fig 65**). There are also Grimsby gravy boats. One type has the coat of arms in a garter, another has the scrolled inscription below with Grimsby named. A third service has a brown rim and the letters GCR in a scroll, but no crest. As stated above, there were many transitional LNER forms. A GCR earthenware inkwell is in existence, together with an egg cup, a five-compartment horizontal condiment holder marked 'GCR Grimsby', a 'Mansfield' marked side plate and 'Guide Bridge' and 'Manchester' items.

The LNWR was very productive indeed with its many wares coming to light since 1986 and now becoming available. Previously, little was known. It had a policy of naming many station refresh-

68 *(right)* Midland Railway vegetable tureen and chamberpot

69 *(below)* NER cup from Harrogate Station

ment rooms on the side, and this adds to its interest. So far, Euston, Rugby, Birmingham New Street, Crewe, Preston, Carlisle , Coventry, Walsall and Greenore are known and there will be others. One brown pattern has the company name in an oval with the station name between, while a second has a triple brown-lined rim with Britannia, but no station. So far, sugar bowls, finger bowls, teapots and milk jugs of many sizes are known (**Fig 66**), the latter in 2in, 3in, and 6in diameter sizes. There are also cream tots with no handles of 2in and 2½in diameter. Butter dishes 3½ x 5in exist along with pint mugs, egg cups and divided cheese/pickle trays.

A third pattern has black script letters 'Property of LNWR Ret to Euston' known in cup form. A fourth, more decorative, is the grey/blue intertwined motif around and inside the rim, with

Britannia in garter at the top. Side plates, dinner and soup plates are in existence, together with teapots and a 6in milk jug (**Fig 67**). A fifth has LNWR in letters at the top of a scroll, with the station name inside, and is light blue. There is also a sixth pattern with two red bands, a seventh with straight sides (only a cup known so far), and eighth with a serrated base to the cup, and a ninth is the (first class hotels?) red and green flowered pattern of which a teapot has been seen. A tenth pattern, found on a hotel hot water jug, has Britannia in a scroll with a gold broad rim top and a narrow base rim of gold.

The Midland Railway has had very little recovered so far. There is a fairly common cup and saucer marked 'Midland' in red in block letters and a small ornate cream jug. There is also a dinner plate with the garter and name in the centre of the plate. There was an ornate service (see **Fig 68**) with intertwined MRC in red letters plus gold rims, seen on chamber pots and vegetable tureens, which must have been for the hotel service, passing across into an LMS successor. There is another design seen in a soup dish, with a black rim and gold band (hotels?) which goes with the ornate MR toothbrush holders.

NER has so far shown quite a variety of station-named ware with York and Harrogate seen so far. Its items are divided into hotel department, refresh-

70 *(left)* NER divided condiment tray

71 *(below)* NER chamber pot with coloured crest

72 *(bottom)* NER dessert dish with coloured crest

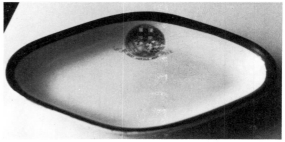

ment department and refreshment rooms. Patterns known are the bold style dull red colour on station tea cups (**Fig 69**). A second has a double and single blue rim with scroll NER between, seen on a soup dish. Two types of divided condiment/pickle trays exist, one marked 'Refreshment Department', (**Fig 70**), the other 'Refreshment Rooms' (horizontal). They are often marked 'York'. These are black lettered and a cup also exists of this type. A chamber pot with coloured crest marked 'NE Hotels Dept.' (**Fig 71**) is known, together with soup bowls, tea cups and dessert dishes (**Fig 72**), a small cream jug and butter pot and a small brown teapot. There was a black letter NER hotels wide water bowl and a well known NER black scroll letter large and small bowl.

The LYR seems to have had little tableware preserved. There are cups and saucers marked 'Return to Liverpool' and 'Bolton' and one service had a blue rim with full crest and the company name in garter on the rim. Of this, a vegetable tureen and a base is known. From the Cambrian Railway, only 'Return to Welshpool' cups and saucers are known, with the company motif. The Caledonian Railway is, so far, sparse, with a cup and saucer marked 'Return to Callender', a 3½in butter dish marked Glasgow Central, and a soup bowl as its few examples. Carlisle Citadel Station Committee produced a marked cup and saucer and 3½in butter dishes. GER items are little known so far, one pattern having a full title scroll of which a soup

dish exists. A cup and saucer and a small, beautiful, light blue crested jug turned up in 1988. GSWR had a blue lettered scroll pattern and examples are known on side and dinner plates, a crested sugar bowl and cup and saucer. Examples are known marked 'Dumfries' and 'Hotels'.

The Highland Railway had a cup and saucer marked with its full title, and a superb crested chamber pot. Examples from the LSWR are also little known so far. Many items were marked 'South Western Railway' (as were its silver items). The name is in red as on 3in cream jugs and egg cups. MSLR is known for coffee saucers with coat of arms and red letters. The SECR produced a fine crested brown coloured cream jug and cup and saucer marked with the company name crescent pattern dessert dish and sugar bowl. The LCDR is known so far for a cup and saucer with crest and name in a vertical oval. The ECJS and WCJS items were of GNR, LNWR or Caledonian pattern.

Apart from pre-grouping transitions, the chinaware of the LMS seems plain and unimaginative. The transitional pieces include a red/green flower pattern of which teapots, and cups and saucers are known and also a large dining club type in a dining club sugar bowl. This was almost certainly a successor to the LNWR pattern 9 (see under LNWR). Another was the Midland pattern interlaced scroll hotel service (see under Midland) with red letters and gold rim. Rex Blaker relates (p113 *Railway Relics & Regalia*) how the Crewe Arms had water jugs, toothbrush holders, soap dishes and basins from this service in every bedroom.

LMS brown cream tots (base mark) were a copy of the Midland type. Red and brown 'Return to Euston' cups are common, a follow-on from LNWR and in Scotland, St Enoch ware was marked LMS (GSWR) until 1925. There are

73 LMS ashtray

black, green, red, blue and brown block-lettered cups and saucers, together with probably similar sideplates, dinner and soup plates. A black block letter steamer-type exists in a soup, side and dinner plate. A more attractive laurel scroll pattern (hotels) exists in black and bold letters. There is a blue seahorse motif type without company let-

74 A collection of railway chamberpots

75 A collection of LNER cups and saucers

76 LNER Kesick/Keswick ware

ters and a sloping scroll letter (bottom left to top right with letters hardly touching) existing in egg cups. (There are at least three different types of LMS egg cup.)

An unusual ceramic ashtray with purple brown rim marked 'LMS Hotels' was a continuation of a Midland pattern (**Fig 73**). One of the few pleasing original LMS designs had the name in garter on the coffee cup and saucer with blue rim. For sheer ugliness, the wooden spoon must go to the brown ceramic teapot with letters LMS crudely written across. Was this for use in company canteens, or during wartime conditions? It should be noted that there were considerable amounts of base marked LMS white-ware, and various flower patterned green/red ware with top name.

One of the acmes of china collecting is

to build up a collection of like items, and we end this section by looking at three such groups. **Fig 74** shows part of probably the largest collection of chamber pots in existence (Rogers' Collection), including two LMS types, LMSR (NCC), Midland Railway, Midland Railway Hotels, LNER, GER and NER Hotels. **Fig 75** shows six types of LNER cups, including three vertical block letter types, scroll and lozenge in blue (Gordon Blears Collection). **Fig 76** shows a group of LNER Kesick/Keswick ware items (Gordon BlearsCollection).

Glassware

Glass railwayana mainly comprises drinking glasses, beer and other bottles, inkwells, ashtrays, condiment pots, etched station and carriage glass and mirrors. Companies known to have

77 *(right)* A collection of railway tableware and glass-ware

78 *(below)* LMS and South-ern Railway drinking glasses, and an LNER spirits tot

produced marked glassware include: GCR, GER, GNR, GN & GEJR, GN & GC, GWR, LMS, LNER, LNWR, LSWR, LYR,

Midland Railway, NER, SR, and in post 1948 times, the Hotels Executive and different British Railways regions especially Eastern Region.

Without doubt the most common articles to have survived are railway bottles and drinking glasses. Old dining car pictures show large numbers of drinking glasses, but pictures of beer bottles in use are rarely seen, probably because the companies did not wish to show them, especially on lines with official company temperance societies, such as the GWR and GNR.

Beer bottles were rare until about 1986 when tip digging began to yield large numbers. **Colour Plate 6** shows clear and green $\frac{1}{2}$-pint bottles from the LMS, GCR, LYR and Midland Hotel, Derby. Almost all were $\frac{1}{2}$-pint and this size can be assumed in this discussion. LMS and LNER (who had three green types and one clear) are very common

79 *(above)* LNER glass and silver salt, pepper and mustard pots

80 *(right)* Midland Railway presentation cruet set

now, although others, even GWR and SR are at present very rare. They are usually green/brown but some are clear. It is very rare for them to be found with a glass stopper, although these do exist. MSLR, LNWR and NER examples are known. Some are station marked, eg LYR Liverpool, GWR Birmingham and Fishguard, but most have no depot. It is clear from the above that railway bottle collecting is in its infancy as we are still classifying and finding, so when any rare item emerges the price for one bottle goes high.

Wine carafes were once common items on hotel and dining car tables. They are known from the GWR (at least three types), Midland Railway, GER, SEC and LNER and there is no doubt whatever that many of the major companies made them and a fair number have survived. Company letters were usually on the bulbous base. Decanters survive marked GCR, LNER and GNR. Ordinary drinking glasses are relatively plentiful and most attractive. **Fig 78** shows 'LMS Cars' with a laurel leaf, 5¾in tall, ¾-pint, and SR garter of which latter there were three sizes, this being the medium.

There were three LMS sizes as well with some having plain letters 'LMS Cars/Hotels'. These LMS and SR types appear to be the most common drinking glasses. LNER examples are much rarer. GWR drinking glasses are also rare and are made of heavier glass marked 'GWR Hotels', etc. There are examples also known from NER, GN & GEJR, Midland Railway, NBR and LCDR.

It is already certain that between them the companies produced most of the glass types to be seen today in ordinary hotels and bars. Sherry glasses are known from the LNWR, marked Euston, and the GWR, while the LNER had a scroll type stem glass. BTH (British Transport Hotels) continued the tradition with a post-1948 brandy glass. A pre-group example of this from the

81 A collection of railway inkwells in glass, stoneware and pewter

Midland Railway is known. Whisky tots or tumblers must have been common. GCR ones are known and of course wine glasses must have been fairly universal both in hotels and dining cars and would have existed in much larger numbers than spirit glasses. There appear to be few survivors; however, GER, GNR and GWR wine glasses have been seen during 1986-7, while a set of six LNER long-stemmed hock glasses have also survived.

Fairly common are the small pepper, salt and mustard pots (**Fig 79**) from the LNER. They are inscribed with small script letters in the EPNS top. Mustard pots had tiny inscribed spoons and some from GSWR, LNER and NER are known. They would have been a standard table item, confirmed by all photographs. We deal with cruet holders below, but many companies had silver condiment sets, glass being in the minority. Presentation glass cruet sets exist, eg **Fig 80**, a four-piece set of Midland Railway vintage. Cruet holders almost invariably lack their original glass/silver pots, having been separated over the years by regular use. Jam/butter dishes were used by the LNER.

A common piece of glassware on the Midland Railway was the seemingly ubiquitous whisky flask. The Midland

Railway was one of the pioneers of packed pre-bookable hamper meals (pre-dating restaurant cars) and from their very common whisky flasks marked 'Mid. H. Derby' obviously did not have a temperance society! There was also a very rare upright pattern flask. Whisky flasks are also known from the MSLR and GCR.

It is still possible to see on today's stations the last survivors of the once common etched station glass windows. A beautiful example is preserved in Bressingham Small Relics Museum with Mersey Railway etched in full. There is a blue 'Smoking' sign etched in GER glass in existence and it was quite common for the glass of the first and second class ladies, and gentlemen's waiting rooms to be etched. Once inside the latter, our forebears were able to admire themselves in company-marked waiting room mirrors of a wide variety. It is now obvious that many companies marked their mirrors, for instance examples from the NBR, Highland and NSR have all been seen recently. Often the initials were in the top of the glass. A common survivor is the compartment mirror, the best being a pleasing LNER oval type. There are other LNER patterns and a common rectangular LMS type.

Glass inkwells, pre-dating fountain

'Landmine'	'Kettle'	Pewter	Porcelain	Glass
GWR	MR	TVR	LMS	GER edge marked
LNWR	LMS	RR		GER top centre marked
LMS	SECR	NER		GER domed etched
LMS glazed	GCR	GCR		LNER domed etched
LMSR	BR(M)	MSLR		GWR 'Go Great Western'
		GNR		GWR
				LMS etched
				GCR domed and lip etched
				GCR domed etched
				LNER Co embossed
				NER Co embossed
				NER Co etched (top cut)
				BR(E) etched under base
				NER Co etched
				MR Co etched lip
				MR Co etched under base (LMS style)
				MR Co with brass top
				GNR

Known types of Railway Inkwells

pens and ball-point pens, were a standard company item, but probably little seen by the public as they were used in goods and booking offices. As so often happened each company had its own pattern. **Fig 81** shows the Chris Atkin Collection of railway inkwells. The two circular GCR patterns were surely the most pleasing. Above is a classification by Mr David Hughes of known inkwells. It must be noted that some of these are in materials other than glass.

The above shows that more companies are absent than present but it is certain that most must have used inkwells as an every day item! Another item of glassware although very few survive, was the flower vase. One example is in the Rogers' Collection showing an SR shipping line flag pattern.

Two other classes of glassware were station lamp names and battery acid containers. Of the latter GWR and MR ones are known. Of the former, company articles are known from NER, GWR, SEC, GCR, LYR & GNR Joint, SR and Garstang & Knott End Railway.

Silverware (EPNS or silverplate)
In general, there was little of this available until some three years ago when Messrs Onslows, the London auctioneers agreed a deal with Travellers' Fare whereby the 'Great Silver Tomb of St Pancras' should be auctioned off. This name arose from the article by Julian Hanwell of Norfolk in *The Railwayana Journal — On The Line* Issue 8, Sept 1986, where he related a visit made to St Pancras' vaults where thousands of items of pre- and post-grouping railway silverware had been sent and stored. He and J.P.A. Mullinger appear to have been two of the very few people to have seen this largely unknown horde, though items from it were sold in the 1970s through Collectors' Corner. As a scene setter, we reprint part of the St Pancras saga by kind permission of the author:

Some years ago I was working in London. By pure chance I met a gentleman who informed me that BR were selling some silverplate from the Hotels. As I used LNER Hotels as a young man in business, I knew of its splendid quality and so bought some.

'Where did you go, Sir?' I asked.

'St Pancras Chambers. The Headquarters of British Rail's Travellers' Fare. Everybody knew about it — there were enough people there'.

'Collectors? Who?'

'Collectors and some Americans. I remember a Yank. This one had cash and he bought a load of silverplate. I bought what you see now'.

'How long ago was that?' I asked.

'About ten years ago. The place was like Egypt'.

During the following six months I could not help thinking about that tomb. Did it still exist? I decided to investigate the possibilities when next visiting London. I did not have to wait long. A deal involving a Southern collector who has also heard tales of glittering relics in the St Pancras vault brought both of us on the trail. My fellow colleague fixed up the necessary appointment and the BR representative told us,

'Yes, there are quite a few items left if you would like to follow me'.

His hand reached far into a drawer and took out a dusty key. He took us onto a stairway which led down. I seem to remember an old-fashioned lift with concertina doors. At the bottom, a quick flick of a switch and the lights were on. We were in a room full of blankets! We walked towards a door at the other end of the passage. The moment had come. Was the tomb intact? The door swung open.

'You've got half an hour. This side Great Western. Over there LMS and LNER. On the right Southern. See you later.'

Our eyes just gazed about us. That little room was stacked high with shelf after shelf of pre-grouping and post-grouping silverplate. Hundreds of pieces all over the place. We had to tread carefully to avoid damaging items left on the floor. I grabbed a GWR Dining Car coffee pot.

'That's a good piece', shouted my friend as he swarmed through the Southern shelves. Next came a GWR Hotels tray with the GWR coat of arms in the centre, then a teapot, jug and sugar bowl, all with the GWR garter with 'Refreshment Rooms' or 'Dining Car' engraved underneath. Other items included an LNER sugar caster, GER milk jug and a GWR condiment stand.

In what seemed only a moment later, our guide

82 Great Central Railway biscuit barrel

83 Southern Railway coffee pot and LMS teapot

once more appeared and told us that our time had run out. Unfortunately there wasn't enough time to inspect the dozens of ice dishes, champagne buckets, salvers, meat dishes, bowls, gravy boats, coffee pots, tea pots, knives, forks, spoons and so on.... And so the great tomb was once more sealed until recently, when Onslows began their Paddington auctions. I believe they will tell you the rest....

Collectors are much more aware of what existed in railwayana silver than is

85 *(left)* LNER silver plate 'Coronation' tea pots

86 *(below)* LNER silver plate spirit stove

the case in china, as a good cross section has already 'come out' via Onslows' auctions. Generally, valuation is by aesthetic qualities and rarity of items regardless of company.

In general, apart from the Cambrian Railway and the M & GNJR, the companies that produced china tableware also produced it in silver.

Share the aura of the GSWR Steamers tureen (**Colour Plate 7**). This is a humble tureen by function, but its design makes it an elegant piece of silverware. The top has the full coat of arms in garter, containing the full company name with letter 'S' underneath denoting steamers. All around is a scrolled leaf pattern, and around the handle a beaded oval. It is very rare to get the handle with the lid. Imagine its daily life in the dining room of one of the GSWR paddle steamers shown in official postcards, rolling around the Kyles of Bute, slipping out of Ardrossan, Wemyss and Greenock with dense smoke pall churn-

ing, GSWR steward in formal dress taking the order from a company menu and you have the essence of the railway scene.

In the same photograph, is shown another Scottish railway item, a Caledonian Railway 1-pint coffee pot with letters 'C' and 'R' intertwined. This is a

87 *(right)* LSWR sugar bowls, and a Southern Railway 'electric flash' soup bowl

88 *(below)* GER silver plate tureen with lid

rarity as there are few Caledonian Railway silver survivors of any sort. Coffee pots are perhaps the most avidly collected of all silverware due to their tall elegance. Also in the photograph is the delightful small LMS menu holder with full company name and central emblem, and the LMS soup tureen. We are looking at works of art in metal: it is no wonder that railway silverware is found a pride of place in many railway lovers' front rooms.

Fig 82 shows one of the most delightful silver antiques, a GCR biscuit barrel with the full company name in a top arc, 'Dining Car' below and the full company crest between, the barrel being set into a rimmed base and with a detachable top. Most GCR silver items have almost lost their crests due to constant cleaning; happily the biscuit barrels have kept theirs. There can only be a tiny handful in existence, the present writer has seen just two. Tall 2-pint coffee pots are shown in **Colour Plate 8** (GWR) and

Fig 83 (SR) both very rare. Neither has figured in any of the Onslows sales of silverplate which *ipso facto* measures their rarity.

Fig 84 shows one of the great range of LNER silverplate. There seems to be more silverware from the LNER than any other pre- or post-group company, for reasons not yet known. The letters were well impressed, so LNER items have 'worn well' in the test of time, unlike other company plate. The two patterns, from two different services, all in script letters can be seen well, with three of the items being different-sized milk jugs, a $\frac{1}{2}$-pint teapot and two sizes of hot water jug.

Fig 85 shows coronation-style $\frac{1}{2}$- and 1-pint teapots with stepped block letters of the late 1930s. There is, of course, a complete service in this style, with various capacity coffee pots, hot water and milk jugs, sugar bowls, and much, much more. While the LMS plate varied widely between hotels, steamers and dining cars, the LNER plate generally seems to be varied only between styles.

A great rarity is shown in **Fig 86**, a spirit stove which dismantles. This was used at hotel tables, and only two LNER examples are known so far. The GER was famed for the breadth and quality of its silverware; **Fig 88** shows an ornate tureen with base and lid both marked and with a top handle. It seems likely that only a handful of complete ex-

89 *(left)* A display of GWR silver plate and chinaware

90 *(below left)* Silver plate LYR jam holder, GNR circular dish, with a tankard and a GWR sundae dish

91 *(below right)* NER muffin dish and lid

amples still survive, as none have been seen in Onslows auctions. The best collections of GER plate are on display at Steamtown Carnforth and at Fawley Railway Museum, Henley-on-Thames.

Sugar bowls and soup tureens are shown in **Fig 87**. Probably every company had sugar bowls, usually with two handles, so they are very common. Soup tureens were used on hotel and dining room tables and are quite rare, especially those of good condition. The example here is of the SR 'electric flash' style used in the 1930s as an advertising symbol on cutlery and large items, but not on chinaware.

Passing now to GWR wares, there are very large amounts of cutlery and salvers of many sizes, sundae dishes, sugar bowls and a fair number of tankards, but far fewer pint and 2-pint tea

and coffee pots. This is due to the low number of GWR hotels, and the far lower number of restaurant car routes compared with the LMS & LNER.

Fig 89 shows a GWR galaxy at the Big Four Railway Museum, Bournemouth and includes the common teapot and a more bulbous and extremely rare second pattern (far left). The juxtaposition of these fully restored memories of yesteryear almost recreates the atmosphere of the diners and hotel rooms. Another great rarity is in **Fig 90** an LYR jam holder resting on a GNR dining car circular dish, and flanked by a tankard and sundae dish. This is how the tables actually looked as perusal of period photographs shows vividly. The pictures of the insides of GWR 1938 64ft buffet cars and twelve-wheel 1938 diners, and the set tables in 1905/14 stock

92 *(right)* LNER silver plate
'Coronation' egg cup and
tray, NER coffee pot, NER
brass measure and LNER
chinaware egg cup

93 *(below)* LNER salt, pepper
and mustard pots, and tea
strainer

speak volumes — see Russell (*op cit* pp 215-7). Especially of interest is Fig 331 showing the place setting per person, namely five forks, five knives, two spoons, wine bottle holder, cruet holder, menu, napkins and tablecloth, with a GWR carpet in Fig 330 plus antimacassars and tablelamps. Figs 320-2 show two patterns of GWR tea urns and platform buffet attendants, as well as GWR teapots, marked jugs and cups and saucers. Fig 321 possibly shows the famous GWR wine bottle.

Fig 91 shows a North Eastern Railway crested and gartered muffin dish and lid, an uncommon conjunction as lids and bases can only normally be purchased separately, and matching by accident is almost unheard of! More rarities in silverplate in **Fig 92**, an LNER coronation ware egg cup with a depression for the salt in the tray base, with another LNER egg cup and a tall NER 2-pint coffee pot, shown together with an NER brass measure. One of the *pièces de résistance* of railway silverplate, is a highly decorated punch bowl, inscribed 'LNWR Queen's Hotel Birmingham'.

This section is concluded by looking at **Fig 93** showing an LNER tea strainer, mustard, pepper and salt pots, all marked with the company's initials and all to be found in the Gordon Blears Collection.

The following is an an inventory of what railway silverplate existed, to enable the serious EPNS collector to build up a large range: asparagus dish with grid and fork, biscuit barrel, bread boat, butter knife, cake tongs/slice, cake stand, cake knife and fork, candlestick holder, chop dish, coffee pot, condiment/cruet stand,. cups, trophies, medals, dessert spoon, divided vegetable dish and lid, egg cup with and without stand, entrée dish and lid, fish knife and fork and fish slice, flower holder, glass holder, grapefruit dish, grape scissors, gravy boat, ham stand, hot water jug, horlicks mixer, icecream dish, ice bucket, jam holder, lobster pick, matchbox holder/striker, meat dish with lid, meat knife and fork, menu holder, milk jug, muffin dish and lid, mustard spoon, nutcracker, oyster fork, pepper pot/mill, pickle fork, punch bowl & ladle, soup tureen, salt pot and spoon, salver with and without feet, soup spoon and ladel, spirit stove, spirit measure, sugar bowl, sugar caster, sugar tongs, sundae dish, sweet bowl, teapots, tea strainer, toast rack, trays, tureens.

A final mention must be made of some of the more remarkable survivors. Several silverplate items marked 'GN & MSL Joint', believed to be from Manchester Central, a Highland Railway soup ladle, GNSR teapot and a gravy boat, together with a GSWR candlestick holder (all marked) are to be found in the Atkin Collection. An LNWR candlestick holder has been found recently.

There is every indication, therefore, that we shall see even more treasures like these come to light in the future.

Kitchen and Dining Car Wares

Very few photographs exist of dining car and hotel kitchens. Some of the best are in Russell *op cit*, pp213-14. The early dining car kitchens were gas fired and gas lit and cooking was done in cast-iron ovens with long panels of gas rings above with all the utensils stacked on a rack up the wall. It is worth requoting a 1914 GWR menu, produced in these dark, cramped, swaying conditions, using wood working surfaces and without any modern electric mixers or cutters whatsoever:

Soup Crème Charolaise
Fish Cod with Oyster Sauce
Roast Beef & Horseradish and Vegetables
Apple Tart. Aromatic Pudding
Cheese and Biscuits
Coffee

Remembering that an early dining car would seat twenty, later ones over thirty, so at one sitting there were that number of four-course meals needed at one time, plus wine, and all the washing up afterwards, prior to a second and sometimes a third sitting and you may well wonder how such an exercise was possible.

94 A GWR restaurant car copper pan

95 A copper pan made by Elkington for the GWR hotels

Plate 5 A colourful collection of wagon cards from the Lancashire & Yorkshire Railway, North Staffordshire Railway, M & GNJR, Southern Railway, LMS, LNER and The Cheshire Lines Committee. *(MRM)*

Plate 6 Half-pint beer bottles marked LMS Hotels, GCR, L & YR, and Midland Hotel Derby. *(MRM)*

Plate 7 Examples of railway silverware. Left to right: Caledonian Railway 1-pint coffee pot, LMS soup tureen, LMS menu holder, and G & SWR Steamers tureen. *(MRM)*

Plate 8 LNER 1-pint water jug and a 2-pint GWR coffee pot, both silver plated. *(Harpenden Railway Museum)*

96 *(below)* Annual dinner menu for the foremen and carters from the GER's Bishopsgate
Goods Depot, in 1922

97 *(above)* Annual dinner menu for the
Bishopsgate Depot's football club, 1923

The array of railwayana concerned is formidable. Soup was simmered in huge, deep two-handled containers; vegetables were boiled either in tinned or copper plated pans of many types. **Fig 94** shows a GWR copper plated pan 10in wide x 5in deep with bronze handle, marked GWR 'Rest Cars', later over-stamped BTHS. **Fig 95** shows a 6 x 7in GWR Hotels Elkington pan stamped 'P'

twice, probably for Paddington. In Moseley Railwayana Museum there is a Midland Hotels 7 x 7$\frac{1}{2}$in pan by Guillard, also of Paris and a GWR hotels tinned pan 8 x 4in with a 9in long handle, made in Italy. These show how much kitchen ware was bought in from France and Italy. The lengths of the handles are of some interest also, showing the widths of the galleys and the need to be able to reach those at the back easily. An LMS copper skillet exists in Bressingham Museum, an unusual article with a curved handle. Kitchen

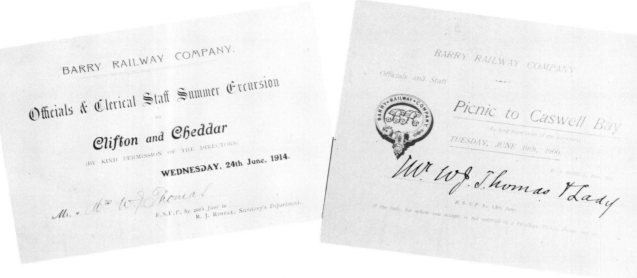

98 and **99** Two invitations to Barry Railway staff outings, 1900 and 1914

copper ware which was almost ignored by collectors 5 years ago is now avidly sought after in auctions, as its interest and rarity has been realised.

Thousands of menu cards must have been used in restaurant cars. Early GWR ones were inside an ornate leather cover, but by the 1930s seem to have been smaller and placed often in marked silver menu holders. The tradition carried on into BR days with the named trains having their own special menus. **Figs 96** and **97** shows two unusual menus from 1922 and 1923, both feature Bishopsgate Goods Depot on the old GER out of Liverpool St. The 1922 menu shows the use of company hotels, the Garibaldi at Great Yarmouth being the venue, 'with all to retire at 11.30pm and Lights Out at 12 midnight'! This occasion was limited to 'Cartage Foremen and Goods Carters', ie just one GER department at one depot! The 1923 Football Club Dinner shows the transition to LNER. At Winchcombe Railway Museum there is a whole book full of

special menus for internal company functions, including the following GNR ones: Police Department anniversary dinner 1899, GNR Mint Street employees, GNR goods department, GNR London agents, also, GWR CME personnel dinner. A 1929 GWR menu is to be found at Harpenden Railway Museum. A whole series of Barry Railways annual staff outing cards has been unearthed, not actually menu cards, but something allied to them (**Figs 98** and **99**).

Besides menus, every place was set with a napkin, usually marked, often in red handsewn letters. Harpenden Railway Museum has an LMS hotels and LMS first class one, together with an LMS coffee pot base cloth, while there are several types of GWR brown lettered hotels/dining cars ones at Didcot.

Stewards and wine waiters would have carried marked glass cloths over their arms while serving, and a reasonable number of these are preserved, although almost all are the various types used by the LNER and LMS, usually with red initials sewn on white.

The marking of company equipment with its name or insignia even went as far as lavatory and toilet fittings, such as toilet roll holders. The well-known ones are those used by the GWR and LMS. The LMS type was almost identical to one used by its predecessor the LNWR, while British Rail had a similar one for a short period. The GWR Thiefproof Dreadnought is far more famous than pleasant to look at, as it was in use to prevent the theft of company toilet paper. A roll of GWR toilet paper exists at Winchcombe Railway Museum, every piece marked. An LNER roll survives in the Rogers' Collection.

First class, and on a few lines, second class passenger backs and heads rested against company antimacassars. The Midland Railway used them and there are plenty of pictures of GWR ones, while the Southern Railway had several different patterns. GWR and GNR types have recently been seen, but to date there are few survivors, which is a cause for regret, as many were *objets d'art* with prominent company motifs.

An addendum to this section is taken from the official *LMS Magazine* for February 1927 where some of the Euston dining car staff are pictured under the control of the Assistant Controller LMS Hotel Services and the Dining Car Superintendent (Western Division) and the Head Dining Car Chef (Western Division). In 1927 there were 138 daily dining car trains on the line. In one year were served, in the cars alone (not counting all the other catering services): 500,000 cauliflowers, 20,000 ducks, 5,000 pheasants, 1,800,000 rolls and teacakes, 150,000 gallons of soup, 10,000 partridge, 400 tons of meat, 50,000 chickens, 5,000 grouse, 500 tons of fish, 500,000 eggs, and in 1935 there were 7,037 LMS employees engaged in catering services alone.

4

Locomotive, Wagon and Carriage Railwayana

It is extremely likely that most of the entire railwayana collecting movement of today was launched due to the enthusiasm for steam locomotives. There is little doubt that if most readers of this book ask themselves for the ten most vivid memories of railways of 20, 30 or 40 years ago they would emerge with ten visions of particular steam-hauled trains. Research into teenage notebooks would produce engine numbers. They would rarely produce any notes on the majority of the contents of this book, not because the latter were not there for the seeing, but because boys, young men and a very few girls and young women went to station depots and track venues to be thrilled at the sights and sounds of steam. So the subject of locomotive railwayana is of crucial importance to the overall theme of this book and it is of some surprise to find just how rare many of these items actually are.

The main items available are as follows: builders' plates, cabside plates, gauges, miscellaneous plates, nameplates, shed plates, smokebox numbers, tender plates and whistles.

Builders' Plates

To illustrate the scarcity of builders' plates data spanning twenty-seven auctions can be used from 1985 to early 1987. This does not include private transactions which would obviously increase the numbers but such a large number of auctions in all parts of the UK involving over 15,000 lots does give an accurate picture. Readers should note that in 1987-8, the sale of builders' plates has dramatically increased.

The numbers of plates from private firms building steam locomotives have been as follows (ignoring for the present private diesel plates and British Railways steam and diesel plates):

Andrew Barclay 0
Armstrong-Whitworth 1
Avonside 1
Bagnalls 0
Beyer Peacock 2
De Winton 0
Dübs 0
Fletcher Jennings 1
Fowlers 0
Hudswell Clarke 3
Hunslet 1
Hawthorn Leslie 1
Kerr Stuart 0
Kitson 0
Manning Wardle 0
Neilson 0
North British Locomotive Co 11
Peckett 2
Robert Stephenson 0
Sharp Stewart 1
Stephenson & Hawthorn 0
Vulcan 0
Yorkshire Engine Co 1

Of the twenty-three builders, save for NBL, only Hudswell Clarke shows as many as three plates with none from most firms. So for virtually half of the firms there was no possibility of acquiring any plate at any of the twenty-seven auctions, though again, many transactions proceed privately. Also there have been sales of diesel plates, eg Andrew Barclay, but the table charts steam only. There have been Fowler plates but not from steam locomotives. De Winton, of course, was only a minor builder of some sixty locomotives during 1869-97.

It is a little surprising that many of these names are so rare as the above numbers cover plates made both for the main line and industrial locomotives, as well as for foreign customers. Excellent colour pictures of some of the above were published in *Railway Relics and Regalia* (1975) showing many of the plates still *in situ*. This situation is of course no longer possible, save for preserved locomotives and re-cast plates. Some examples of recently auctioned builders' plates are given below. The great majority can be bought at under a three figure sum, but very rare old ones occasionally fetch several hundred pounds. Actual value is related to a wide range of factors.

Armstrong-Whitworth, GWR No 6654
Avonside, 1915
Beyer Peacock
Fletcher Jennings, 1877
Fowler, 1942
Hawthorn Leslie
Hudswell Clarke, No 1325
Hudswell Clarke, 1961
Hunslet No 3594
NB Locomotive Co, diamonds
NB Locomotive Co, circular off 48274, built 1942
NB Locomotive Co, LNE off 4612, built 1910
Peckett
Sharp Stewart, off Barry Railways locomotive
Yorkshire Engine Company

Plates from locomotives built by British Railways at present sell for much less than those from private builders, but as reduction of locomotive numbers goes on there is little doubt that the attraction of diesel plates will grow. The plates of the 'Big Four' companies are much sought after especially the LNER engraved examples from Darlington and Doncaster. The collectability of this type of plate was shown in January 1987 when A4 *Guillemot* (Doncaster 1937) was auctioned. This particular example had been re-engraved, some of these plates having had the wording London North Eastern Railway Co filled in during early British Railways days. The popularly known and more prolific 9 x 5in LNER plates, which are identification plates rather than builders' plates in the true sense of the word, but are accepted by collectors under this heading, are cast with raised lettering and incorporate the locomotive number as well as building details.

By far the most illustrious collection of British locomotive worksplates in existence belongs to Keith Buckle of Solihull. His history as a collector has many features in common with the great railwayana collections of Great Britain and is worth recounting. Beginning seriously in 1956, by writing to British Railways and private works, he often obtained plates, either free or virtually so; his Hawthorns & Co Leith Engine Works No 138 of 1856 being a case in point. It is believed to be the only known survivor from this works. In 1958 alone he wrote 1,096 letters! His first plate was purchased by his father for 5s (GWR cabside 3370) and was delivered free to his nearest railway station. He remembers falling over one Beardsmore plate in Derby Works. Official prices in 1956 were 1s 6d for a small Hawthorn Leslie

100 Builder's plate from Andrew Barclay and Son Ltd, Kilmarnock

plate, 2s 9d for North British Locomotive Co diamond-shaped plates and 4s 6d for smokebox plates off Barry Scrapyard locomotives.

Looking at his walls lined with hundreds of plates, the product of over 30 years searching, one sees a 'mini-Barry', the final resting place of the plates once adorning the splashers, boilers, frames and tenders of some of the proudest locomotives to pound the rails of Britain and many parts of the world. The mind's eye sees, re-created in one room, the countless forges and foundries from Glasgow and Kilmarnock, from Vulcan and Gorton, from Sheffield and Darlington — nothing less than the sum total of the greatest burst of locomotive building ever seen; and all from one small island. The collection epitomises the central aim of railwayana collecting which is to reassemble those distant products of the great railway age into a coherent whole.

To illustrate the scale of production of this one class of railwayana, we can consider locomotive building at just one town — Kilmarnock. Journey there now and apart from the Barclay's Works by the station, you would never guess that so many more works existed here at one time.

Andrew Barclay's early plates were

large red rectangles $4\frac{1}{4}$ x $8\frac{5}{8}$in marked 'Son' and then 'Sons'. By 1901, the well known large oval plates were marked 'Caledonia Works' in the centre, continuing until 1947, then replaced by oval aluminium plates. Several other variants exist, such as the rare brass small oval plates made for the Air Ministry's Calshot Light Railway locomotives. Other plates have 'limited' in italic letters, 'Kilmarnock, Scotland', 'Caledonia Foundry & Engine Works', with up to twenty-two different patterns already known, including three types of 'Rebuilt' plate. Also in Kilmarnock was the Kilmarnock Engineering Co Ltd, at their Britannia Works; Grant Ritchie, who made at least two patterns of plate (a brass oval and a rectangle with scalloped corners); Allan Andrews; Barclays & Co (a relative of Andrew Barclay, but a different firm); Barr Morrison: Dick Kerr & Co; Andrews Barr & Co and McCulloch Sons & Kennedy Ltd (**Fig 100** and **Colour Plate 10**).

There were thus no less than nine separate private builders each with very different plates, not to mention the GSWR works there in just one medium sized town. It is worth stressing that, as yet, no major work has ever been written on this very large subject and all one can hope to do is to sketch in a few examples. Fresh patterns are still emerging and there is little doubt that much more is still to be found. Well publicised has been the recovery, by underwater diving in 1986-7, of the worksplate from a Neilson-built locomotive of 1885, which went down in a shipwreck off the Scottish coast en route to Canada.

A few words of caution regarding the total number of plates are needed, rather similar to the points made later regarding handlamp number sequences. In general, the makers' num-

101 Plate from the Caledonian Railway's St Rollox Works, Glasgow

bers are a guideline to actual numbers of locomotives made. For example, Gibbs Hogg of Airdrie are believed to have made only about twenty locomotives; Thomas Green of Leeds only about thirty-eight tank locomotives, but over 200 tram locomotives, so the few steam locomotive plates are part of the general sequence. The plates of John Fowler of Leeds are almost all from diesel engines — works No 4000 10 being the tenth locomotive of type 400. Other examples of these pitfalls are plentiful.

Often the works number is the only way a plate can be linked to a specially famous engine. As we go to print, Christies are due to auction LNER No 1818 of 1935, which happens to have belonged to no less than A4 *Silver Link* and is an engraved Doncaster plate. This will be the second A4 works plate auctioned in the 12 months up to June 1988, and may well make national news media. Early plates, as noted above, are extremely rare, largely due to their being scrapped at the grouping and the lack of preservation in those days over 60 years ago. For example, in the Buckle Collection is an 1885 Caledonian Railway St Rollox plate off a Caledonian 'Pug' which is believed to be one of only two extant (**Fig 101**). Even plates from a very large

102-4 Three builder's plates from the Hyde Park Works, Glasgow, showing the transition from Neilson & Co to Neilson Reid & Co, then to become part of the North British Locomotive Co

105-7 Sharp Stewart & Co kept the same shape of locomotive builder's plate after they moved from Manchester to Glasgow, and the works kept the same design even after they became part of the North British Locomotive Co

concern like the Midland Railway are virtually never seen and the data on the numbers of known GSWR, Highland, NER and other pre-grouping plates is minimal. It is rather more surprising, however, that there are such low numbers of plates appearing in auctions from private builders such as Avonside, Vulcan and the like (see the analysis at the beginning of the chapter). One reason is that a high percentage of the

output of some firms went overseas, where they largely remain. Vulcan plates especially seem strangely rare relative to the fame and size of the company.

It remains to chart some others of the lesser-known early locomotive builders. Lowca Engineering of Whitehaven, for example, began as Tulk & Ley, became Fletcher Jennings and finally New Lowca, closing in 1927, having made about 245 locos from about 1840. There are only known to be four or five of their plates 'in captivity', all with class letters A, B, D, E and T.

Then there were firms like Black Hawthorn and Co and their acquiring firm Chapman & Furneaux, of Gateshead, who themselves had ended by 1902, and other firms such as the Wigan Coal & Iron Co who were basically locomotive assemblers, but who appear to have built a few engines themselves.

Plates were often re-cast or altered when locomotives were renumbered resulting in such inconsistencies as 'London & North Eastern Railway, 65762, Gateshead Works, 1905' — a pre-grouping locomotive bearing an LNER plate showing the British Railways locomotive number! LMS plates are less seen than LNER and are less valued. SR ones are fairly plain oval; the early ones are marked A for Ashford, E for Eastleigh. It is very rare to find pre-grouping works plates offered. Over the last two years there has been a Nine Elms 1893, an LBSCR plate from locomotive No 22 and a GNR from Atlantic No 296 built in 1905; these are eagerly sought after and deservedly so!

Collectors need to know that dimensions and even shapes of works plates from some makers vary widely. A good example of this is the North British Locomotive Company who adopted plates based on those used by its constituent companies. In 1903 when the North British Locomotive Co Ltd was formed, Dübs diamond-shaped plate was adopted for locomotives built at the Glasgow Locomotive Works (later known as the Queen's Park Works); Neilson Reid's oval plate was adopted and became the familiar round plate for the Hyde Park Works and Sharp Stewart's small oval plate continued much as before to advertise the wares of the Atlas Works. Finally, during World War II these plates were superseded by a common diamond-shaped plate which did not show the name of the individual works (by this time the Atlas Works had ceased to be used for building locomotives). In addition, within this framework are to be found several variations of the diamond and Hyde Park Works plates. Some of these variations may be seen in **Figs 102-11**.

Many firms amalgamated. Thus Hawthorn Leslie grouped with Robert Stephenson & Co Ltd to become Robert Stephenson & Hawthorn Ltd. Vulcan Foundry of Newton-le-Willows because English Electric, and many steam firms came to an end in the 1960s or before, eg Fletcher Jennings, Beyer Peacock, De Winton, Kerr Stuart, Kitson, Bagnalls, Manning Wardle, Avonside, Pecketts and eventually even the North British Locomotive Co, the latter having been taken over by General Electric Co Ltd. The standard work of reference on this subject (now out of print) is *British Steam Locomotive Builders* by J.W. Lowe (1975, Goose and Son), while *The British Locomotive Catalogue, 1825-1923* by B. Baxter in eight volumes (Moorland Publishing, 1977 to date) gives full details and history of virtually every pre-grouping locomotive known, and is essential reading on the subject.

108-11 The diamond-shaped builder's plate used by Dübs & Co and their successors the North British Locomotive Co. Note the change in the name of the works

Cabside Number Plates

As the LMS, SR and LNER painted their numbers, and as the cabside plates of pre-grouping companies are virtually never seen, at least not in auction, the field is largely comfined to the GWR. We can surely assume that hundreds of these are in private hands secured on walls and the number entering the market is limited. Under ten have been

112 A cabside numberplate from a locomotive built at Crewe Works for the Dundalk, Newry & Greenore Railway in 1873, sold at a recent specialist railwayana auction

113 A cabside number plate from the GWR's Wolverhampton works

114-15 Smokebox number plates. The lower two were sold at a recent railwayana auction

118 A locomotive shedplate

auctioned in twenty-seven auctions. They are valued by fame of engine, with *Saints* and *Stars* valued at ten times those from say pannier tank locomotives.

Smokebox Numbers

These are of wide appeal as they are remembered by generations of loco-spotters. There is a relatively plentiful supply available on stalls and in auctions. Almost without exception it is the non-famed, non-named ones which are publicly sold. This is true for the fifteen to twenty examples which have been auctioned in the last two years.

Nameplates

There have been two important sources of data on this subject: *Nameplates of the Big Four* by Frank Burridge, (published in 1975 by OUP and re-printed 1985) and *Nameplates on Display* by Ian Wright (1986, published by Pennine). The latter provides data on where names can be inspected, but does not deal with those in private hands

For any beginners starting to collect or invest in nameplates certain guidelines are apparent. Short Jubilee names, eg *Atlas, Ocean, Mars, Revenge* are less desirable than say *Tanganyika*

119 A group of main-line locomotive nameplates. Not to scale

120 Main-line locomotives and numbers which have been sold by auction during 1988, including 60022 from *Mallard*. Not to scale

121 Industrial locomotive nameplates sold by auction recently. Not to scale

or *Impregnable*. This is so also for 'Royal Scots' where a 'double liner' with regimental badge is far more valued than say *The Girl Guide* or *The Lancer*. A badged 'Scot' may even be as desirable as an A4 or a *Coronation*. LMS *Cities* with badges, eg *City of Stoke on Trent* are far more valued than plain ones and the same is true for named V2s.

In the sphere of A4s certain bird names are more evocative, eg *Wild Swan*, *Bittern*, *Golden Eagle* than *Walter K. Whigham*, *Dwight D. Eisenhower*, etc.

Again the long plates (often cast in two pieces) like *Commonwealth of Australia* may be more highly regarded than a short bird name like *Gannet!*

On the GWR with its hundreds of *Halls* and *Manors*, personal name acquisition has always been a possibility, eg one well known collector living in Tudor Road has *Tudor Grange* and many such plates have 'gone back' to their place name origin.

In the period 1986-7 there have been sudden signs of nameplates being on the move in public. Hitherto, since the plates left the locomotives at least 20 years ago, they have circulated privately. However, it is now possible to buy nameplates on the open market and the following have been auctioned or bought privately recently: *Aston Hall, Dalton Hall, Higham Court, Princess Mary, Commonwealth of Australia, City of Hereford, LMS Connaught, SLNCR*

Hazelwood, BR Iseult, Western Pioneer, Western Reliance, Zealous, Moray Firth.

Shedplates

They need not detain us for long. Pioneered by the Midland Railway and LMS and passed across into BR days, the activities of reproducers have greatly reduced their interest and few depots realise very much (**Fig 118**).

Tender Plates

These are usually marked with initials and works number or locomotive number, and sometimes dated but they are rarely seen. Most are cast-iron and some specify water capacity in gallons. Marked pre-grouping examples tend, of course, to be the most valued. There is a story, believed to be true, of an early enthusiast putting his TVR tender plate in a domestic fire to remove the paint whereupon it melted before his eyes — the moral being to remember that Victorian railways **did** sometimes use low melting point aluminium! Probably the most sought after are the engraved GWR brass oval plates complete with builder's number, date, month and tender capacity.

Whistles

A survey of this subject by Frank Soule appeared in the January 1987 issue of *The Railwayana Journal* and the present author draws heavily on the details

122 *(right)* GNR and LNER
locomotive notices

therein. Mr Soule calls whistles 'the
voice of the locomotive' and readers will
instantly recall the high 'soprano' shriek
of a B1, the halting blast of an ex-LNWR
0-8-0 plodding wearily with a coal train,
the bass thunder of a Stanier express
and above all, for most, the tingling
melody of an A4. Behind these sounds
lies the urge to collect whistles!

There are at least nine basic design
patterns with many variations and few
were number marked owing to frequent
changes in the works. Some, however,
were marked as with the Jubilee 5732
sold recently. Collectors should note
that many whistles and hooters are
wrongly described in sales, either by
ignorance or design! So that 'Off a *Coronation*' or 'Off a *King*' is usually a flight of
fancy.

A fair number are becoming available
and appear more easily obtainable than
say a Peckett worksplate! Types sold
recently include Jubilee, other Staniers,
'Gresley', BR Standard 5, LMS Standard
tank, 'Coronation type', 9F 2-10-0, LMS
Crab and GCR Atlantic. These terms
should be treated only as approxima-
tions however.

Gauges
These are usually pressure gauges and
vacuum gauges from locomotive cabs
and were used by the driver and fireman. They are seen from pre- and post-
grouping lines but the class is not much
regarded at present.

Other Collectables
Other locomotive items which are seen
occasionally include tender water
scoops, self cleaning (SC) smokebox
signs, cab mounted shed codes (ex
LNWR, LYR and SECR). GWR locomotives carried a small plate, dated 1909,
warning of the danger of leaning out of
cabsides. There are small plates off
Midland locomotives marked 'Hose Box'
(the hose for washing down the
footplate) and some railways had the
practice of mounting 'Train Following'
notices on the loco front. **Fig 122** shows
two of these from GNR and LNER, and
others are known from the GER, GCR
and Caledonian Railway. Usually the
depot is stamped on the reverse; they
were used in dense suburban traffic to
distinguish between similar trains. On
the LTSR rectangular destination
boards were carried.

Train Headboards
Virtually all headboards which have
been preserved are of the British Railways era and are of aluminium or alloy.
Fig 123 includes *The Aberdonian*. Often the arms of the two terminal cities
were added, as in this case of London
and Aberdeen. There was a back mounting bracket to rest a mounting arm set
on the smokebox door or on the buffer
beam of A4s. On the Eastern and North
Eastern regions there were sets of
named trains stamped on the reverse
signifying a standard casting which was

123 A collection of train headboards. Not to scale

interchangeable. Every locomotive depot providing locomotives for named trains had a supply for each train. The basic shape shown for *The Aberdonian* was used on the London Midland Region for large numbers of named trains, eg *The Comet, The Lancastrian, The Merseyside Express.* 'Flagship' trains like *The Royal Scot* were favoured by special large boards. The latter trains sported a famous wooden tartan design for many years. On the Southern and Western Regions, several individual designs were used for trains like the *Atlantic Coast Express, Golden Arrow, Cambrian Coast Express, Royal Duchy, Cathedrals Express* and so on.

The reason that almost no pre-BR named train boards have survived is that they were mostly made of wood and obviously had a great battering in front of high speed trains. Examples of the ones used on *The Flying Scotsman* (black letters on white board) can be seen on photographs.

Carriage and Wagon Railwayana

Apart from the contents of dining and buffet cars considered in previous chapters, there was a large range of marked furnishings in carriages. Over twenty types of marked carriage fittings exist as follows: door handles, locks and keys, coats of arms, class marks, window straps, blinds, passenger notices, side and roof boards, etched glass, antimacassars, ashtrays, carpets, rugs and footstools, mirrors, electric light shades and bulbs, luggage rack supports, system maps, pictures, footwarmers, toilet roll holders, paper and soap, towels, gas lights, table lamps, vents, carriage worksplates.

Door handles were, and remain, a vital area of safety, hence the need for extreme robustness when they are slammed. There seem to have been few survivals and we do not know how many marked handles existed. A Metropolitan Railway handle inscribed 'Live in Metroland' has been noted. Keys are to be found in abundance. Platform, train staff and, above all, stationmasters were keyholders. To this day the locking of compartments and carriages is an important function. Without doubt, most of the companies had their own keys of many sizes, right down to the Yales in use on company safes and cabinets. There is therefore a distinction between the T-shaped carriage keys and those in use around the station buildings. **Fig 124** shows a group of keys.

Window straps were once universal and are a vivid folk memory of today's collectors. They were partly a safety measure so that doors could only be opened with the window down, using the outside handle. For such a common fitting, few have survived. LMS, GWR, GNR and LNER examples are known. Pull down blinds were also quite common for small and large compartment windows, and may well have been marked. Again, very few have survived.

Coats of arms and class marks are a very large field. Class boards usually had the typical Edwardian shaded letters and numbers. These were usually hand painted, unlike the coats of arms which were usually transfers and are dealt with under a separate heading.

Inside some carriages were various enamel, card and paper advisory notices which can be seen on old photographs. The SECR had a $9\frac{1}{2}$ x $8\frac{1}{2}$in white enamel notice with black letters reading 'In the interests of the public health passengers are earnestly requested to refrain from the objectionable habit of spitting'. The LNWR had a small sign prohibiting throwing of objects out of windows and, of course, there were the universal Smoking/No Smoking signs, often in blue.

Etched glass is not uncommon, tending to have been preserved due to its

124 Railway lock and keys, including carriage door keys

obvious attractiveness. It took the form of first, second and third-class marks, occasionally with company initials. Examples can still be seen in station windows, eg at North Walsham in 1986. Other examples have come through Onslows Auctions — a Caledonian Railway 'Cardean' No 908 and a similar GCR panel of a double headed train. Also sold recently have been a Highland Railway etched 'No Smoking' complete with coat of arms and a Great Northern example.

Carriage boards were, for much of railway history, a familiar feature. Many examples of the small ones which slotted in above end doors exist, usually consisting of destination only, sometimes with 'via', and often being double-sided. Much more noted were the long roof boards, which fitted into grooves on the express carriages. LMS, LNER, SR and GWR ones survive, as well as their BR successors. Original GWR ones are distinguishable by the narrower pattern of letters, with the board having two ridges. The collection of these is in its infancy, but named trains are clearly more desirable. In the late LMS and BR

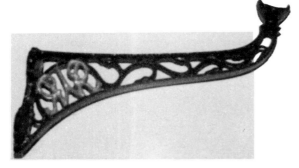

125 GWR luggage rack support

days the tartan patterns on the *Royal Scot* boards were famous. Have any survived? Do pre-grouping roof boards exist?

Antimacassars and ashtrays are discussed elsewhere, but rugs and carpets were widely used in carriages, although they were found in other areas as well, eg waiting rooms, offices and board rooms, and also hotels. There were several GWR patterns. Two patterns of NER, a GNSR and SECR carpets also exist.

Many of the compartment light shades and bulbs were marked with the company name. The LMS had bakelite shades and holders marked, as well as the bulbs. Bulbs made by Siemens and marked with the LNER initials are also known. Behind the lights were company marked mirrors, of which the elegant oval LNER types are quite common, as are the LMS rectangular ones with the letters etched into the glass. Many other mirrors are extant, although the company names are often only branded into the wood surround, eg on the Highland Railway, North Staffordshire Railway and GWR. **Fig 125** shows an example of a luggage rack support. Similar items from the Midland Railway are known to exist and there may be others.

A widely collected feature of compartment stock is the carriage print and map

of the company's lines. Exquisite ones survive from East Coast Joint Stock, illustrated in George Dow's section in *Railway Relics and Regalia* (p 125). The most famous are the GER coloured maps; the practice was followed by the LSWR, SECR, LNWR, GCR, Midland Railway, NSR, GWR, NER and GNR although very few in good condition have survived. The work of George Dow in this field is crucial- in the later steam period as he commissioned Hamilton Ellis to paint twenty-four scenes of LMS subsidiary lines. These exist in large numbers as they are quite recent, and are frequently for sale. They show scenes set as far back as the 1850s, such as an NSR train at Stone Junction, a green Midland Railway locomotive on an express and the Coniston Branch Furness Railway rail motor. They are based, of course, on artistic impression and published colours.

Footwarmers are items which are rarely seen as they were superseded by train heating; they were used mainly in first class carriages and were based on

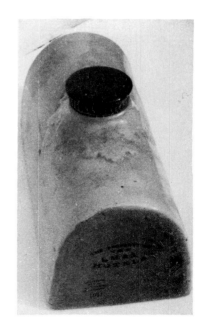

126 A hot water bottle from LMS hotels

127 A selection of railway towels

heat released from soda crystals. The modern successors to these are also seen very occasionally, in the form of marked railway hotel bed warmers. **Fig 126** shows an LMS example. Also in existence are company marked rubber hot water bottles.

A much more common type of railwayana is that associated with railway toilets, both on and off trains. Toilet roll holders have survived in numbers, including the well known LNWR, LMS and BR 'hand' pattern. The GWR had various types especially the allegedly thief-proof 'Dreadnought', inelegant but functional. Most companies did not mark the toilet roll holders, but many marked their tablets of soap. The GWR had at least four sizes, all marked with the company initials in large and small rectangles and ovals. The GER also marked its soap, in common with its successor the LNER.

Some pieces of GWR toilet paper survive and we need little imagination to visualise marked towels, roller towels etc, although, as the companies did not take promotional photographs of loos, evidence of this is awaited. There would certainly have been marked mirrors, while the fold up washbasins may also prove to have been marked sometimes. **Fig 127** shows some examples of company towels, of which the LNER had many different sorts. They were of course used in restaurant cars, hotels,

dining rooms and kitchens. The small ones are 'glass' cloths. The LNER red/black check pattern were also signal lever cloths to prevent chafing of hands. The GWR had several script designs and we may be certain that they must have existed for pre-grouping railway companies.

Marked carriage ceiling gas lamps are also in existence, with company initials on the brass holders. GCR and GWR ones have been discovered recently. Brass air vents and wall grilles were also marked by some companies, eg the SECR. The Pullman Company had a standard fitting of ornate table lamps, but as yet there is little evidence of other company-marked lights surviving.

Wagon Plates

Well over one million railway wagons, owned by both the railway companies and privately, bumped and clanked their way around Britain for much of the railway era. With 21,000 miles of route (excluding thousands of miles of sidings and the like), there were over forty-seven wagons for every route mile, whereas today you will do well to see one freight train on an average length of 47 miles. Most of the old names have gone, never to come back. Names such as Butterley & Bristol, Ince & Claye, Bolton, Baker & Burnett, Thomas Moy & Thomas Hunter, Brown Marshall, the embracing G & C of Gloucester, Chorley, the eight-pronged Midland style most like an eight-limbed octopus and the eight-spoked wheel of Darlington.

As an example of the concentrated use of freight wagons the author remembers one of his local scrap yards at Norton Canes between Bloxwich and Pelsall at Norton Canes Junction, on the now lifted Walsall (Ryecroft Junction) to Brownhills LNWR line, as it was in the early 1970s. It must have had well over twelve roads, each holding probably thirty wagons and every road was choc-a-bloc. Seen from the passing buses, they appeared as a sea of wood and iron carriers, line on line, jammed one against its neighbour. And now where they once languished is a grassy site. The three controlling boxes are gone, the very junction is gone, as is the main line itself. Scarcely a vestige of a big yard can be seen and there are certainly no fallen off plates around. But 17 years ago these lines contained a fair selection of the wagon makers listed below, for we can recollect Midland Railway and LNWR four-plank wagons with makers' plates in position. Unfortunately in those days, private builders were neglected in preference to pre-grouping main-line railways, and what without any doubt could have been bought and preserved for a few pounds, was ignored in the pre-occupation with rare cast-iron trackside notices.

The subject of wagon plates is much neglected and virtually nothing has been written, save for books on wagons of specific companies and a brief two-page article in *The Railwayana Journal — On the Line*, issue 15 of June 1987. The first proper classification of wagon plates by Frank Soule appeared in the July and September issues (26 and 27) of *The Railwayana Journal*. The author would like to record his thanks for much of the data below to Andrew Cutcliffe whose collection of these objects is without parallel.

Each wagon was often equipped with two builders' plates, two star (or speed allowance) plates, 'Generally Repaired By' plates, as well as contents and weight plates, plus wagon labels. Few collectors appreciate just how rare some are and so this analysis features some of those from companies where at present only one or two survivors are known (marked with an asterisk in the list). Wagon plates include those from:

Appleby Frodingham
J. Baker & Co of Kilnhurst
Bannisters & Co of Hull*
Bagnalls
Birkenshaws of Derby
Birmingham Wagon Co
Blake Boiler Wagon & Engineering Co of
   Darlington
Bolton Railway Wagon & Ironworks*
Bristol & South Wales Railway Wagon Co
   Ltd
British Railway Traffic & Electric Co of
   London
British Wagon Co of Rotherham
Brown Marshalls of Birmingham*
Butterley
Thomas Burnett & Co of Doncaster
Cammell Laird of Nottingham
Central Wagon Co of Ince
Chorley Railway Wagon Co Ltd*
S.J. Claye of Long Eaton
Clayton Wagons (Clayton Shuttleworth)
W.H. Davis of Langwith Junction
Darlington Wagon & Engine Co Ltd*
Derbyshire Wagon Co Ltd of Chesterfield*
Wm Gittus of Penistone*
M. & W. Grazebrook Ltd of Dudley
Hall Lewis & Co of Cardiff (Welsh Wagon
   Works, Cambrian, Powell Dyffryn)
Harris & Camm of Rotherham
Hurst Nelson & Co of Motherwell etc and
   Chesterfield
Thomas Hunter of Rugby
Lancaster Wagon Co*

Lincoln Wagon & Engine Co

Metro Cammell of Saltley, Wednesbury, Oldbury and Nottingham

Midland Railway Carriage & Wagon Co

Moreton & Co of Rotherham*

Thomas Moy of Peterborough*

North Central Wagon Co of Rotherham*

Pickering & Co of Wishaw

Principality Wagon Co Ltd of Cardiff

Railway Carriage & Iron Co of Manchester

Charles Roberts & Co

Settle Spakman & Co of Alsager*

Standard Wagon Co of Heywood, Reddish and Stockport

Stanton Iron Works

G.T.R. Turner of Langley Mill

Wigan Wagon Co*

Yorkshire Railway Waggon Co Ltd of Wakefield.

This list is by no means exhaustive, as it does not include, of course, the railway companies themselves, nor companies who were owners/leasors but not builders. Among these were firms like William Rigley of Bulwell, Berry Wiggins, Stephenson Clark of London, Corporation of Hull, West Lancashire Wagon Co, Lancashire Waggon Co and doubtless many more.

There were a total of over fifty firms established at various times, in addition of course to all the railway companies building their own wagons. Many of the latter, however, used the services of the General Wagon Repairs Co with large numbers of branches. This was the origin of the 'Generally Repaired By' plates which are often seen. A little known fact is that these plates were appearing on wagons as late as 1957, still on pre-grouping vehicles!

There have been hundreds of different cast-iron plates, their position on wagons was laid down strictly by the Railway Clearing House whose booklet *Regulation Respecting the Repairing and Rebuilding of Wagons* is revealing read-

128-9 Two decorative wagon plates, from Brown Marshalls & Co and Metropolitan Railway Carriage & Wagon Co

ing. Owners' names had to be imprinted behind the plate in case of loss and standard plates marking rebuilding had to be affixed. Wagon companies were clearly concentrated in certain areas, for example, in central Lancashire was the Central Wagon Co of Ince, Wigan Wagon, Bolton Railway Wagons and Chorley Railway Wagons. In Derbyshire and Nottinghamshire was perhaps the largest grouping of works with Cammell Laird, Derbyshire Wagon Co, W.H. Davis, S.J. Claye, G.T.R.Turner, Butterley and Hurst Nelson. There were two in Rotherham but few, it seems, in the north-east.

A whole number of widely separated towns produced wagons, including Moy of Peterborough, Hunter of Rugby, Gittus of Penistone, Settle Spakman of Alsager and firms in Lancaster and Lincoln.

130-1 Wagon plates from the Chorley Railway Wagon Co Ltd, and the Darlington Wagon Co

It is salutary to realise that this host of builders has rationalised today to Powell Dyffryn, Davis, Procor and Standard Railway Wagon and very few others, ie about 10 per cent of those existing previously. Some of today's firms have lenguiy antecedents, as in the case of the ancestors of Powell Dyffryn in Cardiff. Many names have completely gone, for example Brown Marshall of Birmingham, whose site was given over to Morris Motors when the former migrated to Saltley. The confusing permutations of the Birmingham Railway Carriage & Wagon Co Ltd/Metro Cammell etc is a subject beyond us here, littered with takeovers, site moves and name

changes (**Figs 128-9**).

Although many collectors wrongly believe that wagon plates are common it is worth noting that there are over thirteen examples of plates which at present exist as only one or two known examples and these are starred in the list (**Figs 130-1**). Most of the larger pre-grouping railway companies had their own plates, some of which are very rare indeed, and more valued than those from private builders, for example, plates from the Highland Railway, Furness Railway, North Staffordshire Railway, etc. They are often in the form of registration plates, the standard circular shape with two or four lugs on the side and always with a date and tonnage (**Colour Plate 11**).

In addition, there are very large numbers of LNER, SR, LMS and GWR 'D' plates, taking their name from the shape. These reflect weight ranges, sometimes up to over 40 tons. There are also a wide range of railway wagon workshop plates. Examples from the Cutcliffe collection give an inkling of the range — NER & LNER oval 'To Carry' plates, 'York 1905 12 Tons'; 'NER 2 Tons Luggage'; 'NER 3 Tons Luggage'; 'NER Not To Exceed 5T Distributed Load'; 'LNE $2^{1}/_{2}$ Tons'; 'LNE 3T'; 'LNE 8T'; 'LNE 10T'; 'North Eastern Railway To Carry $1^{1}/_{2}$T'. There were oval plates similar to the above produced by the successor BR(E). Dr Gordon Blears' LNER collection includes 'D' plates of 5, 10, 12, 13, 16, 20, 21, 22, $22^{1}/_{2}$ and 40 tons, ranging in number from a low of 139302 to a high 634321, dating from 1924 to 1947 (**Fig 132**). Note the general caution about numbers; as No 139302 is dated 1924 this does not mean that the LNER has produced that number of wagons in its first year! There is also an LNER 'D' plate of 10 tons dated 1910, number

132 *(right)* A collection of wagon plates

133 *(below)* A selection of wagon plates at the Moseley Railwayana Museum

737241, 'made' at Cowlairs. This may well be a case of an old wagon renumbered by the LNER at Cowlairs, but not built there.

Reference to the tonnage plates above raises the question of how many different tonnage plates existed on this one railway and what were the highest and lowest weights? The 'Big Four' were producing 'Registered By' plates up to

134-5 Railway oil cans and pourers

the end, there being an LMS 1948 12-ton plate No 6345! To show the complexity of the subject, compare this with LMS registered plate 81465 of 1927! Suffix letters are another subject; the LNER used E, C, B, D, N and S, at least. One feature to look for in such items is date and serial number and weight. For example, LNWR No 31 of 1905 may have more to tell than LNWR No 16487 of 1923!

We must also mention axlebox covers, another whole sub-class of wagon railwayana. They are now becoming avidly sought after and it is expected that pre-grouping ones, once quite common, will increase in value. Not long ago, when GER and LBSCR examples came up for sale, there was little interest, but those times have passed. Some most unusual ones were produced by

the Saltley Oilbath & Axlebox Co, around 1911 for Irish narrow gauge locomotives, wagons and coaches, for example, for the West Clare Railway, and also for the Isle of Man Railway amongst others. There are rare ones with no makers' names, from the Clogher Valley Railway and other Irish lines. As this book goes to print, what is possibly the very first example known of a wagon plate box has been seen. This was carried on a Shrewsbury & Hereford Railway wagon and marked 'S & HR' on the top and 'Invoice Box' on the side, all in elegant serif letters, with hinged lid, to contain the wagon route labels

This chapter concludes with **Figs 134-5**, which shows a cross-section of the great variety of marked oil and paraffin jugs, pourers and cans used in servicing locomotives, carriages and wagon axle boxes, signal lamps, road vehicles and a host of other moving parts.

5
Signalling Equipment

A sound remembered by many of today's collectors is the tinkle of the box semaphore code announcing the imminence of a train. But as all-electric long distance and radio signalling is taking over at great speed mechanical signalling will soon be only a memory.

Another archetypal sound is the sigh of the signal wires and the final clunk as a signal is pulled off, particularly as the home and distant signals move together. Many railway enthusiasts recall their favourite station, and the number of minutes from pulling off the signal to the shriek of the 'Flyer' or the mundane thud of a coke train, dependent on length of section and speed of train, and then the noisy rattle as both arms crash down and bounce.

It is these memories that have generated the present interest in signalling railwayana, as well as the realisation that another era in railway history is approaching its end. Just as historic uniforms, carriage fittings, porters' lamps and trespass signs have almost gone, so soon will semaphore signals.

Though this is not a treatise on signalling, we must refer to today's antecedents. The earliest hand signalling by railway policemen developed quickly into plain red and white discs and then into single movable arms, a very few of which have survived, for example, at the Winchcombe Railway Museum. The familiar white vertical bar, or home

arms, and the black V-shaped stripe on distant arms have of course not always been thus. Signal arms have now become a specific area of railwayana collecting, but any save modern BR ones are now rarely seen in auction and are virtually extinct *in situ*, as are wooden arms and wooden posts.

Fig 136 shows a medium height LSWR lattice metal post with a corrugated pattern home arm, capped by an original finial together with 'crow's nest', lamp and ladder at the Big Four Railway Museum, Bournemouth. Remarkably, another of these LSW lattice signals complete with all spectacles, wires and weights was recovered virtually intact from a scrap yard in the last 5 years, and has been re-erected in working order at the Harpenden Railway Museum. Two more re-erected signals may be seen at the Warwick Railway Museum — a GWR centre pivot signal on a tubular post with GWR finial and spectacle glasses and a wooden-posted NER signal.

No less than eleven restored and working signal arms, posts and finials are to be found at the Winchcombe Railway Museum: four from the GWR, one from the Cheshire Lines Committee, NER slotted, NER route indicator, GCR, LSWR and five pre-grouping ground signals. **Fig 137** shows a GCR loft signal with finial and a ground frame made in 1890 by the Railway Signal Co of Liverpool with five ground disc signals. Pre-

136 *(left)* LSWR lattice signal

137 *(above)* GCR signal and
ground frame

138 *(right)* GSWR lattice signal

grouping signals left *in situ* are falling so
fast that the one shown in **Fig 138** and
photographed in August 1986 may be
no more. It is a very tall GSWR lattice
signal complete with GSWR finial, just
north of Girvan signalbox.

Finials are in a class of their own and
a proper written classification is still
awaited. The huge majority were cast-
iron with a small percentage made of
wood, namely some from the Midland
Railway, GWR, GCR and NER. Finials
were located atop signals and on the
ends of some signalboxes, while tall
spirals adorned many station roofs and
outbuildings. Various manufacturers
made them for the railway companies,

obviously decorating their own signalling equipment. Thus the majority are
not marked with railway company initials, and of course big manufacturers
made similar designs for various lines.
The main manufacturers were McKenzie Holland & Dutton's of Worcester,
Railway Signal Co of Liverpool, Holcroft
of Wolverhampton, Westinghouse
Brake & Signal Co, Evans & O'Donnell
and Stevens.

Most finials are not marked with railway company or maker's initials or
name, and identification is a specialist
skill as there were many types used on
the same company lines. For instance
there are ten GWR types on display at

139 A group of tall signal finials

the Warwick Railway Museum, one with a pulley wheel for lifting the lamp up and down from the ground. **Fig 139** shows one of the tallest finials, the McKenzie & Holland 42in, dwarfing even the GCR ball pattern at 34in and the Cheshire Lines Committee at 30in. In the foreground are crucifix types from the LCDR and LYR with a Southern Railway type (far right) and a wooden one from the Midland Railway (far left). Finials are fairly uncommon and very few collectors of railwayana have more than a dozen. At preservation centres they are usually, of course, back on top of signals. Many of them are essays in Victorian and Edwardian fluted elegance.

The following list of finial types has been made available to the author by David Hughes of Chester. The numbers are minima and much is still to be discovered. The second column gives the known numbers of varieties of finial used on that company's lines (large and small versions count twice). The third column is the number known to be marked with company initials.

Company	No	Marked
Barry	2	
B&M	1	
Caledonian	1	
Cambrian	1	
Cheshire Lines Committee	3	2
Festiniog	1	
GSWR	2	
GCR	5	1
GER	5	
GNR	3	1
GNSR	3	
GWR	10	3
Highland	2	
HBR	2	1
IMR	2	
LCDR	1	1
LBSCR	5	
LNER	1	
LSWR	4	1
LTSR	2	
Metropolitan	2	
Midland	4	
M & SWJR	2	
NBR	3	
NER	7	
NSR	3	
SDJR	5	
SECR	5	
SR	2	
TVR	1	
VRR	1	

Thus there is a total of at least ninety-one different types, with at least twelve having company initials.

It should be pointed out that in the LMS and LNER era, finials were no longer made and a post cap sufficed, they are little to look at but are often marked. The Western Region of British Railways continued the GWR pattern virtually unaltered and many of these are still in position. Similarly the Southern Region continued the SR pattern. It

140　a collection of signalling equipment

is believed that Dutton's delicate spear pattern is one of the rarest with perhaps only two known outside the National Railway Museum.

Block Instruments, Repeaters, Tablets, Keys and Staffs

Block instruments were used for communication between signalboxes for the purpose of controlling trains. They are often complex electrical machines with many brass parts in a beautifully made wooden case, and hence have a fascination all of their own. They usually have plungers, a handle or a commutator for transmitting the signals, and the indications appear behind a glass window either in the form of needles or as a miniature semaphore signal, the arm of which is raised or lowered. The latter were introduced for signalmen who could not read needle indications.

There are many different types of block instrument; the GWR and the LNWR made their own, but many companies purchased them from private makers, notably Tyer (established in 1851), Sykes and the Railway Signal Co.

A common variety was the single-needle instrument which came in 'pegging' (ie transmitting) and 'non-pegging' (ie receiving) versions. These were used among others by the GNR, MR, NER, NBR and GCR. Similar instruments were used by many companies for telegraphic communication between boxes; in these the needle struck a sounder, and there was no glass to impede the sound.

Three-wire instruments used a constant current in one of the wires to sustain the indication. The GWR used a distinctive design by Spagnoletti. The LNWR instruments, designed by Fletcher, commonly had needles for both up and down lines, together with the bell, in a single wooden case. The LYR had their own pattern of instrument. The LSWR used a very distinctive design by Preece, with a rounded top and a semaphore indicator, which are quite scarce nowadays. The NER used three-wire permissive instruments made by Tyer; these could count the number of trains in the section. **Fig 140** and **Colour Plate 12** shows a selection

141 A Tyer's No 7 tablet instrument

142 *(above)* A Tyer's No 6 tablet instrument

143 *(right)* GWR block instrument

of signalling apparatus.

Some instruments required only one line wire and were consequently quite complex electrically. They are much sought after by collectors. The SER used a very massive design, now very rare, invented by Walker in 1854; these have enormous coils and a slightly primitive appearance. The Tyers instruments were extremely elegant; their two-position instruments were used by the GER, LBSCR, GSWR and the Caledonian Railway, and the three-position ones by the FR, NSR and GER. The very rare Harpers instrument was used on the LBSCR and in Ireland.

Busy commuter lines, particularly in South and East London, were signalled extensively using Sykes' lock-and-block system, where the instruments were interlocked with the signals and with train-operated treadles. These instruments are very handsome, particularly the 'plunging' variety. They often have the location painted on the face of the instrument. The familiar Midland rotary instruments, introduced after the Hawes Junction disaster, operated in a similar fashion.

Block instruments may be particularly desirable even if they are not of a rare type. Many instruments have unfortunately lost their original brass destination plates and their makers' plates, so those still retaining them are much sought after. The LMSR and GWR covered the brass-work of their instruments by nickel plate in later years, and unplated examples are therefore rare. Other features to look for are exterior terminals on single-needle instruments, and non-pegging instruments

with a handle for sending telegraphic signals. **Fig 143** shows a block instrument designed by the GWR in 1947 as a replacement for the familiar Spagnoletti block instrument, with its two tapper keys and indicator flags. Because of its late date of introduction, many of these instruments were made by the Western Region of British Railways, or the electrical contractors R. E. Thompson. There is also a smaller version for use on permissive goods lines — these have a commutator which shows how many trains are in the section. The 1947 block instrument is still the standard instrument on Western Region lines with mechanical signalling. This example was taken out of use at Cowley Bridge Junction (Exeter) in 1985.

Train describers are much prized by collectors, since they are highly individual, each one showing a set of train types or destinations pertaining to the particular signalbox. They are quite rare nowadays. The type made by Tyers had a typical Tyers case, and a clockwork mechanism driven by a handle pulled out from the side. They were used by the LNWR and GWR. The LNWR also used the impressive Fletcher describers, which had a round iron case, painted green. As in the Tyers instruments the indication was set by inserting a peg into the hole opposite the appropriate destination. **Fig 144** shows a pair of Fletcher describers. Walker describers

were used extensively on the Southern Railway, but are now more or less unobtainable.

Fig 145 shows an LNWR route indicator. Following the adoption of the Fletcher combined block instrument and bell, the LNWR were left with many serviceable instruments on their hands. Many of these were adapted to give route information by the simple expedient of replacing the card showing 'Line Clear' and 'Train on Line' by a similar card bearing the route information.

Block bells were used for communication between signalboxes according to a standard code, with signals such as 'train entering section' or 'train out of section' being sent. The type of train was sometimes described with the 'Is line clear?' signal. Sometimes a coil of wire (called a gong) was used in place of a bell to give a distinguishable tone. There are many types of bells, with some companies having distinctive styles.

Signal repeaters were small instruments which literally repeated the signal indication to the signalman, thus confirming the position of the signal. They were also used to indicate whether the signal lamps were alight, and for track circuits. They come in many varieties; some in round brass cases were mounted on the front of the block shelf, and others had small wooden cases. Some types are quite common, but the pre-grouping companies often had their own designs which are now very rare.

Single-line equipment offers a large field for collectors. The general principle of single-line operation was that there was a single physical object (usually a staff, tablet or token) which the driver had to have in his possession in order to traverse a section. Originally each section had a unique staff, and this system has continued on little-used lines. These 'one-engine-in-steam' staffs can be found in an enormous variety of designs. To give the systems more flexibility, 'staff-and-ticket' working was introduced. Here the staffs were designed to open a solid 'ticket box' containing metal or paper 'tickets' which could serve as the authority to proceed, in place of the staff. The GER used this system extensively. However, this method also had its limitations, and in 1878 Tyer introduced the tablet instrument. Here, each end of the system had an instrument containing a number of

metal tablets, the two being electrically connected such that only one tablet could be obtained at a time. Only one train could therefore be in possession of a tablet, and so have access to the line.

The tablets (about 4in diameter) have the section engraved upon them; the names can be quite evocative, such as 'Hawes-Garsdale'. The earliest tablets were brass or brass and steel, more modern ones being made of aluminium or fibre board. Adjacent sections always had different configurations, for safety. These are indicated by the central cut-out; the usual patterns are round or square, but a triangular cut-out is sometimes encountered. The instruments which contained the tablets are themselves much sought after; they are, however, large and very heavy. Tyer later introduced key tokens which were contained in smaller and lighter instruments. The key tokens were originally of steel or brass, but more recently of aluminium.

The LNWR were unhappy with tablets, and Webb and Thompson designed the 'electric train staff' system in 1888, which was manufactured by the Railway Signal Co. The staffs were made of steel with brass rings, with the section names at one end. They were contained in instruments which were handsome and very tall (nearly 5ft high) and extremely heavy. The staffs frequently had an Annett's key at one end for unlocking a set of points in the section. In later years smaller instruments were introduced which contained 'miniature staffs' which were only 9in to 12in long, compared with 23in for the full-size staffs.

A most useful rough calculation was done by Brian Gell in 1986. He estimated that out of an original 10,000 sections, examples of tokens from only

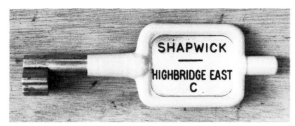

146-50 A selection of tablets, keys and staffs

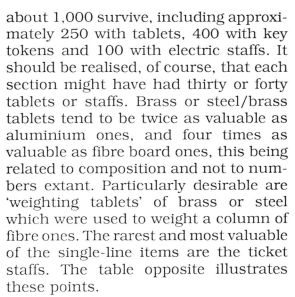

about 1,000 survive, including approximately 250 with tablets, 400 with key tokens and 100 with electric staffs. It should be realised, of course, that each section might have had thirty or forty tablets or staffs. Brass or steel/brass tablets tend to be twice as valuable as aluminium ones, and four times as valuable as fibre board ones, this being related to composition and not to numbers extant. Particularly desirable are 'weighting tablets' of brass or steel which were used to weight a column of fibre ones. The rarest and most valuable of the single-line items are the ticket staffs. The table opposite illustrates these points.

Levers, brass collars and lever description plates are also collected. Warwick Railway Museum has over eighty different ones including examples marked gong, slip, up & down wicket, down fast detonator and barrier control lever. Brass shelf plates are usually marked with the name of the adjacent box and are now often quite valuable. Individual levers are collected, and very occasionally a whole ground-frame block of levers appears for sale. Although not usually marked they can be identified by the expert eye.

Other signalling items that are collected are as follows: internal telephones and code lists, track circuit and lamp repeaters, plungers, winding wheels for crossing and wicket gates. The GWR made several versions of the latter at its Reading Works and BR continued the pattern. Other items found inside signal boxes include: first aid boxes, lamps, stools, sometimes company-marked rugs, clocks, flags,

Type		Material	No of Sections Available
Tyer Tablet	No 1	brass/steel	20
	No 2,3,4,6	brass/steel	65
	No 6	aluminium	80
	No 6	fibre	75
	No 5	brass	12
	No 7	brass	12
Tyer KT	GWR	steel	48
	GWR	aluminium	225
	Type 9	steel/nickel	50
	Type 9	brass	30
	Type 12A	aluminium/bronze	30
Large W&T staff	LNWR		12
	GWR		20
	LBSCR		18
Railway Signalling Co Miniature staff			50
Ticket staff			12
OES staff			50
Point keys			40

Table showing the type, material and number of tablets, staffs and keys

detonators, lay-out diagrams to show signals and points, and gradient diagrams. Some items were works of art with hand-painted designs on carved boards, such as the two remarkable lever description boards surviving from the North Lindsey Light Railway and from the Sheffield & Midland system.

Outside signal boxes were to be found cast-iron or enamel notices fixed to the door to warn against unlawful entry, though very few had company names. Well known ones are the two versions of the GWR, LNWR & GWR Joint, GWR &

151 The interior of Beeston Castle and Tarporley signal box (LNWR)

153 *(below)* A selection of named toe plates from signal box steps

GCR Joint, West London Extension and the LYR. Others had more basic 'No Admittance' notices, as on the LSWR. The steps up to the boxes had toe plates, many inscribed with the company's initials. Known ones are the various patterns from the Midland Railway, LMS, M & GNJR, LYR and NER.

Signalbox nameboards is a vast subject in itself, ranging from the small NER enamel names through to the ubiquitous GWR cast ones with raised surrounds. Most railway companies in Britain were content with wooden boards with screwed on metal or wooden letters. Examples were the LNWR, MR, NSR, and GSWR.

Some railways placed the name along the centre of the box on one side, or on two sides if lines passed on both sides.

Others, like the Midland Railway had names raised at both ends of the box.

Crucial items which are often forgotten are signal wires and pulleys. Many, if not most, important lines marked their pulleys, which were often fixed into the nearest platform edge or wall. Marked ones exist from the RR, LNWR, Midland Railway, LMS, LNER, GWR, SR, LYR, GSWR, LSWR and, amazingly, one from the North Devon & Cornwall Junction Light Railway.

Trackside Equipment

Single line sections and branches often had much trackside equipment, especially those lines equipped with automatic pick up and setting down tablets, sometimes called 'tablet catchers'.

154 LMS, LNWR and GWR signal wire pulleys

155 GWR tablet catcher

These tablets were placed in leather pouches and were collected and set down at speeds of 15mph on the GWR. **Fig 155** shows a GWR catcher in Warwick Railway Museum where the safety net, speed notice and post light are well shown. The pouch was held on an outstretched arm by the fireman, to be picked up by a short tube mounted on a post and set at an angle. An oil lamp was mounted on the bracket and the pick up was reached by an iron ladder. Some GWR locos had automatic tablet catchers mounted on the cabside. There appears to be very few examples preserved.

Men working on the 'way and works' as some lines defined their lines and structure, used many sorts of trolleys, the early ones were hand cranked, the later ones petrol driven, to travel to work. The remains of these trolleys can often be found derelict and forgotten along the banks. By some permanent way huts there were traversers allowing trolleys to be parked at right angles to the track between use. Temporary track rights were gained by men working on

the line by possession of a key or tablet in the same way as those used by locomotive crews. On GWR lines in Cornwall, like the Chasewater, Looe and Helston branches, electrically locked tokens were worked for intermediate gangers huts, as well as from signal boxes at the end of sections and stations.

Fogging Equipment

Fog was a far more serious danger for most of railway history than it is now with colour light signalling and clean air acts. Most well known, and surviving in large quantities, are the detonator tins, invariably company stamped and in varied sizes, some quite large. **Fig 157**

156 An automatic machine for laying fog detonators

157 Fog detonator cans

shows LNER, LSWR, LMS, and GWR examples. Fogmen were employed to place detonators and had either cloth or enamel armbands marked as such, often with the company's name and also special fogmen's lamps. They also had oil filled signal repeaters, eg those made by Sykes.

On some lines, detonators could be placed automatically on running lines direct from signal boxes equipped with one or more foglevers, often at one end of the signal box. Hence the existence of brass lever plates so marked. Also in use were lineside fogging machines like the one shown in **Fig 156** made by the Railway Signal Co of Liverpool, from near Yatton, which enabled a fogman to locate detonators several running lines across without the danger of crossing the lines in fog. Few of these survive.

6
Railway Lamps

The railway lamp is one of the most avidly pursued spheres of railwayana collecting. Perusal of the main lamp collections explains why. In the case of the two biggest, the Pete Rogers and Mike Sharman collections, although both contain between 1,000 and 2,000 lamps, there are very few examples from the majority of the pre-grouping companies. The exceptions may be some of the very large companies, such as the LNWR/NER/GNR/GER. However, even lamps from some of the larger companies, such as the Midland, Caledonian and Great Central Railway, are relatively uncommon. There are very low numbers from some of the medium size companies, eg GSWR, Highland Railway and Taff Vale Railway. Perhaps it is less surprising that there are few survivors from the small companies, including joint companies; or from the early companies which were absorbed in the late nineteenth century. There are only one or two known examples from the following companies: York & Newcastle, Macclesfield Bollington and Marple, LDECR, Sheffield & Midland, Croydon & Oxted Joint, GN & LY Joint, Mid Suffolk Light, Liskeard & Looe.

In short the ratio of preserved lamps to original ones is just as poor as the ratio in other spheres of railwayana collection. Indeed it is worse when compared with cast-iron notices. This is due to the way in which older lamps obviously wore out, or became damaged with constant use over many decades. After grouping lamps would have been scrapped because of the difficulty of finding replacement parts such as glasses and burners. In some cases they would have been cannibalised to make good a better (ie more modern) lamp. Lamps could even deteriorate while out of use, if they were not carefully maintained, and once exposed to the elements they could rapidly rust and deteriorate. As they are so easily displayed on shelves in the average spare room, this further explains why pre-grouping handlamps are so energetically collected.

Many railway companies produced their own pattern of lamps in their main railway workshops, the LNWR at Wolverton or Crewe, GER at Stratford, SECR at Ashford, GWR at Swindon and Cambrian at Oswestry. Some companies not only designed and produced their own handlamps in their works but also employed outside lamp manufacturers, although the GNSR is an example of a company who employed a local lamp manufacturer, Shirras of Aberdeen, to produce their early handlamps and station lamps.

The main firms who specialised in the production of lamps were concentrated in three cities, chiefly Birmingham followed by London and Glasgow. Exceptions might be Whitehead of Blyth who

158 *(above left)* LSWR lamp by Baynton

159 *(above right)* Messenger's corrugated handlamp made for the Rhymney Railway

160 *(right)* Close up of Messenger's maker's plate

produced some lamps for the GNR, or Premier of Leeds who produced acetylene lamps for the post-grouping railway companies. In Birmingham the following firms made lamps: Baynton, Bladon, Bulpitt, Griffiths, Hetherington, Jew, Knight, Levick, Linley, Messenger, Polkey, Poole, Lucas, Rippingilles, Samson, Smith and Chamberlain. **Fig 158** shows a lamp made by Baynton for the LSWR. In London lamp suppliers were Cowdy, Faudels, London Lamp Manufacturing Co, Reform, Risdales, Sugg and Veritas. The Albion Lamp Co gave their address as London and Birmingham while Maclellan stated Glasgow and London as their locations.

Also in Glasgow, lamps were produced by Hendry, Murray and Robb

Moore & Neil Ltd, who described themselves as 'Ship Chandlers of Glasgow, Cardiff and London'. The latter company produced unique handlamps for the LNER, and these were allocated to their GNSR lines. Some of the NBR lamps produced by Bulpitt were plated 'Bulpitt's Patent, Sole Vendors Blackley Young & Co Glasgow'. This indicates that some firms may not have been manufacturers of lamps, but just distributors. Of the thirty firms listed over 50 per cent are to be found in Birmingham. As many of the non-Birmingham listed firms produced only relatively small quantities of lamps we can probably deduce that over 70 per cent of railway lamps, produced other than in the railway's own workshops, were pro-

161 *(left)* GWR copper top hand lamp, with initials on the front glass and on the burner

162 *(right)* Macclesfield, Bollington & Marple Railway hand lamp, note knob for operating a coloured glass

163 *(below right)* NBR signalling lamp

duced in this one city.

Some firms produced a patent lamp which was then employed by various railway companies. An excellent example of this is the remarkable 'Messenger's Patent Corrugated Handlamp', designed to give strength and durability. The most comprehensive collection of these lamps contains examples from the following companies: Furness, Furness & Midland Junction, Cleator & Workington Junction, LNWR & FR (Cleator Joint Lines), Rhymney, Taff Vale. **Fig 159** shows Rhymney lamp No 105, the only known surviving example of the Rhymney Railway Messenger's corrugated lamp. It is a three aspect handlamp with the two large Messenger brass plates and a third on the trigger cover marked 'RR Co 105' which is repeated on the reservoir.

This lamp plus three smaller radius non-corrugated Messenger's Rhymney Railway lamps were saved by one railwayman, Eric Mountford, a former employee and author of a book on the

Caerphilly Works plus other publications on the GWR. Other Rhymney lamps may well surface in the future,

164 *(left)* GWR lever operated signalling lamp

165 *(right)* GCR Appleton's patent handlamp

but if not we shall be indebted to him for saving 80 per cent of surviving examples!

Some railway companies had their own pattern strictly laid down, to be observed by different manufacturers. Perhaps the best example of this was the GNR who employed at least five different manufacturers to produce handlamps of a similar design. The GWR on the other hand, employed at least seven manufacturers to produce a dozen different pre-grouping patterns. After the grouping the GWR employed at least five different Birmingham manufacturers to produce their standard post-grouping 'Paddington' lamp (**Fig 161**).

Handlamps were mainly designed to incorporate a method of signalling either a green or red aspect. In later years some also acted as fog warning lamps, with an extra orange aspect. In order to bring the coloured aspects in line with the lens it was usual for the top to rotate, turning a round drum mounted with curved coloured aspects. An alternative method was to mount the curved glasses in slides, which could be moved, with the aid of knobs, along a brass channel on each side of the lens see (**Fig 162**). Lever-operated lamps were also patented and employed by large companies such as the NBR (see **Fig 163**) and GWR (see **Fig 164**). Linley patented two lamps, one with two levers above which was employed by the East Kent Railway. and a second with the lever within the skirt at the base of the lamp, and these were employed by the Isle of Man Railway. The GCR and the Midland Railway used Appleton's patent handlamp which incorporated a rotating mechanism within the cap, enabling the rest of the lamp to remain stationary (**Fig 165**).

Lamps were often stamped or plated with the station or signalbox name. Companies that had a policy of clearly allocating their handlamps to specific stations or signalboxes include: GNR, GER, LBSCR, Cambrian, LYR, LNWR,

166 NER hand lamp made by Messengers of Birmingham

167 Midland Railway lamp with rectangular front glass

NSR, Cheshire Lines Committee, GCR, MSLR. Other companies which only allocated some of their lamps include, HR, Caledonian, SECR, LSWR & NBR, and NER. Of the post-grouping companies it was the LNER that chose to allocate most of their lamps, using methods employed by the GNR, GER, GCR and NBR. They may also carry a number for that particular railway centre, eg: 'GNRCo HORNCASTLE 5', 'GNRCo WOODWALTON SIG. BOX 3', 'GER MAGDALEN RD 4', 'GN & GE JT CHATTERIS DOCKS 16', 'WISBECH TRAM LINE 11', 'L & NER TATTER-SHALL 5', 'BR(E) SHEFFIELD TRAFFIC 80' (see **Fig 166**, NER, HULL No 434).

As well as being allocated to stations or signalboxes, the following titles have been found on handlamps; 'Porter', 'Relief Porter', 'Grade 1 Porter', 'Inspector', 'Signalman', 'Shunter', 'Station Master', 'Yard Master', 'Fogman', 'Relief Fogman', 'Guard', 'Motorman', 'Driver', 'Permanent Way Department', 'Signal Department', 'Engineers' Department', 'No 19 Gang,' 'Engineers' Department', 'GNR Holton Le Clay', 'Passenger Department', 'Goods Department', 'Loco Department', 'Mineral Department', 'Way & Works', 'Oil Gas Works', 'Railway Works − Ashford', 'Parcels', 'Saloon No 1' for GNSR Royal Saloon Carriage & Wagon Dept, LNWR Northampton Police' (Railway Police). **Fig 167** shows a lamp marked 'M.R.T. [Midland Railway Traffic] (Storm) Settle'.

Sometimes, but only rarely, were personal names stamped on the brass plates. Examples include: 'Guard Baker Highbridge' and 'Relief Porter Christopher' both on SDJC lamps, 'A.E. Green, Redbank Points Cabin, Doncaster Mineral' on an LNER lamp, and 'J.A.

168 LBSCR lamp marked with the name of the user

Jackson, Whitemoor' on an LNER-E lamp. One Southern Railway lamp produced at Eastleigh Works carries three plates on top, base and reservoir all referring to 'F.C. Austin, Motorman, Brighton'. Inspectors' names are perhaps the most common: 'Inspr. Arrand of Grimsby' on a GCR lamp, 'Inspr. Binks of Doncaster Mineral' on an LNER lamp and 'Inspector Mutter of Westbury, Wilts' on a GWR lamp.

Unfortunately only a few companies dated their lamps, and then only some of them. An example includes an LBSCR lamp plated on the reducing cone and base: 'MR FIRBANK, P. WAY DEPT. T.WELLS AND E[AST]BOURNE L[INE]' dated 3.80 on the reducing cone and 8.80 on the base (see **Fig 168).** LNWR lamps were often dated in the floor of the lamp, eg 1870 and a lamp number. A lamp from the LNWR & GWR (Birken-

head Junction) is dated 1884 and one from Huddersfield Junction is dated 1876.

GER lamps were sometimes dated behind the front door, eg '4 C 08', on a GER Saxmundham lamp, '11 D 37' on a lamp from LNER Wisbech, and '8 M 45' on an LNER lamp stamped 'Ipswich'. GNR lamps were often dated on the reducing cone, eg 'GNR W 8.12.89' and the LNER continued this into the 1920s on their GNR pattern lamps, eg 'L & NER 12/25'.

The manufacturer's patent plate may reveal a date, eg a GWR lamp made by Sugg to 'Wrights Patent' dated 1903-4. Bladon dated their post-grouping lamps 'GWR T.E. Bladon 1938', and after nationalisation a BR(M) lamp is plated 'Rippingilles 1949'. Care is necessary as the date may be that of the patent, not the date of manufacture.

In later years it was not unusual for lamps to be re-allocated. An LYR handlamp allocated to Altcar Rifle Range Station was re-allocated when the station closed in 1922. Interestingly it was re-allocated to Hightown, the next station along the line. After grouping the LNER transferred surplus lamps from the GNR and the GCR to their ex-GER lines. A lamp from Stanley Station on the Methley Joint Railway was re-allocated to Middleton Towers in Norfolk. A lamp from the Halifax & Ovenden joint line, plated 'New Bridge Goods Halifax 19' carries an LNER re-allocation plate to Kimberley Park. A GCR-pattern lamp stamped 'LNE-C' has a re-allocation plate 'Bury St Eds'. There are also examples of the reverse flow of lamps — GER lamps plated by the LNER to such GNR locations as Kirton (near Boston) and Deeping St James. A Cambrian Railway handlamp exists which is ex-Welshpool & Llanfair Light Railway

169 MSLR lamp numbered 6911

case of the Manchester, Sheffield and Lincolnshire Railway there are about ten surviving examples, and they are numbered as high as 'MS & L 6911 Maud's Bridge' (see **Fig 169**). If this indicates that there was once over 7,000 of these lamps in circulation then the survival rate is very low indeed. The London, Chatham and Dover Railway amalgamated with the SER at the formation of the SECR. LCDR lamps range in number from 166 to 1373, perhaps indicating that some 2,000 were employed, of which about forty have survived. The SER lamps are again numbered, examples ranging from 429 to 4047, perhaps indicating some 5,000 lamps, of which perhaps forty have survived. The LCDR lamps are usually renumbered as the SECR 6000 series, although many were renumbered a third time by the Southern Railway.

The Somerset & Dorset Railway employed small and large handlamps from the Midland Railway. The Midland-

stamped 'CASTLE CAERENION', then over-plated 'MARCHWELL' (on the main Cambrian network).

The practice of recording serial numbers on handlamps is a feature of considerable interest. While this was considered to be necessary by both the large and the small railway companies it was not universally adopted. Large companies such as the NER and the GER did not number all of their lamps, while the GNSR made provision for numbering their lamps on the large brass plates, they then chose not to number them!

The numbers on lamps from the early companies, which were absorbed in the latter part of the nineteenth century, are difficult to analyse. In the case of the Manchester, Buxton, Matlock and Midlands Junction Railway there is lamp No 1 allocated to Rose Hill. However, the only other surviving lamp from this line is stamped 'M B & M RY E9 P.WAY' which implies another series. In the

170 M & GNJR lamp used by fog men

171 Cheshire Lines Committee lamp from Mouldsworth

style oval brass plates stated 'Somerset & Dorset Joint Railway' usually with a 400 series number. There is a second type of round brass plate with just the initials 'S & DJR' and these usually carry a 6000 series number. Given the evidence of the surviving examples, it is highly unlikely that this indicates over 6,000 lamps in service. The GN & GEJ produced a batch of clearly numbered lamps for their stations on the Lincoln to Spalding line: 'GN & GER 24' allocated to Blankney, and 'GN & GER 41' allocated to Potterhamworth. Other lines used GNR lamps with the 'GN & GE' stamped or embossed into the GNR brass plate, 'GN & GE JT STOW PARK' as well as the re-allocation plate 'Bradfield'. The Norfolk & Suffolk Joint Railway is another example of inconsistency within a joint company. Their northern section employed M & GNJR handlamps and then plated them 'N & S C 47 ROUGHTON ROAD FOGMEN' (**Fig 170**).

However, on their southern section they employed GER lamps, for instance 'Lowestoft North 3' is stamped onto a standard GER lamp which has then been overplated 'N & S C'.

Lamps used by the Cheshire Lines Committee are clearly numbered but it is by no means clear how one should decode numbers such as: '43 PE 24', '52 GE 174' or '68 Ge 1'. The first example is allocated to Mouldsworth and could be 'P' for passenger (**Fig 171**). The second is allocated 'CHESHIRE LINES TRAFFORD PARK SIDINGS M.GDS' and so the 'G' could be for goods.

Numbers might be added by the later company. There is an example of a lamp from the Barry Railways, numbered 6699, unusually high from a small company, and this may well be GWR numbering. One of the few surviving Scottish North Eastern Railway handlamps is clearly numbered '9284', perhaps this is a later numbering as it is difficult to envisage the need for this company to employ that number of lamps before it was absorbed into the Caledonian Railway in 1875.

A further question arises as to how many handlamps were allocated to given stations? Again some light is shed by numbers plated on or imprinted, telling us that at least that quantity was made, though possibly not at one time (these numbers again are taken from the Rogers' Collection). For instance Sleaford 43, Chatteris (GN & GEJ) 16, Ipswich (LNER days) 400, Hallaton (GN & LNWR) 4, Horncastle (GNR) 5, Tattershall (GER) 6, Stanley (Methley Joint Railway) 11.

After grouping the 'Big Four' produced new types of lamps in their thousands and by the end of World War II there may have been 40,000 produced by each company. After nationalisation there was yet another generation of lamps, perhaps totalling some 50,000 lamps. Large numbers of the post-grouping lamps have survived, and it is perhaps not surprising that these latter lamps lack the quality and aesthetic value associated with the pre-grouping era. Southern Railway lamps are marked S(A)R, S(B)R and S(E)R, standing for Ashford, Brighton and Eastleigh respectively, while LNER ones have 'E', 'C' etc for former GER and GCR lines.

At present the value of handlamps is determined by a combination of the following:

1 The general scarcity of items from that particular pre-grouping company.

2 The scarcity plus aesthetic value of a particular pattern of lamp.

3 The condition of the lamp. This is important if there are several to choose from, but it may be of no consequence if only a very small number have survived. If you are offered the only known lamp from the GN & LYJ you are hardly likely to consider it of low value if it does not have the original oil vessel and burner. On the other hand, a GNR collector whose lamps all contain their original GNR vessels, may not entertain another with an LNER vessel. It is naturally preferable to have the original vessel and burner, and to have a less worn example, all of which will attract a premium.

4 The addition of an evocative station name, perhaps from a line which has long closed. There are many collectors who specialise in the closed rural lines of Lincolnshire, and a lamp from the end of a branch line, like Horncastle, would attract a premium.

5 The addition of an attractive company brass plate. The LBSCR produced a large oval brass company plate, but not all lamps had these fitted, and many lost them during service. A missing plate may halve the value of a lamp if there are better complete examples in circulation. In the case of SER handlamps less than five of the survivors have retained their original 'SER Co' brass plates and rape-oil reservoirs.

6 All the basic rules of 'supply and demand' will have a bearing on the value. There may be far more collectors of items from closed lines such as the SDJC or the M & GNJR, while interest in the railways of London may be more limited. Lamps from the Metropolitan Railway may be as scarce as SDJC lamps, but the latter may command the higher price. On the other hand, because there are probably under five surviving North London Railway handlamps, there are bound to be a sufficient number of collectors who are keen to acquire the lamp for their collections, and hence they will command a high price despite the less romantic urban setting.

The table on page 108 is an attempt to correlate the size of some of the pre-grouping companies with the estimated number of handlamps employed. It also gives a rough indication of the numbers that have survived.

Extreme caution is required in the interpretation of these figures; this is only a first attempt to quantify lamps, and it is based on too small a sample to be statistically reliable. It is hoped that in the future much more evidence will become available. At present there is insufficient evidence to conclude that each company that had a general policy of numbering their lamps, started at 1 and ran consecutive contracts.

To conclude, the companies with between 100 and 1,100 miles of single track equivalent, employed perhaps as few as 300 handlamps, or as many as

Company	Size (Miles)	Lamp No (Min)	Lamp No (Max)	No of Lamps Employed	No of Lamps Surviving	% Survival
GWR	6650	68	24418	40000*	300	1.0
MR	5950	5060	23165	40000*	150	0.5
LNWR	5750	6012	36664	50000*	600	1.0
NER	4900	-	-	40000†	800	2.0
GNR	3050	725	18375	30000*	500	1.5
Caledonian	2850	192	1341	4000*	50	1.0
NBR	2700	1176	5805	10000*	250	2.5
GER	2600	-	-	30000†	400	1.5
GCR	2550	348	28146	30000	200	0.5
LSWR	2350	16	5306	10000*	300	3.0
LYR	2200	3700	16112	20000	200	1.0
SECR	1600	50	9227	10000	150	1.5
LBSCR	1250	600	1400	3000*	150	5.0
GSWR	1100	95	3849	4000	15	0.5
HR	650	-	-	500†	15	3.0
GNSR	500	-	-	1000†	50	5.0
NSR	500	-	-	700†	20	3.0
FR	400	-	161	300†	15	5.0
TVR	400	250	1685	2000	15	0.5
CLC	400	?	?	500	20	4.0
HBR	300	-	-	500†	10	2.0
BR	300	180	682	800	20	2.5
M & GNJR	300	1600	2212	2500*	40	1.5
SDJC	200	435	6615	2000	25	1.0
Metropolitan	150	-	-	500†	25	5.0
MSWR	100	17	139	200	5	2.5
MCR	100	-	128	200	5	2.5
PP & W	100	-	151	200	5	2.5
R R CO		105	243	300	5	1.5
CLR		70	170	300	15	5.0
N & SC		47	-	150*GE	10	6.5
CWJR		24	36	50	5	10.0
ANDR		-	138	150	5	3.5
PEEBLES		-	84	100	1	1.0
CAMBRIAN	400	-	-	300	10	3.5

Miles = Total length, including sidings, in equivalent of single track, in 1914.
Lamp number = lowest and highest number found on lamps in the Rogers 'C ollection.
Number of lamps employed:
* indicates that there were lamps which were not numbered
† indicates that it was not the company policy to number.

Analysis of railway hand lamps

4,000 lamps. Today there could be as few as ten known surviving examples, or perhaps, for a few companies, as many as fifty. When one looks at the companies that had less than 100 equivalent single track miles, they may have employed as few as forty handlamps or as many as 300; of these there could be up to twenty known surviving examples, or only one known surviving example.

172 *(left)* Lamp from the Peebles Railway

173 *(right)* Stockton & Darlington Railway lamp

Other railway companies that have not yet been mentioned, but which fall within this range include: Ashby & Nuneaton Joint (under five), Dundee & Arbroath Joint (under five), Dearne Valley (under ten), Eastern & Midland (under three), GC & Metropolitan (under ten), GN & LNW R Joint (under fifteen), Lewes & East Grinstead (five), Penrith Joint (under five), Preston & Wyre (under five), PDSWJR (under three), South Devon (under three), Stockton & Darlington (under ten). **Fig 172** shows the one known example of a Peebles Railway handlamp.

Fig 173 shows a plated handlamp from the Stockton & Darlington Railway. Other companies where only one example is known as yet are the GN & LYJ, MB & MR, Liskeard & Looe Railway.

Comparing the figures above with surviving company-marked cast-iron is revealing. The following companies' signs are 'not uncommon': LDECR, GN & LYJ, Methley Joint, HBR, and Rhymney, while the TVR, SDJC, M & GNJR and Barry Railway are all 'fairly common'. Of course, it may be that collectors of cast-iron were far more successful and observant, or that the lamps have survived but have not yet found their way into the railwayana market. Somehow, we doubt this and believe that far more cast-iron signs from some of these lines have survived. Only the future will tell.

Motive Power Depots and Rolling Stock Lamps

While the previous section dealt largely with handlamps that had been employed to transmit a signal, there were many other hand-held lamps which were designed only to provide illumination. General purpose handlamps and

174 *(left)* GNR goods department lamp

175 *(above)* LMS and LNWR Lucas acetylene lamps

guard's van emergency lamps would have no coloured glasses. Fitters in the locomotive departments or examiners in the carriage and wagon departments all required additional light. Lamps were designed to enable gangers to read the wagon number plates and the destination labels (**Fig 174**), or for the permanent-way staff involved in tunnel work.

While for the purpose of sending a message it may have been sufficient to rely on rape oil during the nineteenth century, and then paraffin during the early twentieth century, the light provided was often barely adequate for such duties as the detailed examination of parts of rolling stock. Alternative fuels included naptha, which was used by the permanent way department on the Cheshire Lines Committee, and this produced a powerful flare lamp. Also the railway companies produced gas, mainly for the lighting of their coaches, and a byproduct of this industry was

'gas oil' which was used in lamps. The Midland Railway platform lamp interiors were therefore marked 'Gas', although they are obviously designed to burn oil. The LNWR found a very much brighter light with the introduction of Lucas acetylene lamps (**Fig 175**) and the GNSR used acetylene for their platform lamp interiors. After grouping, the 'Big Four' all employed carbide lamps, particularly for their engineering works and carriage and wagon departments, where detailed examination of rolling stock depended upon adequate light. It is only since the demise of steam that electric light has made oil lamps obsolete, and are now regarded by BR as redundant assets.

One use of oil lamps on BR which has not yet completely disappeared is for tail lamps on trains. During the steam era trains carried lamps not only to provide a warning light, but also for coding the type of train. Locomotive headlamps and brake van tail lamps could be designed to carry a clear bullseye lens, with the option to secure a red aspect between the light and the lens, giving them a multipurpose use. Drivers of steam locomotives required gauge glass lamps to throw light onto the boiler water level gauge, and these mainly burnt rape oil, as paraffin was too volatile for use so near to the locomotive firebox. O.V.S. Bulleid designed a steam generator to power brass electric lights for his Southern Railway, 'Pacific' locomotives. The Pullman Car Company employed a variety of ornate electric table lamps, usually fitted with scalloped plastic Pullman shades, with the name of the coach, or the number of the trailer car, clearly visible in the ornate brass base. There are a few surviving examples of the early gas-lit coach lights, and also the rape oil lamps which hung in coaches and horseboxes, the burner being enclosed in a large glass bowl. It was often necessary during shunting duties, to leave part of a train standing on running lines overnight. Many companies issued 'train splitter lamps', which were stored in shunter's cabins, and their large hooks enabled the lamps to be hung at either end, on any rolling stock.

Signal Lamps, Crossing Gate Lamps and Buffer Stop Lamps

The pre-grouping companies mostly employed large copper signal lamp cases to house vessels capable of burning for a full week. In some cases the vessels displayed a glass window with an etched flame outline, to ensure that the wick had been properly trimmed and adjusted to enable it to burn for its full shift. These large copper lamps have survived from such companies as the NBR, NER, GNSR, GSWR, LYR and LBSCR. Other companies relied on heavily painted tin lamp cases, the most common survivors being from the GNR, with a similar pattern also used by the M & GNJR, the GN & GE Joint Railway and the West Riding Joint Committee.

176 Buffer lamps from the NBR *(left)* and Caledonian Railway *(right)*

An example of the latter is plated 'W.R.J.C. SKELLOW', 'No 2 To W.R. & Grimsby Full Sdgs', 'H.&B. & GC. SDGS. 15'. An example of a GN & GEJ signal lamp is plated 'Gt. Northern & Gt. Eastern Joint Railway No 199, Stow Park Buffer Stop'. Examples from the M & GNJR are plated 'Potter Higham Up Distant' and 'Murrow Spare'. The SR and LNER produced cast-iron signal lamp cases and the LNER's Welch Patent interiors were usually plated with location of the signal, eg 'LNER Grimsby Docks'. Some of the early signal lamps were hoisted into position with the aid of a pulley; examples survive from the NBR, GNSR, GWR. Signal lamps generally relied on a bullseye lens, either mounted in the case, or on the reservoir, to concentrate the light from the signal's lamp. If the signal was some way out of sight from the box, as was usually the case with distant signals, a heat sensitive electrical contact would indicate the lamp's condition.

There are a few remaining examples

of pre-grouping crossing gate lamps, perhaps reflecting the lower numbers that would have been required prior to the grouping. The GNR produced a similar size round metal case to their signal lamp, but with a long copper tube to engage in the gate timbers below. One example is plated 'GNR No 28257 OLD LEAKE DOWNSIDE SOUTH'. In 1987 it was still possible to find examples of the post-grouping crossing lamps in service. An example of an NBR buffer lamp is plated 'NBR BATTERY END ABERDEEN ROAD, TRAIN RECEPTION ROAD, LEITH WALK GOODS STATION' (Fig **176**). An NSR warning lamp with large red bullseye lens is plated 'N.S.R. 2310'. A lamp of similar design is plated 'LMS CANAL' indicating the railway's interest in this alternative form of transport.

Lamps for Platforms, Waiting Rooms, Offices and Signal Boxes

The pre-grouping companies not only employed their own pattern of hand-lamps, they also displayed their own style of station lamps, either post mounted or wall mounted. While some of the larger companies may have favoured one style of lamp, it was not uncommon to find more than one pattern employed throughout their whole network. Various patterns have survived from stations on the NER, GNR and LNWR. In the case of the SECR and LBSCR while their main design remained largely unchanged, their lamps were modified over many years — the SECR glazed top sections gave way to a single moulded sheet metal section, and the early lead corner pieces were replaced with ornate cast corners and eventually with cheaper cut-metal corners. There are many examples of the pre-grouping pattern being adopted after grouping, as happened with hand-

lamps. The GNR copper scalloped cap lantern was produced by the LNER, and the LNWR's Wolverton wall lamp was produced not only by the LMS but also by the Midland region of British Railways.

While it was unusual for station oil lamps to be converted to gas or electricity, some oil-lit stations survived well beyond the demise of steam. In the south-east Hamstreet Station retained its early oil lamps, even with the original blue etched nameglass, until electrification during the 1970s. Some of the clear glass had been removed from the case to facilitate the use of tilley lamps, to replace the original oil vessel. The Central Section of the Southern Region retained its original LBSCR oil lamps at Cowden Station until well into the 1970s. As one travels into the more remote areas of the BR network it is not surprising to find many more stations retaining their early platform lamps, indeed the Scottish Region have relied on such lamps well into the 1980s.

Many station lamps, which have now found their way into 'mainstream' collections, have come from the residents of villages close to stations that closed during the 1950s and 1960s. It was not uncommon for local residents to purchase the redundant station lamps, and to replant them in their gardens. Many are now in railwayana collections. During the mid-1970s an M & GNJR platform lamp case still with its original 'Tydd' lamp glass was found in a public house car park near Market Rasen. Perhaps an earlier pub landlord had moved north with the lamp? There are examples of pre-grouping lamps being re-allocated, presumably after grouping. A clearly stamped TVR platform lamp was discovered in service at Severn Beach Station, presumably transferred by the

GWR.

It is not surprising that these relics are cherished, not only by collectors of railwayana, but also by the general public who experienced the steam era. Older readers will recall the atmosphere which surrounded their dimly lit rural station, and the welcoming light which greeted the returning traveller. These lamps give so poignant a link to the past that they have become a fashionable reproduction for display in public places, or for use as garden ornaments. One of the manufacturers of pre-grouping lamps — Suggs of Westminster — are still to be found producing these modern reproduction lamps in their factory in Crawley. **Fig 177** shows a Furness Railway wall-mounted lamp complete with FR monogram. Notice the four-scroll holders on which the lamp rested; the normal four-sided glass (one removable) tapered downwards and the four-piece glass top is surrounded by a circular vent with finial.

The lamp standards came in lengths from 6ft above ground level to 15ft above ground level, with the lantern fitted on a four-pronged frog. A horizontal bar formed a ladder rest. An example of this was the GNR's L2 posts, which were fitted with ladder rests marked 'L4 GNR'. Other companies, like the Midland Railway, had their name cast into the stout base of the standard, above ground level. Inverness & Rosshire Railway standards were marked, as were NER crossbars. Many companies employed a distinct pattern of post which was not usually marked with company name, eg the SECR or LBSCR. Many of these posts were produced by outside contractors such as Handysides of Derby, Harwells of Northampton, Smiths of Whitchurch, and the Thames Bank Iron Company of London. **Fig 178**

177 Furness Railway wall mounted lamp

178 GSWR platform lamp, re-erected at a hotel

shows a GSWR example still in use in Ayrshire at the Turnberry Hotel.

Although some of the pre-grouping platform lamp cases were clearly stamped or plated many were only marked on the reservoirs, and some had no markings other than the station name. Cases with brass plates include NBR, Cambrian Railway and GNSR wall-mounted lamps, plus the early MSLR platform lamps. Cases that were stamped with the company name include those from the GNR, LNWR, Midland Railway and Caledonian, although not all cases were necessarily stamped. Platform lamp interiors that were plated include CLC and GNR which also featured the station name, although some of their vessels were only stamped.

GER vessels featured the name of the station on a steel plate, although it is not clear if this was an LNER addition. The NER and Cambrian vessels were plated with the same brass oval which was used on their handlamps. Vessels that were only stamped with the company initials include the SECR, LBSCR, LSWR, LNWR and Midland Railway. In the case of small railway companies, such as the Kent & East Sussex Railway, the variety of surviving lamp cases indicate that they were probably obtained by the company from a number of sources, subject to the price being competitive. Such lamps are not usually marked with the company name, although the station name may have survived on the glass.

Waiting room and office lamps may be wall mounted, hung or free standing in the booking office or station master's office. Brass table lamps from the GER have a heavy ornate brass base with the station name on a brass plate. Brass table lamps have survived from the GN & GE Joint Lines either plated with the

station name, or plated with, for example, 'LNER Nocton & Dunston'. The LMS produced brass table lamps in their Wolverton works, but it is not clear if these were only for dining cars, refreshment rooms, or for office use.

Wall-mounted station lamps were issued by the GWR for their ticket offices, the earliest examples are cast with the patent date of January 1871. The GWR and the Midland Railway produced ornate brackets on which to mount these oil lamps. The NER produced a metal shelf with an integral reflector, on which the oil lamp could be displayed. The M&GNR issued an integral oil lamp with a back plate which could be secured to the wall and which carried the reflector. The glass chimney was secured in an overhanging ornate canopy. The SECR employed rolled brass chandeliers to mount their waiting room oil lamp. An example from Appledore waiting room is plated 'Ridsdale & Co of London'. This manufacturer also produced small hanging lanterns for stations on the GCR's lines, such as at Ollerton.

There are many surviving examples of station gas lamps. The majority had been supplied by the Sugg Lighting Company, their copper 'Rochester' and 'Littleton' styles being suitable for external use. Sugg also produced an enamel 'Westminster' internal gas lamp. Gas-lit stations remained largely unchanged until well after the demise of steam and it is only during the last ten years that they have been rapidly disappearing.

Oil lamps which hung from a ceiling hook were a common feature of pre-grouping signalboxes, and were also allocated to stations and offices. Examples in the 'Rogers' Collection' which carry brass plates with the company name and the allocation include:

179 *(right)* A collection of
hanging lamps used by
railway companies

180 *(below)* GNR lamp yoke

'L & NWR Stores St Helens Junc. No
12071C', 'Cheshire Lines Skelton Junc.
Shunters Cabin', 'M & GNJR Honing
East', 'GCR Passenger Dept. Leicester
Central', 'MET. & GC Watford (**Fig 179**
from left to right). Brass hanging lamps
for the GNSR were only plated with the
manufacturer's name 'Shirras of Aber-

deen'. The NER plated their hanging
lamps with the same brass oval which
was used on their handlamps. The
LNER provided brass hanging lamps,
examples being plated 'LNER Old Leake'
'LNER Wragby' and 'LNER Eastville'.
They also issued metal hanging lamps
for signal box use, with metal allocation
plates. The LMS produced hanging
lamps at Wolverton, but only marked
the reservoirs 'LMS'. The SR provided
tilley hanging lamps and brass hanging
lamps have been found in use in signal
boxes in the Central Section, though
usually unmarked.

Most stations had lamp rooms safely
located some distance from the main
buildings. They were seldom built of
inflammable materials such as wood,
and there are many surviving examples
of the corrugated iron huts in which the
fuels were stored, and the lamps were
trimmed. The doors were either labelled
'Lamps' or 'Lamp Room' with enamel or
cast-iron door plates. In addition there
were often notices prohibiting smoking
or warning of the risk of fire, eg the 1916
'Highly Inflammable Stores' notice by
Chromo of Wolverhampton, which re-

181 Storage cans for lamp oil from (left to right): Inverness and Perth Junction Railway, GWR, Axholme Joint Railway

fers to prohibition of anyone under 16, plus arrangements for locking and the address of the keyholder. In order to facilitate the transportation of several trimmed and filled signal lamp vessels, the GNR issued yokes stamped with company initials and painted with the allocation — 'GNR Boston Pass', and 'GNR Bradford Gds'. The GWR supplied a long wooden carrying pole with slots to engage the top handles of the signal lamp vessels. **Fig 180** shows one such GNR lamp yoke with chain and triple lamp hooks.

The lamp room would also be supplied with storage cans, measuring cans, lamp filler cans and funnels, all of various sizes and patterns. Storage cans may be plated with the location — 'A.J.RY. Ealand Depot Crowle' or 'I. & P. SEC 29' as shown in **Fig 181**. Others were plated 'When empty return to general stores Swindon' or 'Return to Stores Dept. Gateshead when empty'. The measures were typically stamped

'GWR Swindon-Quart' or 'LBSCR 1 Pint'. Filler cans were usually conical or drum shaped and may be plated 'N.&S.C. Hopton Rape Oil' or 'GER Welnetham — Petroleum Oil for Long Burning Lamps'. Funnels may be stamped and plated in the same way as the company's handlamps — an MSLR stamped funnel carries the brass plate 'Manchester Sheffield & Lincolnshire Railway Co — Maud's Bridge'. An LBSCR funnel is stamped, plated 'Pevensey' and carries the 'London Brighton & South Coast Railway' brass oval. Finally there would be wick trimming scissors, wick soakers and wick cans. Even these small tools would invariably carry the company initials.

When one considers that there were 6,683 passenger stations in Britain in 1937 and 6,909 goods stations, and an enormous number of signals, crossing gates and buffers, one can begin to imagine the scale of the lampman's duties!

7
Along the Tracks

Undoubtedly, the late 1960s and early 1970s was the best period for re-discovering and evaluating the artefacts of the railway tracksides. After the ravages of the 'Beeching Axe', thousands of miles of closed lines lay overgrown and temporarily forgotten, gradually being repossessed by farmers and other landowners. Onto these lost lines stumbled the early collectors of trackside railwayana. They could still remember the LNER, GWR and LMS signs, but what were the strange items lettered SYJL or SJS or CCSC or OAGBR? Twenty years after BR took over, signs obviously predating the grouping had still survived. Even today the excitement that gripped these rediscoveries can still be remembered.

In those days of collecting trackside signs, there were many who casually walked a trackbed or rusting railway without knowing who had owned it, especially if they did not possess a copy of the *Ian Allan 1965 Regional Gazetteer* or the later *BR Pre-Grouping Atlas 1972 Edition 5*. At some point on a hot August afternoon there came in sight a gate adorned with a cast-iron gate sign marked 'Midland & London & N. Western Joint Lines', which for a very small price, the local farmer would readily permit to be removed.

Above the tracks, on either side of road bridges, there swung the testimony to the 1861 and other Locomotive Acts:

'Weak Bridge' or 'Bridge Weight Restrictions' signs, and signs warning against trespass onto lines via bridge access points. Along what was the South Yorkshire Joint Line Committee (owned by the MR, LYR, GCR, GNR and NER) were to be seen literally dozens of signs fully titled or sometimes with initials only. And along both sides of the tracks in those days virtually every public and farm crossing was festooned with signs. For example, just one crossing would often have a post-grouping and pre-grouping trespass plate and two more on the other side. If crossings were adjacent, that meant eight signs, all marked. It became clear that what was being rediscovered was the remains of the height of Victorian railways, which had remained virtually intact, with new versions added in post-grouping times.

Older collectors remember the location of old plates marked with the initials of long-forgotten railway companies. While wandering on the GCR near Wrexham, what did the plate with the letters 'CQR' stand for? Research indicated its origins as a 'Wrexham Mold & Connahs Quay Railway' plate with the 'W' and 'M' ground off by the GCR, with the impressions still clearly seen. And anyone walking from Sellafield to Marron Junction in Cumberland in 1969 would have walked past dozens of gates, almost all still enriched with plates cast by the LNWR & FR Joint Lines.

182 A collection of cast iron gate notices at the Moseley Railwayana Museum. All come from railways, although only one (LNER, second from top) bears company initials

In those days of collecting it was possible to stand on a railway bridge and look down the lines and see items that are now avidly collected, fixed on posts at almost every crossing. On the Vale of Towy Railway (LNWR & GWR) between Llandeilo and Llandovery, a new collector stopped his car in a layby and happened to read the name on a nearby sign, and was startled to realise that he had 'found' a new line which no collector at that time had been aware of. When such facts started to become widely known, a great spate of discovery was soon launched. It was not unknown to predict that certain pre-grouping companies would have made marked cast-iron, and to be able to prove this inside a day by lineside research on closed parts of the system.

Suffice to say that by the mid-1980s some 120 different railway companies (pre- and post-grouping) had been proved to have made named or initialled cast-iron or enamel signs and even in 1988 new ones are still being found. It is worth relating the history of sign collecting as other sections of railwayana collecting, eg china, are still in the stage passed through by cast-iron ten to fifteen years ago.

Gate and Stile Notices

There were a wide variety of gate and stile notices, some warning of penalties, others only extolling users to shut and fasten; some with a please, others more curt (**Fig 182**). The great majority of railways used long unmarked gate signs like these. Not surprisingly, some exist whose origins are not really known. The two central ones show how the heavier, solid Midland Railway 'Shut & Fasten Gate' was copied by a lighter thinner LMS type below.

Even more collectable are those

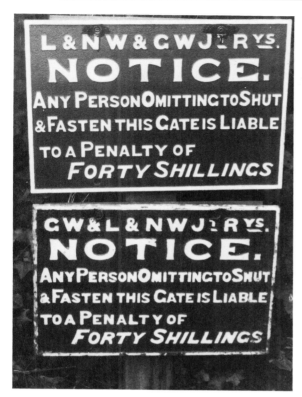

183 Two versions of gate warning signs from the LNWR & GWR Joint Lines showing the inconsistencies of railway initials

184 Gate notice from the West Cornwall Railway

former were on the Lancashire Union lines, the latter on the Preston & Wyre Railway and others. Many Welsh companies used gate signs which are now much sought after, including the RSBR, the Rhymney, the Cambrian, Brecon & Merthyr, the GWR in several forms, and amazingly the Gwendraeth Valleys Railway, which produced at least two different patterns of signs. The famous GWR pattern had varieties marked West Cornwall, GWR & Mid J and GWR & GCR Joint. **Fig 184** shows one example.

Two other points should be made. The Railway Executive, British Transport Commission and British Railways Board all continued pre-nationalisation types, with their own names or initials, both in cast-iron and enamel. Few companies produced enamel signs due to poor weathering, but the beautiful blue ones by the Furness Railway are an exception.

Boundary Markers

Boundary markers are one of the richest, and still only partially tapped, sources of railway relics in existence. Why they are so fascinating is that they still perpetuate long forgotten company names which have left no other trace, save perhaps on a few items of paper. **Fig 185** shows a cast-iron LNWR post *in situ*. A very old NER type was a circular bollard with letters around like a collar.

where company letters or names topped the gate notice. Prominent examples include the LNWR and all its jointly owned lines. Hence there exist GN & LNWR, Midland & LNWR, LNWR & FR, LNWR & LYR, LNWR (in old and new styles) all dated Euston 1883, the ponderous wording referring to 'Carriages, cattle or other animals' and with the threat of 'forfeit or pay any sum not exceeding 40/-'. It should be noted that this exceeded total weekly wages in many cases, so was meant as a great deterrent. Another type of gate notice was found on the LNWR & GWR , cast in two forms, as **Fig 183** shows.

On the LNWR & LYR Joint Lines two types were made, one the very heavy LYR, the other the light LNWR type. The

185 *(left)* An LNWR ground-level boundary marker still *in situ* near Ashbourne

186 *(right)* Boundary post from the GWR & GC Joint Lines

187 *(below)* A selection of GNR boundary posts

The GWR used a triangular section boundary post.

Many of the earliest boundariy markers appear to have been made of stone, with examples known from the Bodmin & Wadebridge, Liskeard & Caradon, Cockermouth, Keswick and Penrith, LYR, HR, Preston & Wyre and North Staffordshire Railways, but as few boundaries are dated, it is difficult to be sure. Many others were of road milepost type with vertical backs for locating against walls and buildings as in the case of the GWR triangular design and those used by the Brecon & Merthyr Railway. Later ones range from the well known circular GWR, Severn & Wye Joint, GWR & GCR Joint (**Fig 186**), LNWR & GWR Joint and GW & RR types, to the 'tombstone' LNWR type. The latter type was used for a range of LNWR joint lines, notably Midland & LNWR, LNWR & FR and possibly GN & LNWR, for the North Union Joint on canals and for the Preston & Longridge Joint Railway.

Some of the most attractive are illustrated here. A well-known and common pattern is the GNR type. **Fig 187** shows a whole selection of these. Some had letters impressed, others raised, giving rise to many slight variations. The pattern was used for the GN & GEJ, West Riding & Grimsby, M & GNJR, Norfolk & Suffolk, and most remarkably the Gar-

ston & Liverpool Railway. It is thought that examples from other pre-GNR companies are still to be found.

For some reason South Wales was one of the areas which had most boundary posts. It appears that almost all the major railway companies planted their legal demarcations and new ones are still being found. Examples are known from the GWR (three main types with serif, non-serif and date differences), GW & RR, Cambrian, Monmouth Railway & Canal Co, Forest of Dean Railway,

188 *(above)* A collection of boundary posts, mainly from South Wales

189 *(right)* Boundary post from the Central Forest of Dean Railway

190 (above) Boundary posts from the Pontypridd, Caerphilly & Newport Railway, and the Alexandra (Newport & South Wales) Docks & Railway Co

Alexandra (Newport & South Wales) Railway & Docks Co, Severn & Wye Joint, Brecon & Merthyr, Neath and Brecon, Rhymney, Taff Vale, Barry Railway, Rhondda & Swansea Bay, South Wales Mineral Railway, Pontypridd Caerphilly & Newport, Mid Wales Railway, Port Talbot Railway & Dock Co, and most recently, discovered in October 1987, Fishguard & Rosslare Railways & Harbours.

This plethora is still to be explained; it is possible that due to the criss-cross of lines in adjacent valleys, legal demarcation was of great importance in this area. **Fig 188** shows examples from the TVR, Cambrian, RSBR, BMR, Severn & Wye Joint, MWR, PTRDCo and MRCCo. **Fig 189** shows what is arguably the most pleasing example of a Victorian cast-iron boundary post, from the Central Forest of Dean Railway. **Fig 190** shows an example from the long winded

Alexandra (Newport & and South Wales) Docks & Railway Company, plus one from the Pontypridd, Caerphilly and Newport Railway.

Other designs seem so far to have been 'one-offs', such as the tombstone type from the NSR and the GC & MJ; only three of the latter type are known so far. The circular bollard type, one of the four known NER designs, is currently believed to be the earliest type and is only found around the Hartlepool area. Other companies whose marked boundary posts are known are the LDECR, HBR, BER, GER, Midland and LSWR, while in the London area the Hammersmith & City, Metropolitan, and Watford Joint put small markers into their pavements. The LNWR, SMJR and MSJAR placed small oval signs

190 Rhymney Railway bridge weight restriction sign

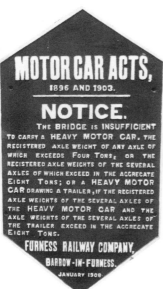

192 Furness Railway bridge weight restriction sign

stamped initials into the ends of rails. There is one BR design, perpetrating the GWR circular type, with BR(WR) letters.

This is an area of railwayana where much remains to be discovered, and where other able-bodied walkers equipped with determination will find previously unknown examples.

Bridge Signs

On most bridges across their tracks railway companies usually installed either bridge restriction diamond- or rectangular-shaped signs, almost always at both approaches, or inset into the parapet on both sides. The wording was a variation on the common theme of barring locomotives/heavy motor cars from passing over the bridge without the consent of the company. The diamond-shaped signs specified either maximum tonnage or maximum weight on any one axle, and often refer to 1861, 1896 and 1903 Acts of Parliament. **Fig 191** shows one of the most attractive weight restriction signs from the Rhymney Railway with two borders and five different type styles.

The superb Furness Railway elongated diamond-shaped sign, only one of which is known, has the bonus for the collector of having the company's name in full as well as 'Barrow-in-Furness' and 'January 1908' (**Fig 192**). **Fig 193** shows the largest type of diamond, in the SMJR group, and refers also to weights of trailers.

The large diamond-shaped signs were cast to a general pattern, many by the Coalbrookdale company where some of the originals are still on display. Railway company address, title and specific weights were added as needed. There is no doubt that damage to bridges must have been of major concern and bridge notices are therefore a

either on fences or in pavements by bridges.

There are, of course, post-grouping boundary posts of many sorts. The LNER continued the GNR type, while the LMS had at least three concrete designs. Nothing is so far known from the Southern Railway, although the SDJR

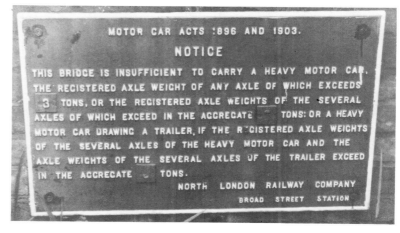

193 *(above left)* Weight restriction sign from the Stratford-upon-Avon & Midland Junction Railway

194 *(above right)* Weight restriction sign from the North London Railway. Note the changed weight limits

195 *(right)* A collection of bridge numbers

very interesting aspect of railwayana. Relatively small companies were as assiduous as the large companies: there are impressed aluminium ones from the Derwent Valley Light Railway, cast ones from Isle of Wight Central, NBR, WMCQR and many others. **Fig 194** shows one of perhaps only two or three to have survived from the North London Railway.

Bridge numbers were located on the left-hand side of bridge piers, facing trains. Almost every company used them, a major exception being the GWR. They were usually cast-iron, with each bridge normally having a pair. However, with large companies, several lines had their own number sequence, so there

were often multiple examples of the same number. Many lines included their initials round the border. **Fig 195** shows some of the rarest in existence at Moseley Railwayana Museum; note the variety of shape.

Initials after the number indicated one bridge with abutments, while those in the middle column with cut-away corners were viaduct numbers. At one time, the Carlisle Citadel Station Committee's bridge numbers were the rarest known but others were sold off the station walls by BR in the early 1980s. Probably the rarest bridge number in existence is from the Wakefield Joint Passenger Station (WJPS); only one is known to have survived. Even in the late

196 *(left)* NBR mileposts

197 *(right)* A milepost from the Cheshire Lines Committee. The initials represent London Road, Manchester

1980s, it is still possible to see pre-grouping bridge numbers from LBSCR, LBR, CLC and a few other railways. A favourite last resting place of BR bridge numbers is as house numbers.

Mileage and Gradient Posts

These were usually placed on one side only of double-track railways. Both these areas of railwayana have never been catalogued or recorded, yet both are passing very rapidly from the scene. Due partly to the legal requirement to provide accurate distances relative to fares, railway companies were meticulous in locating their posts. The early ones were often wood, especially gradient posts, although it is hard to generalise, as some companies appear to have used cast-iron from the outset. On the other hand, lines like the Furness Railway and the Maryport & Carlisle Railway used wood until the end and the last surviving examples were still to be seen as late as 1986. **Fig 196** show a complete set, restored, at the Winchcombe Railway Museum from the NBR . They were bolted at an angle for ease of viewing from engines.

It must suffice to mention outstanding general features of other lines. **Fig**

198 *(right)* Milepost from the South Eastern and Chatham Railway, indicating 69¼ miles

197 shows one of the more unusual types, a CLC 16¾ milepost with a D-shaped top. Generally one two or three dots were used for ¼, ½, or ¾ mile. **Fig 198** shows such a milepost from the SEC. Sometimes the railway was indicated by name or letters. The distance to London Road, Manchester on the MSJAR & CLC was shown on the very attractive mileposts of that company.

It is still possible to see whole series of ex-LNWR wooden mileposts along some lines. It was normal to have a specific shape for each ¼ mile, with the largest reserved for the full mile. **Fig 199** shows a selection at the Moseley Railwayana

199 A collection of mileposts and gradient boards

200 Maryport & Carlisle Railway wooden mileposts

Museum. The $44\frac{1}{2}$, $69\frac{1}{4}$, $69\frac{3}{4}$ and 70 (clover leaf) are LMS mileposts of concrete, cast at Irvine in the GSWR style.

The series of NER posts with 'ears' above or at the side of the distance can be seen. The NER marked junctions and main stations on some of their posts, as did the Midland Railway, but this was not general.

Finally, **Fig 200** shows full mile and $\frac{1}{2}$ mile painted wooden posts from the Maryport and Carlisle Railway. **Fig 199** also shows a variety of gradient posts. Although they were vital in steam days, these are now falling out of use. In the foreground stands a fine MSLR cast-iron gradient post (1 in 100/1 in 163) not having angled arms. The post indicating 1 in 220 with delicate shaped ends is from the Maryport & Carlisle Railway (perhaps the only one saved?), while the example with rounded ends showing the 1 in 200 on both arms is one of the few from the Furness Railway to be preserved. The large 1 in 672/1 in 99 was used on the NER, and the 1 in 102/ 1 in 184 was the standard Midland Railway design.

There are very few marked gradient posts with names. Exceptions were the GCR and CLC. Some of the latter's posts had both arms marked as well as the post. Some exceedingly early examples have survived. A recent one to appear was off the Manchester, Bolton & Bury Railway, whose full title was the Manchester, Bolton & Bury Canal Navigation and Railway, which amalgamated with the Manchester and Leeds Railway in 1846 and became part of the Lancashire & Yorkshire Railway a year later. In general, however, both gradient and mileposts remain little known and perhaps this book may help to draw attention to a fascinating field for collecting.

Trespass Signs

It will be remembered that at least 115 railways have left their memorial in cast or enamel signs with company initials or names. A sizeable percentage of this number is found in trespass warning signs or advisory notices located by subways, culverts, company canals, goods or locomotive depots. **Fig 201** shows one of these signs, taken when it was still *in situ* on a wooden post on one of the Cardiff Railway stations, with coaching stock behind. A similar one is preserved at Winchcombe Railway

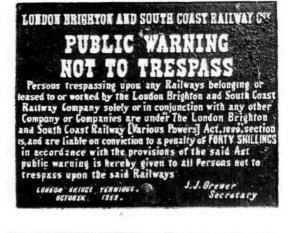

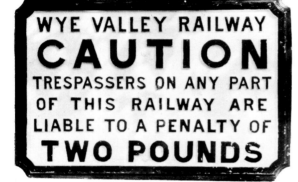

201-4 Trespass signs from the Cardiff Railway, LBSCR, Wye Valley Railway and Carlisle Citadel Station

Museum, and appears to have been the only cast-iron sign from this railway to have survived.

Fig 202 shows a cast-iron LBSCR trespass sign, a good example of railway typography, with five type styles. Only some half-dozen examples are known to have survived, and there is doubt as to their correct colours. The earliest one seen had already been re-painted with artistic licence in what were believed to have been the likely colours. Collectors need to know that the SR, on grouping, exercised a vendetta against the LBSCR and appears to have removed most of their signs (unlike the SEC and LSWR,

great numbers of whose signs survived up to the early 1980s) and hence their extreme scarcity. Some LBSCR diamond-shaped bridge signs did survive, but they were overplated with SR.

Fig 203 shows another very rare trespass notice, from the Wye Valley Railway so rare that when the first one re-emerged, collectors could not believe that such a sign could have survived. The style, totally different from the LBSCR, is large, bold and simple. Similar ones were made, without the company name, for the Monmouth Railway and Canal Company. Yet another unique sign, recently seen at the 1986

205 *(right)* A collection of rare trackside signs

206 *(below)* Trespass warning sign from the Hull & Barnsley & Great Central Railways Joint Committee

centenary of Carlisle Station where it formed part of a display, is a trespass sign marked 'Carlisle Citadel Station and Carlisle Goods Traffic Lines'. It was known from old photographs of Carlisle Citadel Station that LNWR-style trespass notices at one time adorned the forecourt as well as the CCSC viaduct plates noted earlier. But what intrigued collectors when this sign was seen was that it was issued jointly by the Station Committee and the Goods Traffic Lines (alternatively referred to in the fifth line as the Goods Traffic Committee) (**Fig 204**).

Fig 205 taken at Winchcombe Railway Museum shows a group of rare trackside signs. The MSLR sign was erected at crossings and elsewhere (and this company also used a relatively common canal bridge warning sign of similar size). By contrast, the GWR & LSWR sign (GWR style) is a unique survivor from the Isle of Portland Joint Railway. It was readily visible from the road which avoided Weymouth town centre, by the car park on the site of the joint station, until the mid-1970s before being bought for preservation. On this short joint line were also trespass signs and several boundary posts, all in GWR styles. This illustration also shows part of both a Dundee & Arbroath Joint and an Oldham, Ashton & Guide Bridge Railway trespass signs (both in LNER style).

A further style of trespass notice is shown in **Fig 206** with an HB & GCJ sign signed 'By Order The Committee'. A much commoner version is signed by 'Oliver S. Holt, Secretary'. Hull & Barnsley Railway trespass plates were of similar design. Often these trespass plates were located adjacent to bridges as well as at crossings, and used to be bolted onto posts of great length, some at least 12-15ft tall so that they poked

208 *(above)* A very early Midland Railway trespass sign threatening prosecution 'as the Law directs'

209 *(left)* Cast iron LSWR signs

Fig 208. Signed by J.F. Bell, the secretary of the Midland Counties Railway and the first secretary of the Midland Railway, it must date from about 1838-46 and it is believed to be one of the oldest cast-iron railway notices to survive, although there is alleged to have been a Birmingham & Gloucester Railway trespass sign in Camp Hill Goods Station, Birmingham before demolition.

Whole series of cast-iron signs were produced, covering many locations, using the same basic casting pattern with varied wording. **Fig 209** shows an LSWR 'family' of signs, all heavy, with rounded corners and secured by large nuts. The 'Beware of Trains' sign was a very common one, while the 'Cross Line by the Bridge' sign was bolted below platform edges to warn against crossing station running lines, especially electrified ones. Some of these can still be seen. The other two were much rarer.

Another similar group were the trespass signs from the LNWR and its joint lines like Midland & LNWR Joint, GN & LNWR Joint, LNWR & GWR (Vale of Towy) and ordinary LNWR & GWR Joint from lines in the Birkenhead area. For the LNWR & FR, an LNWR style 'Beware of Trains' was cast but, as yet, no joint trespass sign is known. On the GWR, the standard serif and non-serif trespass signs were used for a great number of owned and part-owned GWR subsidiaries, like the Port Talbot Railway & Dock Co, Rhondda & Swansea Bay Railway, GW & LSWR Joint, West London Extension and GWR & GCR Joint.

Enamel Signs

Alongside the tracks of a few companies could be seen examples of enamel trespass and other signs. These were often enclosed in a wooden frame to protect

up above the bridge to give warning to would-be trespassers.

An extremely early sign is the Midland Railway trespass notice shown in

Plate 9 Two decorative name-plates from mainline loco-motives: *Great Northern* (BR Eastern Region), *Nederland Line* (SR Merchant Navy Class), and a train headboard from *The Royal Duchy* (BR Western Region), on exhibition at Fawley Museum open day 1987.

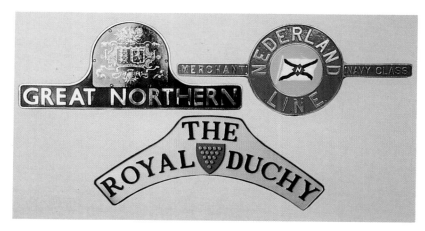

Plate 10 Locomotive builder's plate from Barclays & Co, Kilmarnock, dated 1883. *(Keith Buckle Collection)*

Plate 11 Standard circular wagon registration plates from the LMS, LNWR and LNER. *(MRM)*

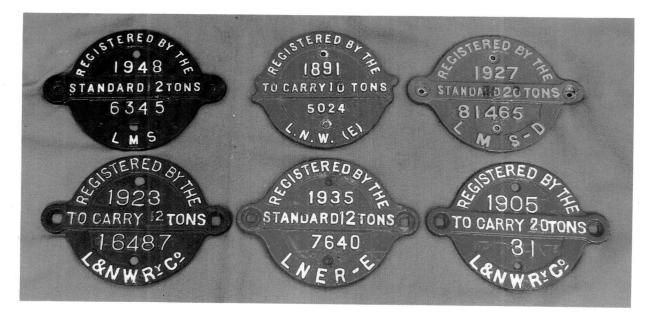

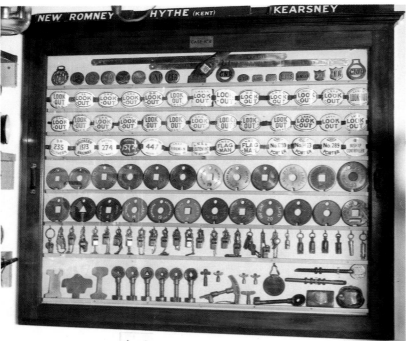

Plate 12 Railway signalling equipment top row, two Midland Railway rotary instruments flanking a Great Northern Railway pegging instrument and a GNR telegraph instrument; second row, various repeaters; with various bells below. *(Alexander Knapton Collection)*

Plate 13 An impressive collection of small items of railwayana: row 1, horse brasses; rows 2-4, enamel arm bands; rows 5-6, signalling tablets; row 7, whistles; row 8, signalling keys. *(Peter Rogers Collection)*

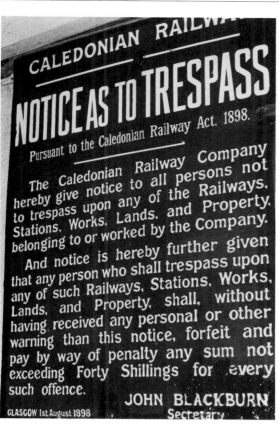

210 Enamel trespass sign from the Caledonian Railway

211 Enamel sign from the Selsey Tramway

the edges, as on the Caledonian Railway, whose trespass notices were usually at the ends of platforms and by bridges on paths leading to the station. Quite a lot have survived (**Fig 210**). There was also a version of this sign used by the LMS. Also, in Scotland, was a very rare Dundee & Arbroath Railway enamel trespass sign and it is possible that a GSWR one existed, as its impressions on the underlying wood have been found. In the north-east of Scotland were numerous Great North of Scotland Railway enamel trespass notices signed by Mackintosh, the company secretary, and made in distinctive brown with an off-white background. The NBR also produced enamel trespass signs.

In England, companies known for their enamel signs included the GWR with both vertical and horizontal patterns, the LMS and the LBSCR, the Vale of Rheidol Railway, the Kent & East Sussex Railway and the Weston, Clevedon & Portishead Railway, but on the whole the practice was quite unusual.

Other famous enamel signs include a beautiful Midland Railway blue enamel notice warning against the practice of interfering with posters and advertisements on its stations and the unique survivor from the Selsey Tramways (**Fig 211**). Several companies had signs under their bridges to warn against the posting of bills. The NLR had a small enamel, initialled sign, while the GWR & GCR had a very well laid out wooden one. The GCR and LNWR both had cast-iron ones, with the GWR having metal letters on a wooden sign.

Trackside Signs

A whole range of occasional trackside signs must be summarised. On the LNWR & LYR Joint Railway small marked signs were located by signal boxes at crossings, regarding the tampering with warning bells (**Fig 212**), while the Dearne Valley Railway had a similar, but larger, notice. Very common were the wooden 'Whistle' signs, usually mandatory before crossings. The GWR had a plain 'SW' (Sound Whistle) in cast-iron, while the LSWR used wood. Wood was also used for the famous GWR sign

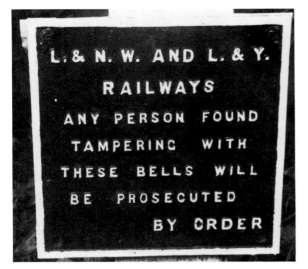

212 LNWR & LYR Joint Railway trackside sign

advising goods trains to pin down brakes.

Other Trackside Equipment

Along the tracks were the once ubiquitous linesmen's huts. Some had marked cast-iron stoves, but survivors are exceedingly rare. Inside these huts could at one time be found billhooks, scythes, axes, forks, grassrakes, spades, buckets, track-gauges, spanners, hammers, screwdrivers, mallets and lamps all marked with the company's initials, while outside there was often a grinding wheel and quite often, a traverser to get onto and off the rails with a gangers' trolley. **Fig 213** shows some of the above.

Padlocks and keys marked with railway initials were an integral part of trackside equipment and have survived in some numbers. **Fig 214** shows the Moseley Railwayana Museum collection which includes examples from the LNER, GWR, Cambrian and LSWR, and

213 A group of buckets, shovels and fork used by the trackside

214 Padlocks marked with railway initials

a small brass lock from the Midland Railway.

Finally, it should be noted that in this chapter we have tried to deal with items actually found along the tracks. Other signs, for example those to be found at stations and goods depots, are elsewhere in this book.

8

Railwayana of Railway Workers

Uniforms

Uniforms are a most interesting aspect of railwayana, and we are indebted for some of the data on this to the recent book by D.J. Froggatt *Railway Buttons, Badges and Uniforms* (Ian Allan, 1986) which has by far the largest collection of pictures of this subject ever assembled.

Unfortunately for the collector only a fraction of uniforms originally issued have survived; although many old photographs of railwaymen have survived, their uniforms have not. This is largely due to the practice insisted on by the railway companies of handing in old uniforms. Indeed, the GWR had over fourteen standard forms for uniform requisition. In the case of ordering new canvas aprons, clogs, oilskins, etc, the worn out article had to be sent to the General Stores at Swindon.

1 May and 1 November were the last days for measuring up for new winter and summer garments on the GWR, ie 6 months ahead of when needed, to give the contractors plenty of time. There were most detailed rules for procedure for men re-graded after uniform issue for the half-year and for men transferred in the meantime. In the GWR official *Standard List of Uniform, Caps & Clothing, Traffic & Goods Departments* of 1929 there were seventy-seven pages of types, rules and photographs. The following is an extract from page 6.

9. MISCELLANEOUS

The undermentioned Forms are used in connection with the requisitioning of Uniform Clothing and Caps, also for the issue of Surplus and Misfit garments, supplies of which can be obtained from the Stationery Department, Paddington, on application.

	No.
Summary of Requisition for Clothing	3132
Number and sizes of Caps required	2635/1
Summary of Boots required	1160
Misfit Clothing	2673
Self Measurement and alteration required	2673/1
Misfit Caps	2673A
Misfit Macintoshes and Leggings	2673B
Surplus Clothing	2673C
Deductions from original requisition	2673D
Certificate for Uniform Clothing ordered in anticipation of changes of grade	5844

10. STATION EQUIPMENT

In connection with the issue of Miscellaneous items such as

    Canvas Aprons

    Clogs

    Oilskin Clothing etc.

supplied as 'Station Equipment', arrangements must be made in case of renewals, for the worn out article which requires to be replaced, to be sent addressed to the Storekeeper, General Stores, Swindon, immediately on receipt of the new article, an advice note forwarded at the time of despatch, giving particulars of the articles returned. Divisional and District Officers must sat-

isfy themselves that such articles which
require to be renewed are unfit for further
use. When ordering Station Equipment the
form provided for the purpose must in every
case, whether for 'first issue' or 'renewals'
accompany the requisition.
In the case of 'renewals' the requisition to
the Stores Department must in every case be
accompanied by a certificate from the Divisional or District Officer to the effect that
the circumstances in which the first or
subsequent issue was made remain unchanged.
JUNE, 1929.

A.C. COOKSON,
Stores Superintendent.

The range of items produced for just
one company now seems staggering. On
the GWR the basic issue was: cap, overcoat, pea jacket, tunic jacket, vest, trousers, breeches, frock coat, black or
brown macintosh, coat, leggings,
sou'wester, cape and either leather or
brown macintosh leggings. Many of
these were available in different cloth
standards (serge, cloth, jean, etc). This
booklet could not have been the only
catalogue of uniform as it does not specify all the grade 1-4 station masters.

There were fifty clothing 'groups' each
with specific issues. Group 50 for example included GWR hotel hall porter
and hotel front entrance attendant.
They were allowed Cap No 4, overcoat
and serge frock coat, vest and trousers.
Frock coats were available from 35-43in
to suit GWR employees from 4ft 10in to
6ft 3in tall. Group 45 was for road motor
attendants and horse parcel vanboys.
Group 41 was for omnibus inspectors
only. There are over forty photographs
in the book, which lists no less than
thirty-four styles of cap, not counting
black silk hats and firemen's brass helmets.

An extract from page 45 includes:

215 LMS guard's jacket

MISCELLANEOUS

Patt. No.

M.2 Khaki Drill Dust Coat double-breasted,
chocolate coloured cuffs. Badged 'G.W.R' in
chocolate coloured worsted both ends of
collar. Brass buttons.

M.4 Blue Jean Jacket, single-breasted.
Badged 'G.W.R' in red worsted both ends of
collar.

M.5 Blue Jean Trousers, Fly-front.

M.10 Blue Worsted Guernsey. Badged
'G.W.R' in red worsted across front.

M.13 Undressed canvas Jacket. Single-
breasted.

M.28 Brown Holland Cap Cover.

M.29 Black Waterproof Cap Cover.

Black Paramatta Macintosh, single-
breasted, fly-front, plain collar. Brown Twill
Macintosh, single-breasted, fly-front, plain
collar. Black Leather Leggings, steel spring
fastening, strap and buckle at top.

Black Leather Leggings (Napoleon shape)
with spat to cover lace holes of boot. But-
toned at side.

216 *(left)* Southern Railway dining car steward's jacket

217 *(top right)* NER porter's cap and LNWR sailor's hat

218 *(lower right)* Buckle from a Midland Railway guard's belt

Black Oilskin Coat, double-breasted, plain collar.
Black Oilskin Leggings with strap at side to fasten to Trouser button.
Black Oilskin Sou'wester. Brim 2¹/₂ inches all round.
Black leather ankle clogs, strap and buckle fastening.
Black Oilskin Bib Apron.
Black Leather Gauntlet Gloves for Private Car Drivers.
Black Pegamoid Combination Overalls.
Brown Twill Macintosh Leggings with strap at side to fasten to Trouser button.

It will be seen that there were no less than four types of leggings: brown twill, two sorts of black leather and black oilskin. M.4 and M.5 were supplied to 'Men who clean Cars' and to at least fifteen other grades. M.2 was for motor bus conductors.

Fig 215 shows a well preserved LMS guard's jacket with red piping, fancy scrolls on the lapels, and silver buttons. This is fairly typical of later guards' apparel as only a small number of companies had metal badges denoting rank, which was usually indicated either on a metal cap badge or in woven

letters round the lapel. A few lines like the GCR had metal rank badges on the tunic. A Southern Railway dining car steward had a scroll name but plain buttons, this being a fairly common practice for the grade (**Fig 216**). One of the commonest of uniform items to have survived is the GWR porter/signalman jacket.

An example of a cap is shown in **Fig 217** which is an LNWR sailor's hat with LNWR in the ribbon. This is a relatively common item as a cache of them survived into recent times. An NER porter's cap is also shown.

Fascinating insights into the pride and standards expected of employees survive in rulebooks. For example in 1847 the LNWR stated that 'all staff appear on duty neat and clean' and station masters were to inspect staff daily who were to be 'clean shaven and with shoes brushed'. On the Arbroath & Forfar Railway enginemen were supplied with white coats, and it was a company regulation that 'any driver who reported for duty on a Monday morning with a soiled coat would be fined 15/-.'

Survival of railway uniforms has been so rare that nowhere in Britain is there any substantial collection of uniforms, either pre-grouping or post-grouping. At Bressingham Small Relics Museum is a group of several CLC jackets with red and gold letters and one marked just 'C.L.', together with an LNER vest and jacket with red lapel letters, plus an LMS overcoat. At Winchcombe Railway Museum there are some ten items including a GWR horse department carman's jacket. At Didcot Small Relics Museum there is a jacket from the Taff Vale Railway. Harpenden Railway Museum has a 1941 LNER police cape and at Warwick Railway Museum there are a rare stationmaster's pill hat, a red-piped porter's hat, a brown paramatta mac and leggings, a canvas apron, a porter's jacket, a yard inspector's jacket with yellow roundels, and eight-button overcoat and an ambulance man's helmet, all from the GWR.

At Chris Atkin's Collection in Spalding are an LNWR sailor's hat, a GNSR cap, a GNR porter's hat, a GCR hatband, an LNER red-lettered cap, an M & GNJR tunic and LNER gaiters. At Moseley Railwayana Museum, Birmingham, there is a full porter's uniform of waistcoat, trousers and jacket, and a steward's jacket (both from the Southern Railway), three LMS items including a Carriage & Wagon Department jacket and guard or steward's(?) jacket with blue piping, various GWR items including a long greatcoat with red collar, plus an LNWR sailor's hat. In Froggatt's book there are over sixty pictures of uniform items including those for LNWR gas meter inspector, GCR carters, GCR superintendent, and guards from a number of different railways.

It seems that, station masters, station inspectors and messengers apart, passenger guards were probably the most lavishly attired of any grade due to their high profile in the public eye. They were initially regarded as successors to stage coach guards and were often attired in green frock coats, as in the early LNWR days for example. They had a diagonal leather bandolier with badge and clasp, often in silver, with a pouch containing a railway watch. Pictures of passenger guards exist (see Spence *Railway Travel* for Cambrian, GNR and LNWR guards). The LNWR men had a cap with two braided bands with 'Guard' between. The knee length coat had double rows of six buttons. LNWR initials were along the lapel, the most striking feature being the leather sash slung over the right shoulder with a large buckle with metal letters 'LNWR' supporting a leather bag, while trousers had a stripe down, thus the passenger guard was a finer figure than a ticket collector who had no marked buckle.

Station Staff and Uniforms

To give some idea of the number of staff employed at stations we will consider a few examples at random. At Byfield on the Stratford-on-Avon and Midland Junction Railway, there were four staff and at Towcester on the Northampton & Banbury Joint in 1900 at least seven as shown in photos in Arthur Jordon's book on the SMJR (OPC, 1983). At Cuddington on the CLC there were ten. These examples were fairly small rural stations and were not exceptional.

Jeffry Spence's *Railway Travel* (Batsford, 1977) shows many stations and staff scenes, eg Oakham Station (MR) in 1890 with nine staff. Bishops Stortford in the 1870s had over twenty staff, while Retford in 1867 had over sixty. Euston Hotel (LNWR) in 1908 employed at least seventeen hotel porters alone. It should be realised that many of these photographs only show one shift of staff and often do not include signalmen, linesmen, fogmen and so on, employed at the station, so the numbers are understated. They do give an idea, however, of the numbers even at small places, and often mean more than just requoting the number of LMS employees in 1935 as 222,220.

Railwayana collectors should study these pictures of staff to build up an idea of the range of buttons, cap badges, uniforms, buckles and sewn-on insignia which originally existed. It is difficult to say how much has survived as whole uniforms are still being discovered.

The study of old photographs and the items surviving shows several general points. On most uniforms, the company's initials were sewn on rather than being in badge form, usually on both collars along the neck. This was true especially for the GWR, the Cambrian Railway, the Highland Railway and for some LMS uniforms. The grade was likewise often sewn in gold or yellow letters along the lapel. Some lines had cap badges in chrome letters, notably the GCR, LMS, CLC (metal), Cambrian, SMJR, Alexandra Docks & Railway, SR and LBSCR. Others had only sewn letters, with or without the coat-of-arms. Excellent pictures of GWR guards can be studied in *GWR Company Servants* by Janet Russell (Wild Swan, 1983, pp133-6). Early pictures show GWR in large letters above the cap peak. Most later ones had no initials but the grade sewn on with a GWR roundel near the buttonhole. GWR dining car attendants (shown on pp215-20 of the same book) wore black jackets, waistcoat with white

shirt and black bow tie and had the grade sewn on the lapel, as had dining car chefs. Female GWR World War I ticket collectors had the words on a hat band with GWR on their collar (*ibid* p222). GWR telegraph boys, messengers, platform buffet boys and the like had grades around the neck but no initials.

At the other extreme was the splendid attire of the GWR station master with his pill-box hat replete with gold braid and GWR roundel. There were three separate station master grades, depending on the status of the station, shown by ornate black braiding on the sleeves. Apart from the hat, the rest of the garments do not appear to have been marked in any way.

Very few female uniforms have yet come to light, although they certainly existed, especially during both World Wars. Pictures exist of Southern Railway female employees marching past, with SR badges prominent.

Buttons

'Once on the railway, always on the railway' was once an adage of railway service and one of the strongest testimonies to the loyalty of the company were uniform buttons featuring the company's initials. These have lasted in very large numbers as they were often kept as mementoes of employees' life-long service on the railway. Although uniforms were required to be handed in after usually 1-2 years' use (and the companies were very strict about this), when men retired they sometimes kept them. This, as well as the durability and smallness of buttons and the fact that one uniform set often had as many as ten buttons (TVR police overcoats had twenty buttons on the one garment!), has ensured their widespread survival.

Buttons are a most interesting section of railwayana as they are sometimes the only marked items to have survived from some of the very minor companies. Moreover, new ones are still turning up, for instance a remarkable one from the Neath, Pontardawe & Brynamman Railway which never actually operated under this name as its powers were transferred to the GWR almost immediately after its authorisation In the Chris Atkin Collection at Spalding there are marked examples from over ninety separate railways including the Cardiff, C & OJ, CER, EMR, ELR, D & AJR, ECJS. LDECR, M & SWJR, SMJR and WCJS.

To give would-be collectors an idea of what is available on the open market the following marked buttons were auctioned in the period January 1985 to June 1987: M & SWJR, TVR, GWR, LNER, SR, LMS, MR, LYR, Weymouth &

Portland, NER, Bristol Joint Station, HBR, M & GNJR, GNR, AJR, Mersey, GE Steamship, GER, Metropolitan, HR and LNWR. The amount of highly detailed data on buttons has been enormously increased by the publication in 1986 of David Froggatt's book *Railway Buttons, Badges and Uniforms* (Ian Allan). Perusal of the list of known buttons, abstracted below from this book gives insight into what has survived. It should be studied with the proviso that it is only a selection of what is known and con-

219-23 A variety of railway buttons

Aberdeen Joint
Station
Arbroath & Forfar
Ardrossan
Arpley Joint Station
Ashby & Nuneaton
Joint
Axholme Joint
Aylesbury Joint
Station
Barnsley Joint
Station
Birkenhead, Lanca-
shire & Cheshire
Junction
Birkenhead
Birkenhead Park
Station Committee
Birmingham &
Gloucester
Bishop's Castle
Blackpool & Lytham
Bristol & Exeter
Bristol Joint Station
Blythe & Tyne
Bolton & Leigh
Bradford, Wakefield
& Leeds
Carlisle Citadel
Joint Station
Carnforth Joint
Station
Chard Joint Station
Chester & Holyhead
Chester General
Station
Cleator & Working-
ton
Cleobury Mortimer
& Ditton Priors
Light
Clifton Extension
Cockermouth Joint
Station
Colne Valley &
Halstead
Cornwall
Corris

Croydon & Oxted
Dumbarton &
Balloch Joint
East Anglian
Eastern Counties
East Kent Light
East Lincolnshire
East London
Eastern & Midlands
East Union
Edinburgh & Glas-
gow
Felixstowe
Festiniog
Furness & Midland
Garnkirk & Glasgow
Glasgow, Barrhead
& Kilmarnock Joint
Glasgow, Paisley &
Greenock
Glasgow, Paisley,
Kilmarnock & Ayr
Grand Junction
Great North of
England
GW & LNE Joint
GW & SR Joint
Isle of Wight
Isle of Wight Central
Jersey Eastern
Jersey
Kent & East Sussex
Light
Knighton
Lancaster & Carlisle
Leeds, Dewsbury &
Manchester
Leeds Joint Station
Leeds
Liverpool, Crosby &
Southport
Liverpool & Man-
chester
Liskeard & Looe
Llanelly Railway &
Dock
London & Birming-
ham

London & Greenwich
Lynton & Barnstaple
Macclesfield, Bol-
lington & Marple
Maenclochog
Manchester &
Birmingham
Manchester &
Milford
Manchester, Bolton
& Bury
Manchester & Leeds
Market Harborough
Joint Station
Mawddwy
Methley Joint
Midland Counties
Midland & South
Western Junction
Mid Wales
Neath, Pontardawe
& Brynamman
Newcastle & North
Shields (police)
Alexandra (Newport
and South Wales)
Docks and Railway
Nidd Valley Light
Normanton Joint
Station
Northampton &
Banbury Joint
North Midland
North & South
Western Junction
North Wales Narrow
Gauge
Nottingham Joint
Station
Oswestry & Newtown
Oxford, Worcester &
Wolverhampton
Pembroke & Tenby
Pensnett
Perth General
Station
Plymouth, Devonport
& South Western

Potteries,
Shrewsbury &
North Wales
Preston & Wyre
St Helens
Scottish Central
Scottish Midland
Junction
Scottish North
Eastern
Sheffield, Ashton
under Lyre & Man-
chester
Sheffield & Midland
Shrewsbury &
Hereford
Shrewsbury Joint
Station
Sirhowy
South Devon
South Staffordshire
Stalybridge Joint
Station
Stockton & Darling-
ton
Stockton & Hartle-
pool
Tewkesbury &
Malvern
Tottenham & Forest
Gate
Tottenham &
Hampstead Joint
West Lancashire
Weymouth & Port-
land
Whitland & Cardigan
Whitehaven, Cleator
& Egremont
Whitechapel & Bow
Worcester Joint
Station
Yarmouth & Norwich
Yeovil Joint Station
York & North Mid-
land

Railways and stations known to have issued marked buttons

centrates on the more unusual and interesting lines, hence does not include many of the less surprising survivals, eg M & GNJR, SDJC, MSJAR and so on, nor does it include Irish or London Transport lines. In no sense should the list be read as exhaustive.

In a few cases, eg the Manchester & Milford Railway, it is known that buttons were made and worn for a time, but it does not mean that one has survived. Further details can be found in the work cited. It is known that the East Lincolnshire Railway ordered sets of high quality silver buttons, but was taken over by the GNR before opening. Probably the buttons may have been worn by the officers of the company before and during opening only.

Considerable duplication of identical initials exist. For example 'AJ' stands for both Aberdeen Joint Station, Axholme Joint Railway, Arpley Joint Station and Aylesbury Joint Station! CJS stands for Chard Joint Station, Carnforth Joint Station, Churchdown Joint Station, Cockermouth Joint Station, as well as Carlisle Citadel and Chester Station!

224 A variety of cloth and enamel armbands

225 LNER fire brigade enamel armbands

However, the initials and patterns were of course all different. There is also NJS (Nottingham Joint Station and Normanton Joint Station) and four joint stations all labelled generally BJS.

It should be noted that on many lines, different qualities of button were used according to the employee's grade with gilt silver, brass and nickel being used in that order. Black horn was also used, and pewter on some early lines. Copper and copper alloy buttons are also known. Buttons specifying sections of the railway were often used to designate police, marine (steamships), hotels and dining cars.

Enamel and Cloth Armbands

Several grades of railway workers normally wore permanent armbands denoting grade, and sometimes rank. The most common are the oval enamel 'Look Out' armbands, almost all red on white with red surround, secured by leather or elastic straps round the sleeve and worn by men whose job it was to blow a gangers' horn to warn track workers of approaching trains (**Colour Plate 14**). The design was almost standard, except that the company initials were either at the top, bottom or both sides. Various types are shown in the photograph. It is certain that most, if not all of the pre-grouping companies had these armbands, most of which are not uncommon. Examples are known from the Midland Railway, LNER, LMS, GWR, SR, LNWR (two types), GNSR, Furness Railway, GSWR, SECR, Caledonian Railway, MCR, LYR, LBSCR, M & GNJR, CLC, LSWR, GNR, NBR and GER. A rare square LMS type exists, while the NBR and LNER also had a 'flagman' armband. In addition there were also fire department enamel armbands, although these are extremely rare. There

226 *(above)* LNWR porter's badge

227 *(near right)* Midland Railway badge, probably an outside porter's

228 *(far right)* Midland railway steward's lapel badge

exists LNER 'Fireman Fire Brigade' as well as LNER 'Lieutenant Fire Brigade' (square shape with blue letters on white background) **(Fig 225)**.

Outside porters, often private porters for holiday traffic who were not railway company employees, had armbands. Some of these were enamel, others brass. These occurred on the NER, GWR and LNER notably. A 'Keswick No 7 Out Porter' armband exists. The LNER had an oval armband marked 'Porter' with the LNER in lozenge style and the number inside in black on white. There are also various others such as Southern Railway porter and the design passed into BR days with regional colours. There is even a BR 'Mishap Controller' in red and white. The cloth 'Pilotman' armbands are much rarer than the enamel 'Look Out' armbands, probably as they were far less durable. These were worn when piloting 'foreign' drivers over strange territory.

Most companies needed these armbands, and they must have once been everyday items as examples from small companies exist, eg the Severn & Wye

Joint Railway, and M & GNJR. They are standard white letters on red background. Unnamed examples also exist.

Badges and Medallions

It is convenient to divide lapel badges into the purposes for which they were issued. Our forebears were little different from people today in that they liked sporting their allegiance, though the number of badges surviving seems very small and the same badges rarely turn up twice, save for Rail Service ones.

Sports badges were produced by the GER for running and cricket, the former being issued for the 1927 Great Eastern Amateur Athletics and for later LNER athletics badges. The GER also produced badges for boxing and bowls.

229-31 Midland Railway long-service ambulance medals, silver *(left and centre)* and gold *(right)*

There was a GWR official rugby football XV which had a tasselled cap with GWR coat of arms, which is preserved in the Didcot Small Relics Museum, as well as a cricket team, for which there were almost certainly badges. On the Midland Railway, a medallion was struck for the rifle club in 1913-14. On the LNWR, a Frank Ree silver medal existed for a rifle club and it is known that railway clubs existed for angling, chess, debating, gardening, art, music and drawing.

In 1938 the GWR issued silver, gold and bronze medals for its Annual Music and Drama Festival. It is very likely that these were cast annually, but the details of these many societies remain very obscure. There were also official choirs (GWR Swindon), and on the LNER and there are stamped music sheets. It must be stressed that any of the above badges are extremely rare and usually exist only as 'one-off' items at present.

With the next group, that of ambulance items, it is a very different story. From when the very first railway branches of the St John Ambulance Association were set up by the Midland Railway and the GWR in the decade 1886-96, large numbers of badges were produced by many different companies.

232 South Eastern & Chatham Railway St John Ambulance Association badge

Details can be perused in Froggatt (*op cit* pp112-23). Of the two main types of St John's badges, the smaller circle badge had the company name inside an outer circle, while the larger had the company name in a scrolled addition at the base of the medal. Many of the pre-grouping lines used these two sorts (**Fig 232**). In addition, there were badges specifying certain depots. For example, there is one marked 'GNR Doncaster Ambulance' and another 'M.S.L.R. Ambulance'.

Another type is the long service ambulance medal, of which there is a very wide variety, though each is rare or very rare. They were commonly made of bronze, silver or gold. The LNWR and Midland Railway had silver medals, the LNER a 20-year gold, the GWR a 25-year first aid gold, the Southern Railway a 7-year bronze, 14-year silver and a 21-year gold. Some companies added metal bars above the medal for periods of service, while others depict twelve specific acts of conspicuous first aid service.

Medals were also struck to commemorate special incidents, like those by the LMS for employees who maintained service during the 1926 General Strike. The LNWR struck a white metal medal and gave it out to Crewe children in 1887 for Queen Victoria's fiftieth year of reign and to celebrate the fiftieth year after the Grand Junction Railway reached Crewe. The Southern Railway presented 50-year service medals to employees, and the GER presented all staff with a medal in 1923, thanking them for their service, before the company was amalgamated at the grouping.

During the Boer War there was an LNWR Regiment with special collar tabs. At the openings and anniversaries of lines, a great number of special medallions were cast such as for the LNER centenary in 1925, and a Barry Railway medallion marking the cutting of the first sod in the docks.

Certainly the most common of all lapel badges are railway service badges. These, especially during World War I,

had to be worn by employees as a protection against being given the white feather for not being in uniform. World War II ones are common, World War I examples less so. Rarities exist from the Hull & Barnsley Railway, Isle of Man Railway and even from Colonel Stephens' lines as well as for most of the pre-grouping lines. LMS, LNER, SR and GWR examples are all very common, as are those from certain other lines like the GSWR. Froggatt suggests that badges from over thirty companies have so far been located for World War I.

Other types of badges were for railway convalescent homes, while others merely had the company name, as with the delightful blue LNER lozenge-shaped badges. Yet another group are the railway temperance society badges such as the GWR Temperance Union, established in 1883, and the LMS Temperance Union. Several lines, such as the GWR, also had official staff associations with badges.

Police Railwayana

Police departments were probably run by most of the early companies as their earliest duties included the hand signalling of trains. As is generally known, signalmen to this day are called 'Bobbies' for this reason. Early railway police truncheons are very decorative and are marked with company initials. Examples are known from a number of railways including from GWR, South Devon Railway, South Western Railway, Cornwall Railway and Bristol & Exeter Railway. They are notably similar in style for obvious functional reasons, and this similarity extends to their decoration, colouring and serrated grips. Examples exist both in the National Railway Museum at York and in various private collections. It should be appreciated that many of them, along with wax seals are some of the earliest pieces of railwayana to have survived.

Much more familiar are police helmets, although fewer complete examples have been preserved, even from fairly recent times, than have antique truncheons. A rare picture of a group of twenty-one LNER police, illustrated on page 150 of Froggatt's *Railway Buttons, Badges and Uniforms*, shows what is perhaps a police inspector, or higher rank in the middle of his men. Page 135 of the same book is a picture of police cap badges from the District Railway, Metropolitan Railway, GCR, GER, GNR, GWR, LYR, LMS, LNER, LNWR, Midland Railway, NER, NLR, CLC, SECR, and Southern Railway.

Pay Checks

Pay checks were issued as wage collection tallies for a wide range of railway departments. Checks were issued for goods, stores, steam shed, locomotive, cartage, wages, motive power, traffic, permanent way, running shed, locomotive & carriage, docks, carriage & wagon, engineering, joint traffic, parcels cartage, maintenance and passenger departments. Many of these, of course, were the names used by different companies for the same department. The great majority of pay checks were brass with a few of copper, and some of pewter. As **Fig 233** and **Colour plates 15-16** show, the shapes were diverse. The great majority were circular, and many were oval of various sizes. There were a fair number of rectangular and hexagonal shaped checks, but very few were square. Some had wavy tops (LNER) and several were circular with straight bases, eg some NER and LNW motive power depot checks which also show the number of the shed. Rectangular

checks were used by the Rhondda & Swansea Bay Railway and sometimes by the GWR, while the GWR Cardiff Docks check had a very particular shape, see **Fig 233** (row 6, second from the left) and the GWR sometimes used a pear shape. St Pancras parcels had a triangular design, while the LNWR included an octagonal shaped pay check.

Almost always, the front bore the initials or name of the company together with the department and usually the depot and the number of the employee. Some had a hole to hang the check on a holder when out of use. It is of interest to see the continuity inside one depot despite change of company, eg three from Curzon St Birmingham marked LNWR, LMR and BR(M) maintain the same shape and material. The MR goods style passed into the LMS as examples from the Leicester and Derby areas show.

It is also true that shapes fluctuated more inside the departments of one company than they did between companies. In other words, we cannot make statements about distinctive company styles, though certain patterns seem to be limited to a few companies, eg GWR locomotive department checks.

Very few paychecks from the smaller companies appear to have survived. Occasional ones are seen from the Rhymney, TVR, RSBR, Cardiff, LTSR, GNSR, M & GNJR, Festiniog and Barry Railways but the vast majority are from the major pre-grouping lines like the MR, NER, LNWR, etc and from the 'Big Four'. An exception is the considerable number of survivals from the MSLR. It seems that most survivors come from a fairly small minority of depots and stations. For example in the West Midlands, there are large numbers from Saltley, Curzon Street and Lawley

233 A collection of pay checks, showing the large range of shapes in which they were made

Street, but almost none from all the other depots, save a few from Walsall and Wolverhampton.

Due to the relative cheapness of acquisition, it has been easy to build up very substantial collections. One at Spalding totals over 900.

Fire Fighting Railwayana

The major railways maintained their own fire services complete with the following pieces of equipment, all of course marked with company names or initials:

a Fire tenders of many sorts, hand, horse and petrol propelled. (The LYR had its own 2–4–2T locomotive stationed at Horwich, in steam, to rush the LYR fire train to any part of the system.)

b Hoses etc, with brass marked nozzles, which very occasionally emerge in auction.

c Firemen's clothes and helmets. Rare photos show the insides of depots with racks of helmets, etc (on the LMS for example).

d Standpipes and hydrant keys.

e Extinguishers.

f Firebuckets.

g Notices.

h Badges, buttons and lamps.

A fire tender built by BR to a GWR design was still in use at Swindon Works Fire Station in 1986. At the rear was a multi-directional nozzle for attaching to hydrants, and two BR tall hand-held extinguishers. Items of fire equipment in Moseley Railwayana Museum include a tall LMS fire extinguisher, which was probably a standard guard's van fitting but is now very rare. GWR extinguishers are quite common and have an inverted cup on top. **Fig 234** shows an LMS wartime hard hat and air raid notices. Perhaps the latter were put up at the entrance to stations in case passengers had not heard the sirens. It is worth recording that the LYR, NER, MR, LMS, GWR, SR and certainly others, had their own fire brigades. Fires on the NER were reported to the Fire Department at the Central Fire

234 *(left)* LMS hard hat and air raid notices

235 *(below)* A brass GER fireman's helmet

236 *(left)* LYR fire hydrant notice

and keys. Nozzles marked LNWR, GCR and LNER are known. Winchcombe Railway Museum has a wrought-iron hydrant key stamped ECR and an LNWR one.

Clothing and helmets are very rare (**Fig 235**). One of the few helmets to have survived is at Winchcombe Railway Museum. An armband, white on blue marked 'Fire Guard' of LNER origin is known, but buttons and badges are very rare indeed, those known being from the LMS, SR and LNER and are modern and wartime types. There is also an LNER fire brigade armband in existence. There are, happily, a moderate number of extinguishers surviving. The GWR is by far the best known with at least eight patterns, all numbered. For details of types see Petchey (*op cit*).

Station, Kington Street, Hull, and defects in equipment to the Mechanical Engineers Department, Alfred Street, Hull.

The GWR laid down very specific guidelines to be followed with a wide variety of enamel notices (see previous chapter). One has survived from Bala Junction (see *The Railwayana Journal — On the Line,* No 6 May 1986, 'Railway Fire Fighting Equipment' by Tim Petchey) and refers to alarms, turning on water, appliances, hose, buckets, winter, keys, persons to be summoned etc, and is dated 1923. **Fig 236** shows a very rare LYR fire brigade notice which would have guarded what must have originally been a vast store of nozzles, connectors, stand pipes, hydrant covers

Ambulance and First Aid Equipment
'GWR First Aid Equipment List No 2' from inside a first aid box lists the following items (those indicated with an

Plate 14 A GWR pilotman's cloth armband, enamel 'Look Out' armbands from the LNWR, LNER and Midland Railway, and a ganger's warning horn marked BR(M). *(MRM)*

Plate 15 Pay checks: top row, left to right, LNER ('Loco. Dept. Hitchin'), GWR ('Loco W'hampton'), LMS ('Sandon & Canada Dock Goods'); bottom row, L & YR ('Methley Junction'), L & SWR, LNER ('Grimsby Docks, Port Masters, Fish Dept, Clerical Staff'). *(David Scudamore Collection)*

Plate 16 Pay checks: top row, left to right, CLC ('Huskisson Station'), NLR ('Pay Check'), Eastern Counties Railway; bottom row, L & YR and LNWR ('Ansdell'), LB & SCR, Midland Railway Company ('St Mary's, Derby'). *(David Scudamore Collection)*

Plate 17 Four Midland Railway posters(1902-3). On the lower left is a decorative poster for their express services from London and the south of England to Scotland. The others are letterpress posters for passengers' luggage, a Swansea-Birmingham timetable, and parcel rates. *(Roy Burrows Collection)*

237 Ambulance boxes from the LMS, GWR and LNER

asterisk were marked with the GWR's initials):

antiseptic tablets, bandages rolled* (1in, 2in, 3in), bandage triangular*, bicarbonate of soda*, boracic lint and ointment*, castor oil*, cotton wool & mops, eye patch, knife*, measure glass*, petroleum jelly*, plaster*, safety pins, sal volatile*, scissors*, smelling salts, splints*, swansdown bandage*, iodine*, tourniquet*, tweezers, washing bowl*.

The contents of these first aid boxes were prepared for the railway by contractors whose name appeared on the packets, usually with LMS, GWR, etc stamped over. Bottles and hardware and glass were usually only stamped with the railway's initials, as were splints and tourniquet boxes. Practices differed with time in this matter as the larger companies had many separate first aid boxes. It is very rare for anything like the complete contents to be preserved and invariably the contents have a mixture of original and BR items. It is rare for pre-nationalisation contents lists to have survived. The contents of LMS boxes were similar to that listed above. **Fig 237** shows various ambulance boxes from the LMS, LMS Ambulance Stores, LNER (wood), Midland

Railway, and GWR.

Other known marked company first-aid boxes include examples from the LBSCR, LYR (long and narrow), LNWR, GNR (wood), Leeds Central, Caledonian, SECR, GNSR, and Axholme Joint Railway. Pre-grouping boxes were usually wood, post-grouping ones usually metal (except LNER). All except examples from the LNER, GWR and LMS are extremely rare and very few pre-grouping ones have survived.

A few stretchers and patients' wheelchairs exist. The commonest of the former are Southern Railway marked stretchers, themselves taken over from the LBSCR. Vertical stretcher boxes still adorn many SR stations as they were once a standard SR fitting. They are stamped SR in the wood and on small plates. The other companies must have had similar items for emergencies, just as they had wheelchairs for infirm and disabled passengers. A good photograph of this exists on page 132 of Russell (*op cit*).

It is worth remembering the various World War I and II ambulance trains, which were built or converted hurriedly at the outbreak of war, must have contained much marked railwayana in-

238 LNER enamelled water jugs

cluding some of the various company blankets which survive, although of course these emanate chiefly from hotels and sleeping cars but are dealt with here. There are single and double size, some hotel marked. Examples are the various colours of LMS (buff, dark grey with red letters) and various patterns of GWR and LYR, usually with hand stitched letters.

The major source of first aid railwayana is badges for which detailed coverage is given in pages 112-23 of *Railway Buttons, Badges and Uniforms* by David J. Froggatt (Malaga Books 1986) from which some of the following information is taken. The GWR formed the first St John Ambulance Association in November 1896 and issued first aid medals from 1899, although the first of these was actually issued by the Midland Railway in 1886. Other railways quickly followed suit and marked insignia are known from the Furness Railway, GER, GCR, GNSR, GNR, GWR, LBSCR, LCDR, LMS, LNER, LNWR, LSWR, LYR, Mersey Railway, Metropolitan Railway, Midland Railway, M & GNJR, MSLR, NER, NLR,

SER, SECR and SR.

There was a fairly standard pre-grouping pattern of oval enamel arm badge with the St John Ambulance star in the centre, with the words 'The St John Ambulance Association' in an outer circle. Below this was a small curved plate with company initials. The CLC and GCR had a similar version with 'Ambulance Corps' and the company's initials only. As well as these there were 7, 14, 21, 20 and 25-year service badges in bronze, silver, gold, gilt and occasionally copper and pewter, sometimes as medals on ribbon, or medallions, some as lapel and arm badges.

Some companies added year bars to be worn above the medal, eg 5, 10, 15 and 20-year bars. In addition, there were many medals struck and presented for special instances of bravery or skill in first aid. Examples of these are the medals presented by the LNER and SR during World War II, and the Midland Railway for first aid rendered at Woodhaven Mill, February 1902. Many were marked 'Ambulance Corps' and sometimes were marked with the depot, eg 'GNR Doncaster Ambulance Corps'. Others were awarded after a minimum number of tests had been passed.

The LNER, almost alone it appears, made a series of enamelled water jugs and billy cans used in such places as hotels and staff canteens. There were a variety of different designs of which three are shown in **Fig 238**. They are included in this chapter on railway workers as they were for the use of employees, and not passengers.

9
Railway Documents
& Publicity

This huge arena of railwayana has for convenience been divided into a number of categories, although goods invoices and letters have been dealt with in Chapter 2.

Departmental Letters and Memoranda

Many of the various railway offices and officials issued their own headed notepaper and these included the audit office, chief mechanical engineer, engineer's office, general manager's office, goods manager/office/superintendent/agent, legal or deeds department/solicitor, parcels department, registration office, company secretary, signal & telegraph department, superintendent of a line or station, as well as memoranda for internal correspondence.

Fig 239 shows examples of early railway correspondence. That from the General Manager of the Wirral Railway dated 1894 includes the company's crest. This style of notepaper with a printed heading in copperplate script and with a logo is much more attractive than those that have just the company initials and no crest.

One of the few surviving documents from the short and short-lived Hoylake & Birkenhead Railway (which had its name changed to the Seacombe, Hoylake & Deeside Railway in 1881) is illustrated. It refers to the need to 're-charge' for the carriage of a perambula-

tor and was a tear-off slip with a counterfoil copy as the serrated edge shows. An examination of the date shows that old stationery was still being used six years after the company changed its name.

The interest of paperwork lies partly in the insight it gives into railway traffic, now hardly imaginable, such as the memo from Cleator Moor (CWJR) to Altrincham and Bowdon (MSJAR) on the subject of a parcel.

Some railway companies had London offices despite being of very modest size. The letter from the Didcot, Newbury & Southampton Railway shows this and refers to 'Sufferance Roads', that is private roads which had to be closed one day a year to demonstrate legal ownership. Other railways were strictly local, as in the example from the Dundee & Arbroath Joint Railway, which had a combined office for the secretary and manager.

Fig 240 shows the full title of the East & West Junction Railway and the serial number of that item of paper (190 in brackets). The volume of forms produced even on small lines was quite remarkable and although there is no proof that there were ever 189 others, evidence from other small lines supports this. The same illustration shows one of many Cockermouth, Keswick and Penrith Railway paper items, this form being unnumbered.

239 Early railway
correspondence

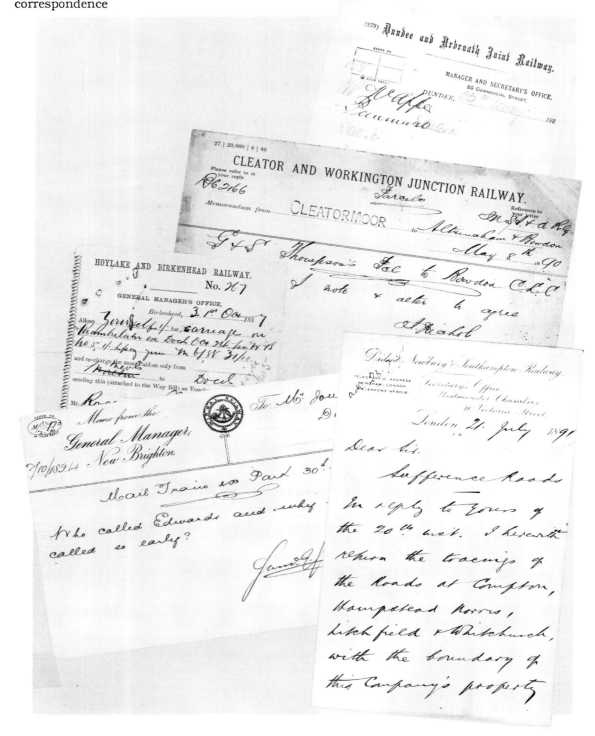

240 Railway memos and other documents

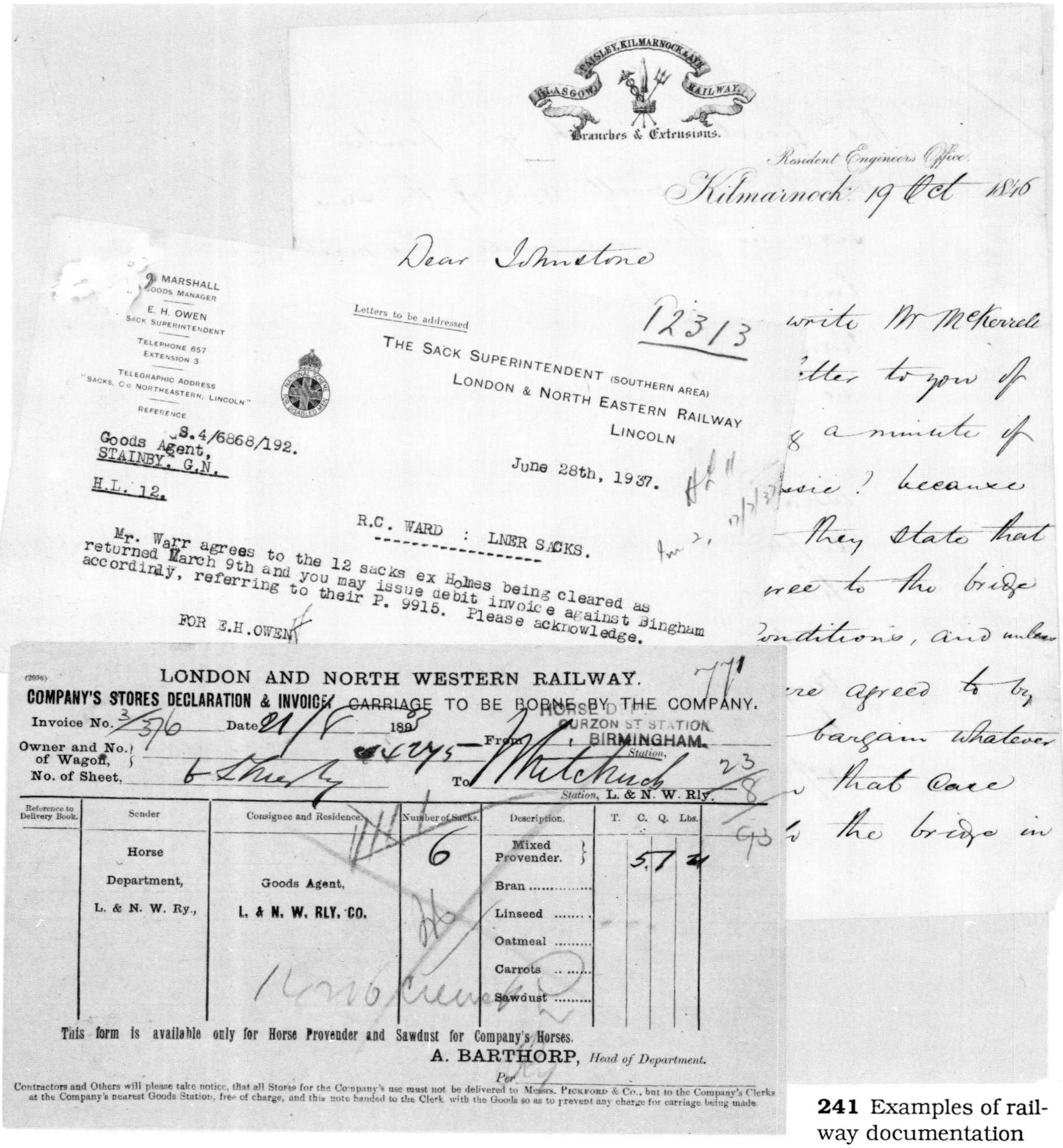

241 Examples of railway documentation

Another attractive crested notepaper was produced by the Cambrian Railways (**Fig 239**). It refers, unusually, to a 'Trains Department'. The great majority of Cambrian Railway items had no crest and therefore this is quite rare. A feature of some railways, especially those last-

ing a long time, was the changes in print style reflecting change in company policy. Also show are three examples from the Furness Railway, all dated between 1896 and 1906. The company was also known for a time as 'The Furness Railways' and cast-iron signs with and without the 's' exist.

Careful collecting of paperwork throws up great insights into the scale of railway activity at one time. One document in **Fig 240** might at first sight appear to relate to marriage of company employees, but actually refers to a change of name on marriage for the registration of shares at the GWR's Registration Office. The clue is in the words 'Dividend Warrant' towards the bottom.

There are also many surprises for the collector of paperwork. Several Scottish railways for example had 'Resident Engineers' offices' (for construction of the line), with notepaper. **Fig 241** shows a very early example dated 1846, for the 'Glasgow, Paisley & Kilmarnock Railway, Branches & Extensions', which includes the armorial design which was later used by its successor the GSWR. The LNER had at least two sack superintendents, each with their own office and notepaper as scrutiny of the illustration indicates, and again shows the importance of paperwork in recording this otherwise unrecorded detail. Of interest is the number of other companies who had forms of various sorts linked to sack hire. The same illustration shows a little known area of railway operation, the horse department of the LNWR.

Fig 242 has a selection of letterheads, some of which are the rarest railway documents to survive, including from the Holsworthy & Bude Railway Works, the Stalybridge & Saddleworth Railway, the South Devon Railway and the Cornwall Railway.

The scale of railway operations is evident from studying the serial numbers of documents. Many companies did this, and in the case of large concerns like the GWR and LMS, very high num-

242 A collection of early railway letterheads

243 A small selection of the vast number of official forms used by the GWR

bers exist. **Fig 243** for the GWR shows a range of their large buff forms, the highest serial number here being No 5398A. Most of these have very comprehensive instructions on the reverse as to how they were to be completed. The LMS had official forms with numbers in the range 30,000 and 50,000 as early as the 1930s, although, as in the case of numbers on lamps, we must not assume all numbers were used.

Fig 244 shows unusual GWR documents headed 'Chief Accountant's Office' giving a 'one occasion only' horse rate. 2174-1 is an engine lubricant requisition and 2079 covers slipped carriages with additional portions for the head guard, slip guard and driver. There were even LMS forms dealing with the return of company clocks for repair, and daily conductor's bell punch statements from LMS road motors on the Garstang & Knott End line (form 3540).

Documents with counterfoils were produced in large quantities and many have survived. **Fig 245** has a selection and includes an LMS station master's receipt for the 'Conveyance of Mares and Stallions for Breeding Purposes'. **Fig 246** dated 1860 is one of the very few documents extant from the Oxford, Worcester & Wolverhampton Railway, and refers to their standard practice of sending horses and carriages by train.

Railway Share Certificates

Fig 247-8 show two especially artistic Victorian share certificates, from the Shrewsbury & Hereford Railway (9¾ x 6½in) and the Midland Railway (8½ x 5½in). Typical dimensions of others are: Fleetwood, Preston & West Riding Junction Railway 10 x 6½in; Darlington & Barnard Castle Railway 10 x 7in; GSWR 9¾ x 7in and LCDR 8¾ x 5½in, although almost every company had a different

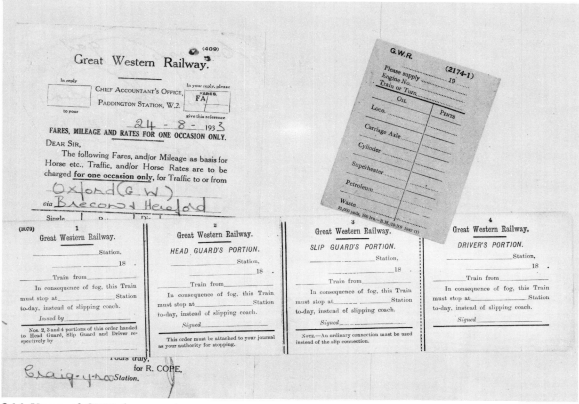

244 Unusual GWR documents

245 Railway receipt counterfoils

246 An early receipt from the Oxford, Worcester & Wolverhampton Railway

size of certificate. The degree of excellence of the engravings speak for themselves, often with delicate rural idyllic

scenes nestling below the titles.

Shares varied from a normal minimum value of £5 up to £20 and £25. They were numbered and usually signed by the company secretary himself, and sometimes by the directors as well as in the case of Buckley Railway shares. The company seal was usually embossed bottom right or left, the Fleetwood Company's seal, for instance, was in red with full title and crest. Many examples are dated 1846, the year of the 'Railway Mania'.

Some shares were 'Preference', eg from the LCDR while others were 'Guaranteed Preference Consolidated Stock'. Shares have survived from extremely early times probably due to the retention in deed boxes in legal offices. Shares dated 1833 are known from the London & Birmingham Railway.

It is arguable that early share certifi-

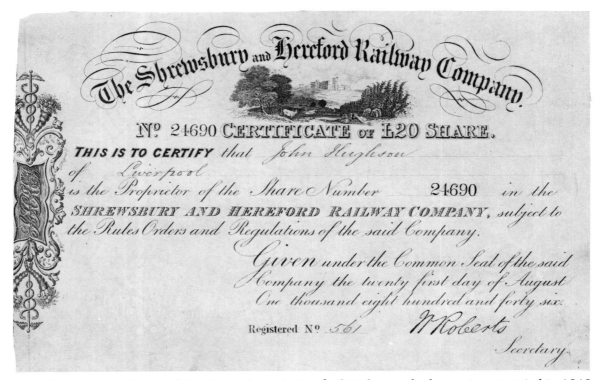

247 £20 share certificate of the Shrewsbury & Hereford Railway, which was incorporated in 1846

248 Midland Railway preference share, 1878

cates are among the most delicate pieces of art contributed by the railway age. At present, interest in this type of railwayana is low, although there are one or two specialist collectors. There is tremendous scope for anyone wishing to begin a collection as the number of companies from which shares have survived is lengthy, including such minor lines as the Sittingbourne & Sheerness Railway, the Paisley, Barrhead & Hurlet Railway, the West Somerset Minerals and the Rugby,

249 *(above)* Notice to Lancaster & Carlisle Railway shareholders advising of the amalgamation with the LNWR

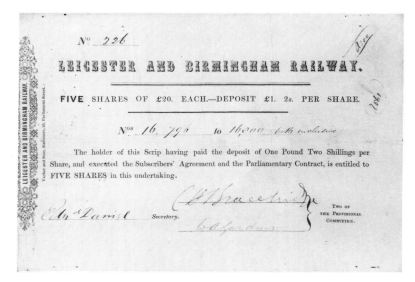

250 *(left)* Receipt for five £20 shares in the Leicester & Birmingham Railway, which never existed in more than name

NEW £32. SHARES—FOURTH CALL of £8. per SHARE.

No. 50

LIVERPOOL, 8 April 1846

Received on Account of the London and Birmingham Railway Company, the Sum of One Hundred Four Pounds, to Account for on Demand.

For the Bank of Liverpool.

£ 104

CHESTER AND CREWE RAILWAY.

Third Call of £5 0 0 per Share, due 9th of November, 1838.

No. of Receipt, 31 Liverpool, 2 Nov 1838.

Received the Sum of Fifty Pounds to be placed to the account of the Directors of the CHESTER & CREWE Railway.

For THE BOROUGH BANK.

W Kershaw

SECOND CALL, £5. per SHARE.

No.

1 March 1837

Received on Account of the Midland Counties Railway Company, the Sum of One hundred Fifty Pounds, to Account for on Demand.

For The Bank of Manchester

R Greenough

£150

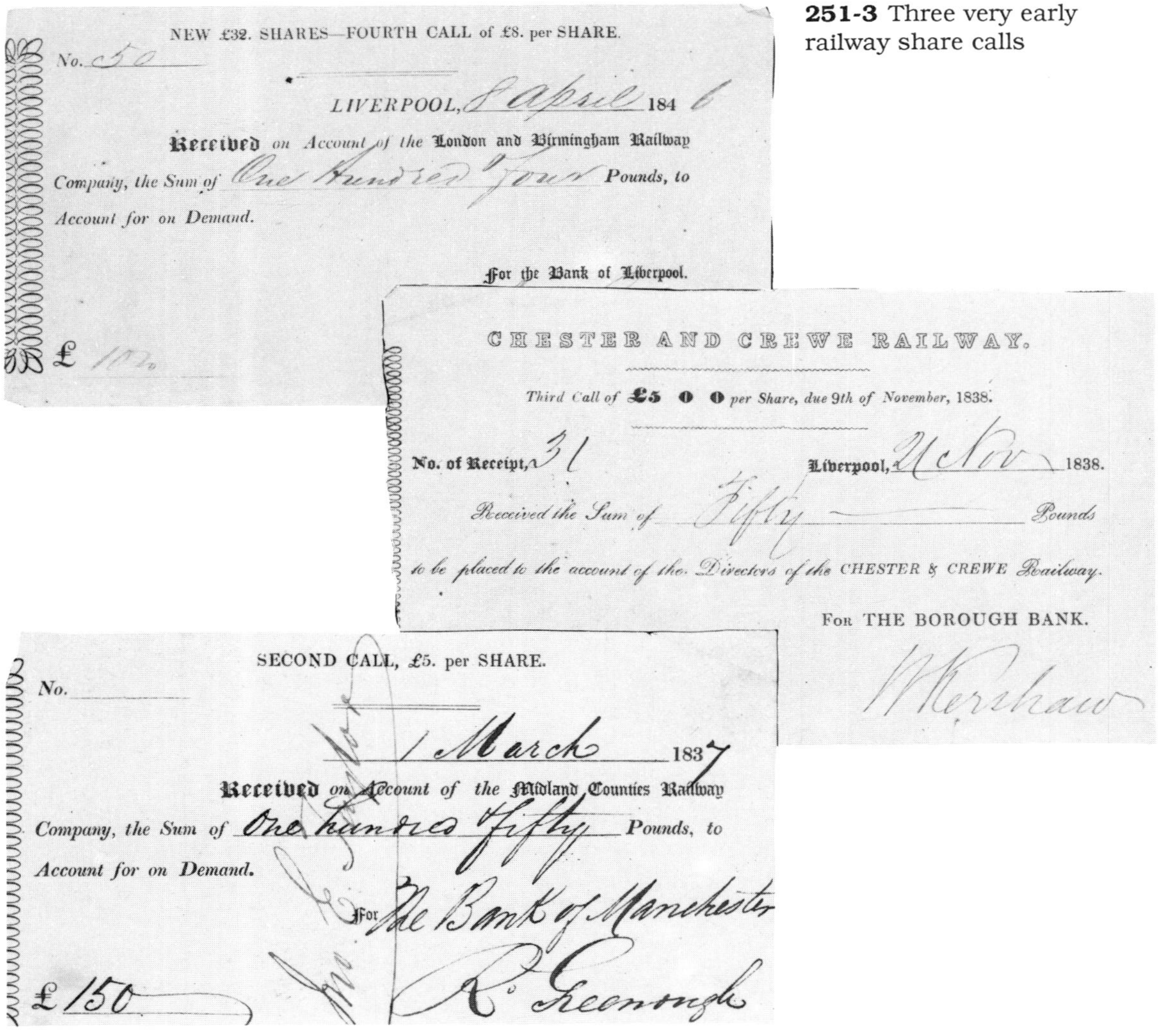

251-3 Three very early railway share calls

Derby & Manchester Railway, which existed on paper only.

Remarkably early examples of railwayana as well as share certificates survive from legal departments, including, receipts for or requests for share capital and circulars regarding meetings and notices. The latter are not so attractive as they usually lack the ornate scripts used in shares and receipts, but they often have fascinating data. An example is shown in **Fig 249** where Lancaster & Carlisle Shareholders were advised of the amalgamation with the LNWR in 1878. Share certificate receipts are often ornately designed masterpieces of lithography and they also exist for long forgotten projected railways which never became reality. An example is shown in **Fig 250** from the hoped-for Leicester & Birmingham Railway which never existed in more than name.

Fig 253 is a second call on a £5 share from the Midland Counties Railway dated 1 March 1837. **Fig 252** is a third call on a £5 share from the Chester & Crewe Railway dated 9 November 1838,

254-5 Two LNER handbills

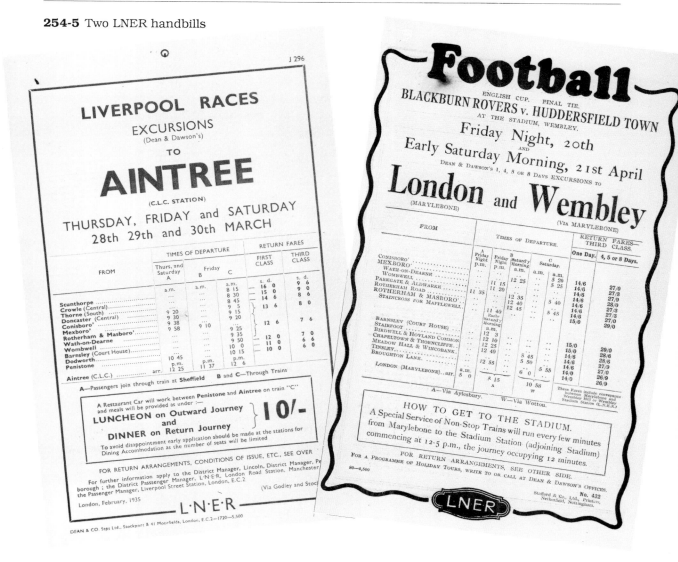

which is just as rare as the 1846 London & Birmingham share call in **Fig 251**.

Handbills

Ever since the very first excursion train ran on 20 July 1840 on the Midland Counties Railway between Nottingham and Leicester, production of handbills for special day excursions has been a major part of the railway scene. Of course, many bills relate to two-day, three-day or longer combined tours by rail, road and sea. Their value to the railwayana collector is that they convey the aura of what the railways were in business for, namely to persuade the public to travel to distant parts and to savour the leisure attractions available on Bank Holiday weekends and other holidays.

These bills survive in large numbers and are easily collectable. They have a wide colour range, but are fairly standard in shape and size. Usually they were impaled on a hook (originally a nail) and hence often have a hole in one

256-7 Excursion handbills

corner. By far the most common are from the LMS and LNER, probably due to the large number of resorts served by these lines. SR and GWR examples are less common. Bills from pre-grouping lines are fairly common with examples from CLC, Midland, GCR, SEC, GER often seen. They usually comprise full day, half day and evening excursions and cover coastal and inland holiday resorts, race meetings, football and rugby matches (FA Cup Finals were a favourite). **Fig 254** show a 1928 cup-final handbill for Huddersfield Town v Blackburn Rovers with special trains to

Marylebone from Yorkshire. It was established practice for the LNER to run cup final specials down this line.

Other features on these bills are the one, four, five or eight-day stay allowed, and the issuing agent for the train ticket, namely Dean & Dawson, 1 Gallowtree Gate, Leicester. This was Thomas Cook's original office which still stands as a listed building (see picture in Maurice Bray's book *Railway Tickets, Timetables and Handbills* (Moorland 1986) page 123). Often the year is not shown on the front of the handbill as they were fairly current items and the year would have been obvious. It is worth studying the graphics of handbills as a number of typefaces were often used.

Handbills are sources of reference to long vanished lines in the same way that wagon cards and goods invoices are. **Fig 255** shows an example of this. The excursion to Aintree (CLC) via Penistone (1935) used the now-lifted line through Woodhead Tunnel and the CLC extension to Aintree; train C had a restaurant car. Typographical change to the LNER initials can be noted.

Fig 256 shows a much earlier handbill of 1894 with at least twelve typefaces. In 1894 the return trip from Birmingham to Blackpool for a day cost 5s, whereas by 1928 (as shown above) 5s was sufficient for only a half day from Yorkshire to Bridlington. Very often, as these handbills show, a longer visit was encouraged. No luggage was allowed except on the 'extension ticket' trains.

Another pre-grouping handbill, this time of 1901, is shown in **Fig 257** to 'North of England Watering Places' via the Midland Railway. This was run by Thomas Cook for 3, 8, 10, 15 or even 17 days.

Race specials have, until quite recent times, been a standard railway offering with trains running to large numbers of venues. If a list of English racecourses were drawn up, with nearby railway access it would encompass dozens including Newbury, Wolverhampton, Aintree and Uttoxeter. A handbill for Uttoxeter Races in 1929 stipulates that cancellation notes must be received by the LMS in time for the train to be cancelled. Of great interest is the mention of long closed lines and stations, namely Warwick (Milverton) and

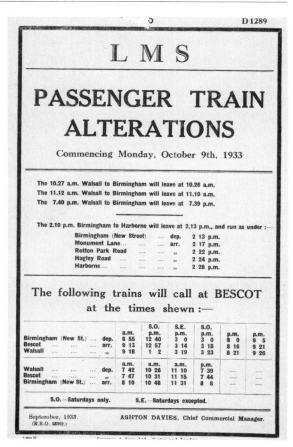

258 LMS handbill announcing train alterations

Brownhills (High Street).

Another type of handbill was that giving local alterations. **Fig 258** shows alterations via the Harborne branch in 1933.

Railway Posters

This area of railwayana is dominated by post-grouping examples. Analysis of five sales of railway posters by Onslows (London) in 1985-7 shows that 80-90 per cent of posters on the market are from the LMS, LNER, GWR, SR or BR and over the last two years there have been no more than one or sometimes two examples of Midland Railway, GNR, LNWR, LYR, LBSCR, SECR, Highland

259 LNER poster by Alexeieff

260 Poster of 'The Night Scotsman' by Robert Bartlett

Railway, GNSR, Caledonian Railway, NBR or NSR posters offered for sale. It is significant that this rarity is *not* reflected in poster values. In 1985 a selection of the above pre-grouping posters in good condition was indistinguishable in value from post grouping ones.

The market is controlled by art buy-ers in London and the south of England, by the National Railway Museum for the National Poster Collection and is only 'broken into' from time to time by specialist railwayana collectors, making this class of railwayana very different from any other. Also virtually all the supply so far has been channelled

261 *(left)* GWR letterpress poster of 1879 for its steamships to Ireland

262 *(below)* Midland Railway lithographic poster of 1903 extolling the scenic virtues of its Settle and Carlisle route to Scotland

through one London auction house.

It appears that art content and style is as crucial in most posters as actual railway content and it is of some importance to understand the major artists who produced posters for the railways. The list below shows some forty artists whose works are frequently seen:

Alexeieff, Bartlett, Beck, Montague Black, S.R. Brealey ('Sunny South Sam'), Lesley Carr, G. Clausen (LMS 'Best Way' series), Cooper, Cuneo, V.I. Danvers, Stanhope Forbes, Gawthorn, Richard Jack, T.D. Kerr (Southern), Ronald Lampitt (GWR and BR), Littlejohns, John Mace, Mason, Fortunio Matania, McCorquodale Studio, Ralph Mott, Charles Mayo, Merriott, Frank Newbold, Charles Pears, Tom Purvis, Leonard Richmond, Septimus Scott, Shoesmith, S.R. Shepherd, Clodagh Sparrow, Fred Taylor (LNER and BR), A.R. Thompson, Maurice Toussaint, Edmond Vaughan (1929 'South for SR Sun'), Wilkinson, S.R. Wyatt, Vic Welch.

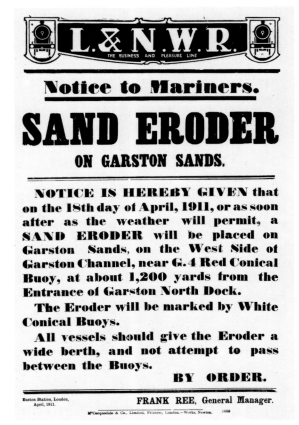

263 Poster from the LNWR ('The Business and Pleasure Line') announcing the use of a sand eroder on Garston Sands in 1911

Though it is already obvious that several hundreds of different railway posters survive, it is not possible as yet to state very much about relative rarity, as poster sales are in their infancy. Values fluctuate wildly. For example, in recent sales examples of the same GWR letterpress poster of 'Steamships on the Limerick and Waterford Route' were valued at £90 and £410 while exactly the same Wilkinson poster of the Isle of Man made £90 and £170. Similarly the LBSCR poster 'Cheapest and Quickest Route to the Continent' sold for £50 and £360. Such fluctuations rarely happen in other areas of railwayana and suggest short term influence from outside rail-

wayana collectors; the latter at present give the impression of not yet having worked out how to appraise posters.

The GWR had a few dramatic posters; especially famous is Charles Mayo's 'Speed to the West', which makes a vivid stylistic contrast with 'Cornwall' and its impressionistic dimpled blue sea.

There were some poster series given over to famous trains, and the docks, works, or industries that they served. Examples are the LMS 'Best Way' series showing steelworks, permanent way, a Stanier Pacific on shed and coal mines etc, and the LMS view of the *Coronation Scot* and LNER *Coronation* crossing the Royal Border Bridge. The imposing GCR series of Immingham Docks at their opening are of this type. On the whole however, the railways concentrated on advertising resorts and leisure activities in their areas and these are the single greatest class seen in auctions. Every east and south coast resort was covered, some several times by different artists. Lowestoft was painted by Newbould and Purvis for the LNER. Devon, Somerset and Cornwall as an area was extolled by the GWR, rather than individual resorts.

In the 1930s some railway posters were influenced by abstract and modernistic styles favoured by some artists. The LNER, for example, produced a whole series of silhouetted bathers adorning the eastern beaches, designed by Tom Purvis and titled 'The Drier Side of Britain'. Posters illustrating the outlines of *The Flying Scotsman* — inside and out — by Alexeieff, Bartlett and Beck produced British all-time poster-price records at Onslows in early 1987 (**Figs 259** and **260**).

It must be said that the railways, with a few exceptions, rarely seem to have fully exploited the grandeur of their natural scenery. Shap, Beattock, Ais Gill and Rannoch Moor figure little, if at all, though the Midland Railway and the LMS produced some striking posters of the Peak Forest route, Scafell, the Settle & Carlisle line and the Lake District.

Interesting examples of pre-grouping posters include 'The Garden of England' showing LBSCR train times to the Isle of Wight on a scroll, while the 'Riverside Excursions' of the LSWR portrays an idyllic rural scene on the Thames. 'England's Greatest Poet' bestrides the east coast, extolling visitors to Stratford-on-Avon to use the much advertised shortest and quickest GCR route. An attractive early script GWR Devonport poster promoted the greatest naval dockyard in the world. The contrast in style of the Alexeieff ones with these could hardly be greater. Which is to be preferred is highly subjective. Certainly, the impact made by the thrusting speed of the LNER Pacifics must have been considerable.

Whereas colour posters were usually printed by lithography single-colour posters were printed by letterpress. **Fig 261** publicised the steam sailboats from New Milford to Waterford, reassuring passengers that they would not share the boat with pigs, sheep or cattle, except on Saturdays. An LNWR example refers to a sand eroder at Garston railway docks (**Fig 263**), while another example is the remarkable £5 reward offered by the Dundee & Arbroath Joint Railway in 1884 to the apprehenders of signal wire tiers!

Despite these attractive and interesting examples it must not be forgotten that the majority of such posters were of course the one-time ubiquitous time-tables displayed at stations inside poster boards.

Publicity Material

A wide variety of objects were used to publicise railways in ways scarcely credible today. Though most of this chapter concerns documents, the theme of publicity takes us into other media which carried company titles, arms, maps, times and fares. This publicity material included sweet tins, enamel advertisements, matchbox holders and strikers, ashtrays, bookmarkers, dining car postcards, playing cards, compartment maps, luggage stickers, jigsaws, booklets and books.

Fig 264-5 shows examples of publicity books. The LNER was by far the most copious producer. Its book *On Either Side* describes the routes from King's Cross to Aberdeen, Inverness and Mallaig with outlines of an A4 locomotive under Edinburgh Castle and Westminster Abbey on the front cover, with St Paul's Cathedral on the rear. Inside includes photographs of the *Coronation*'s all-electric kitchen and the inside of the 'Beaver Tail' observation car. Folded in the back is an excellent map of the LNER system. *The Track of The Royal Scot* was a similar LMS booklet and the company published a whole series of route books. The GWR had a great array of brochures of which its *Holiday Haunts* is most familiar. Also illustrated is a pre-grouping publicity guidebook by the LBSCR to the South Downs. Probably the most common items were the guides giving places of interest accessible from the nearest stations and some of these had lists of accommodation, though some of them were offered as separate booklets, for example by the GCR.

The LNER, was unique in the range of luggage stickers it produced for its named trains. They were light blue and deep blue with gold circular borders and

264 *(left)* LBSCR guide book to the South Downs (no date)

265 *(below)* *The Track of the Royal Scot,* an LMS route book from London to Carlisle (1947)

blue, red or gold segments. The centre contained a dark outline in Art Deco style of an A4 locomotive. The *Coronation* stickers had a clear red background and the *Dominion of Canada* nameplate can be seen. In BR times a similar design was used for some named trains on the Eastern Region. See page 167 for details of the more conventional type of luggage label.

Advertisements of tinplate were sometimes spectacular. The GWR's new route to Ireland via Fishguard led to the famous GWR maps of the system being produced as advertising maps of differing sizes, with the GWR system allegedly spreading to Folkestone, Brighton, Felixstowe, Ely & Sheffield! It was red on cream set in an azure sea with Ireland in green, plus blue lettering and the top and bottom panels had black lined letters on green. It was made in large and small sizes and there was also a teatray with the same design. There were also red and black tin trunks acting as sweet boxes with 'LNWR London' in cream on the top. These were not actually made for the railway and occurred in about four sizes.

The front and back covers of timetables were ideal for publicity material. The LNWR one for 1898 measuring $7\frac{1}{4}$ x $11\frac{1}{4}$in, showed the system map on the front with engravings of ten of its hotels (Crewe, Euston, Holyhead, Birmingham, Liverpool, Dublin, Greenore, Perth, Preston and Glasgow) on the rear (**Fig 266**). Bookmarks were made by several lines, especially the GWR, LNWR and GCR and were always packed with pictures and information about the company's lines and virtues.

Like so many other types of railwayana, the once common railway ashtray is now a rarity. The number surviving seems to be very small indeed and totally unrelated to the vast numbers originally produced. They were of two main types: swivelling coach mounted and the flat ashtrays used in hotels and refreshment rooms, etc. The brass ones normally have a serrated lip for striking matches. SR and GWR types are relatively common, the others are rare to very rare. There were many which were limited to a specific hotel, the Charing Cross and Midland Bradford are examples. White pottery ones also exist from Preston refreshment room. The base of glass ashtrays carried hotel names so were mobile advertisements. As this area of collecting is in its infancy general statements are hazardous, but we can say that the Midland Railway brass type was continued as the LMS brass pattern with MR and intertwined LMS letters. It also appears that the most common to survive are various types of SR ones. At least five are known as follows: Charing Cross type, upright chromed, brass round with 'sunshine' letters and ship flag, brass swivel and china round crested type. Another white pottery type is a leaf-shaped one from the Midland hotels (and the successor LMS hotels) with the names clearly

266 LNWR timetable, 1898

marked. There is also in existence a GWR long-crested china type and another GWR white china design with green edges and GWR in a centre roundel.

Limited numbers of match cards and combined strikers survive. Combined strikers are not uncommon and are known from the LYR, GEWR, LMS, LNWR, GNR, Midland Railway and MSLR.

There are dozens of survivors of company and hotel matchboxes in the form of both ordinary boxes and in small card packs with tear-off matches. It seems likely that many, if not most of the railway hotels at one time or another advertised themselves with matches

267 A collection of GWR jigsaw puzzles

and they are a rich source of data on the hotels themselves. Inside the LMS for example the change in lettering style in the 1930s is reflected in its book matches. Known examples of match-boxes include CLC books in a silver matchbox holder, a GER tin matchbox with crest, LMS and GWR hotels pattern of book matches and three types of LNER hotels book matches advertising the East Coast Route, Harwich and the *Silver Jubilee*.

Jigsaw puzzles were made in large numbers by the GWR, but are virtually unknown from any other railway company. **Fig 267** shows a selection of these famous GWR puzzles, including a 150-piece puzzle with intertwined GWR initials on a black and white box (front), a 200-piece puzzle in an orange-fronted box and a 375-piece puzzle with a blue fronted box. There are also 300- and 400-piece types and from 1937 onwards some of the boxes have the GWR initials in a roundel. The subjects are exclu-sively of GWR terrain: castles, famous locomotives and trains, historic places like Ann Hathaway's cottage, Caerleon or King Arthur on Dartmoor.

The boxes normally carry a small colour print of the subject and were sold on GWR station bookstalls so that trav-ellers could engross themselves on the journey. They survive in very large numbers. They were made by Chad Valley, the world famous Birmingham toy firm. It is fairly certain that over a million were made (750,000 were sold by 1934 with some 30,000 during Christmas 1930 alone). There were forty-three designs made, plus some for juveniles and one limited to GWR staff only. As they were hand cut no two are exactly the same. The first ones were in flat rectangular boxes, but in 1932-3 they were changed to free-standing boxes and in 1934 the final form was made, with pink mottled labels and the title on the side. Some views were used several times, eg Windsor Castle (Nos 4, 23, 41), *King George V* (Nos 10, 13, 32). Several of the pictures were taken from current paintings for GWR posters, chiefly by Claude Buckle, Fred Taylor and Ronald Lampitt and Fred Moody. A full account of GWR puzzles was written by Ian Wright in *The Railway Magazine*, January 1985.

Luggage, Route and Merchandise Labels

The lack of many very early labels is in contrast to the occurrence of other fields of railwayana such as tickets or buttons. Apart from the supposed existence of a label from the London & Greenwich Railway (D.A. Bone in *Railway Relics and Regalia*, 1975) and the fact that labels from the Somerset Central Railway (1854-62) are known, most early ones appear to date from the 1860s.

In earlier times, the fixing of a label on luggage was mandatory before entrainment was allowed; hence the importance of label racks where labels were stored ready for use.

The variation of size, colour, typography and data enscribed make labels of great interest. The greatest variation in typeface was practised by the LBSCR. **Fig 268** shows four different type styles, not to mention size, colour and design differences used by this company. Colours are red on white (Crystal Palace), black on white (Eridge), black on green (Annerley) and black on buff (Brockley).

There is hardly a colour that has not been used by one company or another. The Great North of Scotland Railway used pale yellow, some CLC ones are light green, some SDJR ones are pale blue, while pink was used for some GNR labels. Coloured diagonal crosses appeared on LBSCR Isle of Wight destinations and LYR parcel labels were a deep purple. One of the most striking designs was to be found on labels used by the Metropolitan Railway and the Metropolitan & GC Joint Railway, where four red triangles were used in the middle of each edge with print in large red letters. The purpose of this was, of course, for quick identification by railway workers. **Fig 268** shows other features. The LBSCR ones have 'From' and 'To' on some, 'Destination' only on others, while Nutfield and Caterham (both black on orange) show the SEC practice of putting the destination only without reference to its own company title. The two SDJR labels of 1927 were route labels, one to the south, the other to the north. The Nos 817a and 824 were stock numbers.

The NLR label is of great interest, reflecting the brief period in the early 1900s when through-expresses worked from Broad Street to Birmingham to compete with the new GWR direct cut-off route which had just opened to avoid the Oxford detour.

Fig 269 shows some GWR types. The GWR Isle of Man label (3in x 3in) and the later standard label (eg 'Windermere', $2\frac{1}{2}$ x $2\frac{1}{2}$in) were square. Several GWR constituents had square labels, eg TVR (3in x 3in) with the Barry Railway and Bristol & Exeter Railway almost so, although the South Devon Railway and the Cornwall Railway's labels were rectangular. Some of the GWR route labels used colours (the GC through route label is red on white and the Midland Railway one green on buff); however, the ordinary GWR ones were white. The 'With Care' and 'Eggs With Care' labels were both very common on many railways for obvious reasons and were always red on white as were 'Glass' and 'Fragile' labels. The GWR 'Combined Rail and Air' label obviously dates from the start of the Railway Air Services in the 1930s.

Fig 270 illustrates several of the points already made. The South Devon Railway was one of only a few lines to print 'Passenger Luggage' on its labels (as did the Highland Railway and the GNSR). Some companies put their name in full on labels, eg the LBSCR; others used initials and title in turn (like the

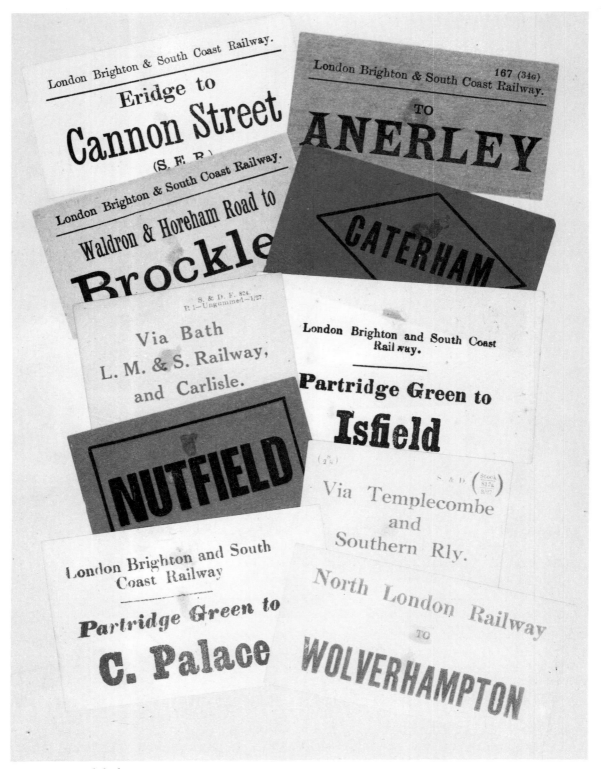

268 Luggage labels

269 Luggage and goods labels

NSR and the GWR). Some parcels were marked 'Pre-Paid' others 'To Pay' as the Macclesfield Committee parcel label shows. The square GWR pattern occurs in the GWR & GCR label indicating GWR parentage. The NER label has reference to two other lines, and many route labels show this feature as in the GNR and Metropolitan Railway examples shown here.

The examples shown in **Fig 271** exhibit several features not so far discussed. At $2\frac{1}{2}$ x $1\frac{1}{2}$in, the Dundee & Arbroath Joint Railway label is one of the smallest produced. The Dunlop and Sorbie labels illustrate that the transition of one design to its successor company. The Dunlop label refers to the GSWR subsidiary, the Glasgow, Barrhead & Kilmarnock Railway, while the Sorbie label is clearly inspired by the GSWR design and refers to the GSWR section as well as the Portpatrick & Wigtown Railway section. The LYR parcel label in deep purple is marked 'To Pay' while the examples from the LNWR & GWR Joint Railway, the Cambrian Railway, the GER and the LSWR reflect the way that luggage labels in general after the grouping of 1923 tended to

270 Luggage and parcels labels

become narrow rectangles.

Fig 272 shows a TVR label to Neath using the Rhondda & Swansea Bay Railway line, while the Barry Railway label to Cardiff used the Taff Vale Railway. The GNSR and the Highland Railway labels use the word 'Luggage' while the North Staffordshire Railway had a specific 'Left Luggage' label. The four NSR labels all have serial numbers (C400, 372, 379, 343) and the last a date (1920) making it one of the latest NSR labels as well as being rather unusual in that it denotes that a 'Higher Value' charge had been paid for the transportation of valuable animals and birds. **Fig 273** shows a few of the large number of LMS labels which can always be iden-

tified by the ERO number (although early LMS ones have transitional GF (goods form) numbers inherited from the Midland Railway and other transitional types from its constituent lines.

Other Printed Items

It remains to give an outline of the great volume of other railway printed items not mentioned already in this chapter or elsewhere in this book. One fascinating field for collectors are the cards specially printed for the company or for railway societies. The history of railway clubs and societies has received little attention and would be an interesting area for research. **Fig 274** shows a menu card for a CLC staff dinner; on the back of the

271 Luggage and parcels labels

menu the sweet course includes a 'Cheshire Lines Pudding'.

Special timetables for royal trains are another interesting area of railwayana. As royal trains at various times travelled on so many of the pre-grouping lines, relatively large numbers must have been printed. There appear to be few survivors, which often come to light in the form of collections kept as souvenirs by particular drivers. One such complete collection came to light in the estate of a deceased Saltley driver. **Fig 275** shows the front cover of a 1919 royal train timetable. There are of course many official books on a wide variety of topics including company rulebooks, telegraph codes, fire regulations, books of company uniforms, inventories of station equipment, goods

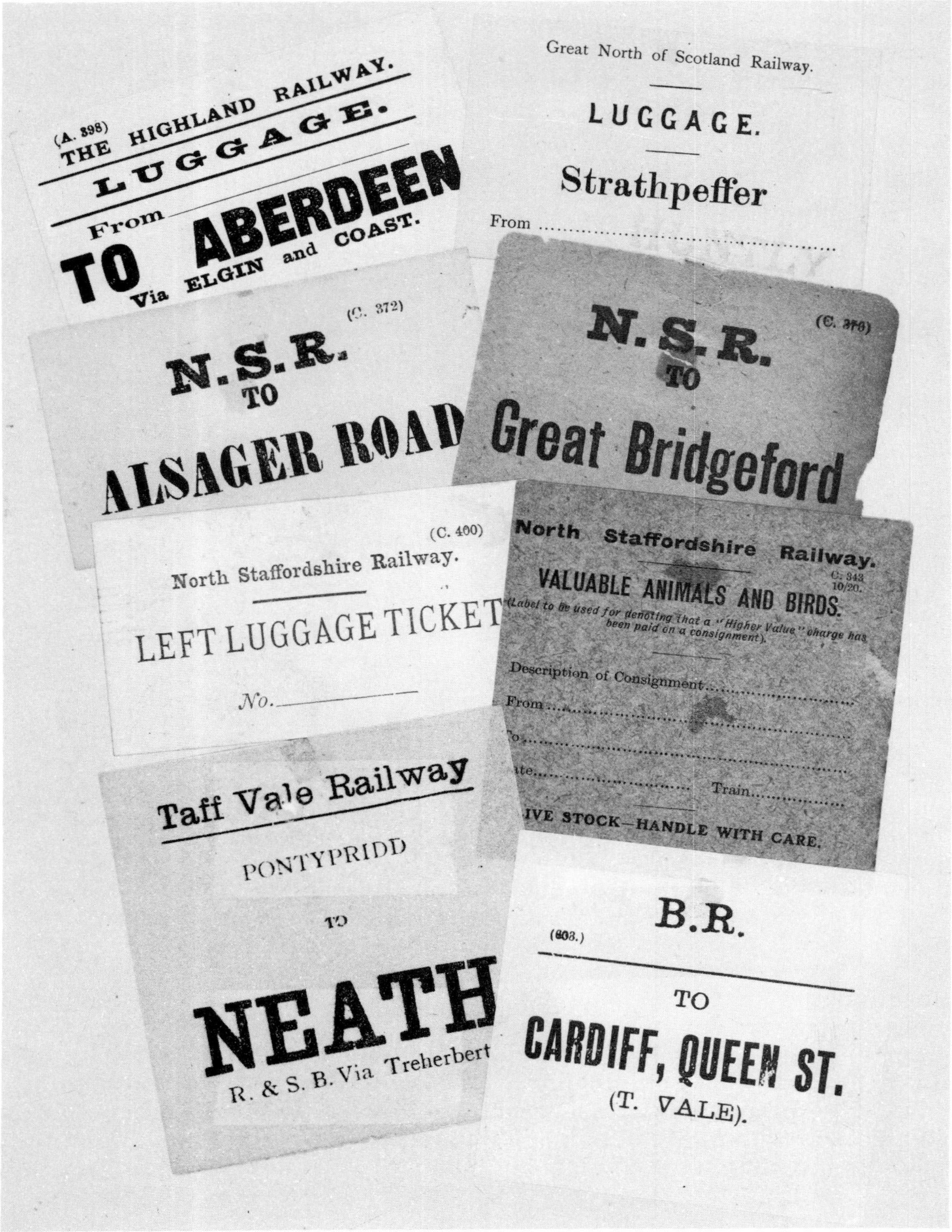

THE HIGHLAND RAILWAY.
(A. 398)
LUGGAGE.
From
TO ABERDEEN
Via ELGIN and COAST.

Great North of Scotland Railway.

LUGGAGE.

Strathpeffer

From ....

N.S.R.
TO
(C. 372)
ALSAGER ROAD

N. S. R.
TO
(C. 378)
Great Bridgeford

North Staffordshire Railway.
(C. 400)

LEFT LUGGAGE TICKET

No. _____

North Staffordshire Railway.
C. 343
10/20.
VALUABLE ANIMALS AND BIRDS.
(Label to be used for denoting that a "Higher Value" charge has been paid on a consignment).

Description of Consignment ....

From ....

To ....

Date ....   Train ....

LIVE STOCK—HANDLE WITH CARE.

Taff Vale Railway

PONTYPRIDD

TO

NEATH
R. & S. B. Via Treherbert

B.R.
(803.)

TO

CARDIFF, QUEEN ST.
(T. VALE).

272 Luggage and goods labels

URGENT ERO 34206

SHIPMENT ERO 34206

LMS-INSURED GOODS. ERO 33853.

No.

From

To

Date Train

E.R.O. 33900

URGENT

Via L M S

E.R.O. 21564/7

LMS

TOWN DELIVERY

PAID

FROM

No. of Packages

LMS E.R.O. 21981.

FRAGILE

LMS E.R.O. 21524

GLASS

L. M. & S. R. E.R.O. 21524

GLASS

L.M.S. E.R.O. 21523 O.P. 3

EGGS

WITH CARE.

273 Goods labels

274 Menu card for a Cheshire Lines Committee staff dinner, 1907

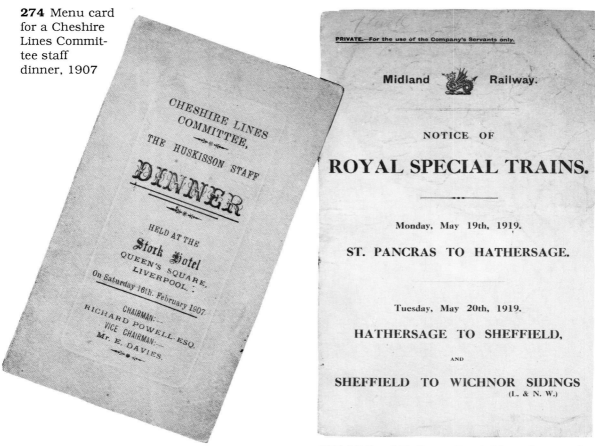

CHESHIRE LINES
COMMITTEE,

THE HUSKISSON STAFF

DINNER

HELD AT THE
Stork Hotel
QUEEN'S SQUARE,
LIVERPOOL.:
On Saturday 16th February 1907.

CHAIRMAN:—
RICHARD POWELL ESQ.
VICE CHAIRMAN:—
Mr. E. DAVIES.

PRIVATE.—For the use of the Company's Servants only.

Midland   Railway.

NOTICE OF

ROYAL SPECIAL TRAINS.

Monday, May 19th, 1919.

ST. PANCRAS TO HATHERSAGE.

Tuesday, May 20th, 1919.

HATHERSAGE TO SHEFFIELD,

AND

SHEFFIELD TO WICHNOR SIDINGS
(L. & N. W.)

275 Midland Railway timetable and general instructions for a royal train, 1919

rates, gradient diagrams, company remembrance books of employees killed in World War I (issued by the LNWR and Midland Railway among others).

Over and above these there are many items which are difficult to classify like 'Best Kept Station' certificates, 'Length of Track' certificates, awards on retirement and certificates of appreciation to loyal workers during strikes.

Railway Tickets and Passes

We propose to illustrate why the collecting of this class of railwayana attracts a following allegedly greater than any other single group of people by referring to the Swan Collection of medals and passes auctioned in London in April 1986. Almost all are in ivory with the

company name in full in the outer rim, sometimes with a number inside, and often on the reverse a personal name and/or title. They are usually round, sometimes oval and occasionally quadrafoil. It should be realised that they are the transitions between paper hand-issued tickets and Edmondson cards, and although most of these were in expensive ivory or even silver (in the case of the passes for the Newcastle & Carlisle Railway's director and solicitor), others, of brass, were issued as 'ordinary' tickets or tallies and of course were carefully re-collected. Their successors, on a mass scale, were the brass or copper 'checks' issued to numerous railway grades as tallies to collect wage packets. It is interesting to see some actually described as a 'ticket', eg the London & Birmingham Railway director's ticket of 1837, the Eastern Counties Railway director's ticket No 3, the LBSCR, the Grand Junction Railway and Somerset & Dorset Railway tickets. The durability and obvious historical interest of these articles has ensured that many have survived from a wide variety of early lines, in some cases when all other remains of the railway have perished. They were recognised as 'collectors' pieces' within a short time of their issue. Some of the most prized of all passes are those inscribed with the personal names of legendary figures like George Stephenson.

They were not always limited to first class or to directors. For example, both the Kendal & Windermere Railway and the Newcastle, North Shields & Tynemouth Railway issued brass second and third class brass season tickets.

Examples exist from the Maryport & Carlisle, London & Brighton, Eastern Counties, Grand Junction and Stockton & Darlington railways. Less expensive and less easily lost, season tickets soon emerged in the form of small

276 A very early Midland Railway ivory ticket

leather-bound passes, often embossed with the company name in gold letters and they are basically the same today.

Fig 277 shows a leather-backed first class free pass issued by the West Midland Railway for travel between Leominster and Kington. The rarity of this is attested by the fact that the company only existed between 14 June 1860 and 1 August 1863 when it amalgamated with the GWR. As the pass was issued after the merger old stock was clearly used. Some Edmondson card tickets command values of several hundred pounds to specialists who are aware of their great rarity. A number of factors can influence rarity, such as a station changing its name early on thus giving only a limited number of years of issue or the closure of stations and lines, not 20 years ago with the 'Beeching Axe', or even in the 1930s when buses had a severe effect on suburban lines, but 100

277 West Midland Railway first class free pass, 1863

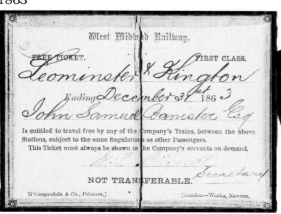

years ago. As a general rule, most tickets with dates in the 1870s and 1880s are regarded and valued as very rare so that even tickets from major companies like the Midland Railway and LNWR may be much sought after.

Single tickets are generally much more prized than return tickets as they are usually intact, whereas used returns are in halves. **Figs 278-9** show Birmingham area Midland Railway and LNWR singles all dated in the 1890s and early 1900s. Careful scrutiny reveals a wealth of data such as the Parliamentary fare rates on 3583 and 4793, the exact location of the New Street Station booking office ('Bridge' on 7128), and 'No 1 Perry Barr' on 4114. The stations at Moseley, Willenhall, King's Heath and Broom Junction are all of course only memories today. The Midland Railway 7128 (stamped 'Return' on the rear) was printed on white, the LNWR singles on green. However, earlier Midland singles of the 1860s were of other colours, eg yellow, and these are much rarer and more valuable.

The Midland Railway third-class single from King's Norton to Church Road illustrates in the latter name one key to ticket rarity, namely a station closed in 1925. Further examples of tickets from closed stations are 265 and 7460 (King's Heath and Moseley, both closed 1941) and the Midland third-class return (green) from Camp Hill to Moseley No 1935 of 25 October 1883. Camp Hill Station is now a builder's yard although just recognisable as a former station, while Camp Hill Goods Station (once the terminus of the Gloucester & Birmingham Railway) is now an industrial estate. The buff-coloured Midland Railway return from Selly Oak of 26 June is to Somerset Road, a long-closed station on the original Birming-ham West Suburban Railway. The green Midland Railway third-class return No 273 of 26 October 1883 is from Church Road to Granville Street which was, at one time, the first station from New Street, literally a few hundred yards out and one of the rarest station names to survive on Birmingham tickets.

Examples of special rates are shown in the return halves Nos 274, 765 and 2640. Leicester to Moseley of 1891, in red, was valid for Saturday to Monday only. The Scarborough excursion (possibly for train number six) is in green and white vertical stripes. The 'Pleasure Party' ticket of 1894 is in purple with white horizontal band. The post-grouping LMS green single ticket of 1937 lists four long-closed stations, namely Hazelwell, King's Heath, Lifford on the Lifford Loop) and Bourneville. This shows zonal pricing as there is a distance of several miles between these stations and the 3d fare was the same to all of them. The LMSR Smethwick platform ticket was still being issued in 1966 as shown on the rear.

Before leaving tickets it is worth mentioning that the LNWR green singles Nos 4647 and 5897 both have stamped on their plain backs company advertisements, the first having 'Scotland for the Holidays. Travel by The Royal Route. L & NW & Cal. Rlys. Frequent Cheap Excursions' and the second 'Euston and Edinburgh in 8 hours 15 mins'.

Platform tickets are some of the most eagerly sought after tickets, especially pre-grouping ones as they were only issued between about 1903 and 1923. It is worth pointing out to the non-specialist that very large numbers of stations issued platform tickets in an attempt to stop fare evasion. Hence tickets from places like Buntingsford, Marks Tey, Derby Road, Ponders End, Woodbridge,

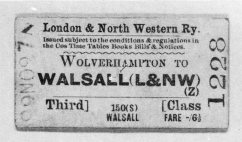

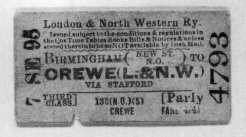

278 NWR and Midland Railway tickets from the Birmingham area

279 Midland Railway and LMS tickets from the Birmingham area

Chertsey, Ramsey, etc. The most recent extensive book so far on tickets is *Railway Tickets, Timetables & Handbills* by Maurice Bray (Moorland 1986) where more details can be found.

The well-known GWR ticket for 'Shipwrecked Mariners ...' and others was only one among a range of special groups for whom tickets were printed. The GWR printed them for ocean passengers, the LNER for mill workers between Renfrew and Paisley (and doubtless for other areas as well), and also household removal tickets. The Highland and LMS produced tickets for passengers on goods trains in areas like the Scottish Highlands where traffic and

passenger trains were both sparse. The LNER had group tickets for ships' crews (minimum party of twelve) for crews transferring between ships at different ports. The LMSR issued fishworker's tickets and also sold tickets to sea bathers going to Exmouth.

As in the case of headed notepaper and waybills, many of the early railways have had their tickets preserved as ticket auctions quickly demonstrate. So examples from the Corris, Liskeard & Caradon, Hull & Barnsley, Severn & Wye & Severn Bridge, Axholme Joint, Southwold, Westward Ho! & Appledore, Shropshire & Montgomeryshire, London, Tilbury & Southend, Mid Suffolk

280 Reward notice from the Dundee & Arbroath Joint Railway, 1884

DUNDEE & ARBROATH JOINT RAILWAY.

£5 REWARD

WHEREAS, at or about 10.45 p.m. on Saturday, the 26th January last, some evil-disposed Person or Persons did maliciously fasten, with a cord, the Wire of the Distant Signal about 600 yards west of Arbroath Station, thereby interfering with the working of the said Signal, a REWARD of FIVE POUNDS Sterling will be paid to any party giving such information to the undersigned, or other Official of the Joint Railway, as will lead to the Conviction of the Person or Persons concerned.

Head Offices, Dundee, February 1884.

E. GILBERT, Manager.

JOHN LENG & CO., PRINTERS, BANK STREET, DUNDEE.

Light, Cockermouth Keswick & Penrith railways are not especially rare. After all, there is no reason why they should be, bearing in mind that many of them have also left hardware with names and initials. When we consider the Edinburgh & Glasgow Railway, Monkland Railways, North Pembroke & Fishguard Railway, North Wales Narrow Gauge Railway, Thetford & Watton Railway, Wisbech & Upwell Tramway, Wantage Tramway, West Somerset Minerals Railway, we can see the wide range of interest and diversity to be found in railway tickets.

In closing the section on tickets we would reiterate that as well as 'rare' companies, is the question of little-used stations and unusual uses. For example, the BR ticket numbered 0000 for an 'Early Morning Single Shap to Shap Summit', ie to the granite works from Shap Station, was issued for just a six-day duration. Then there is the LMS ticket from Leicester West Bridge to Glenfield (closed 1928) on the Leicester & Swannington route, or the LMS Jura or Islay to Edinburgh Princes Street (joint with McBrayne's steamers), or a Caledonian Railway 'bicycle, pram or mailcart' ticket from Lochawe to Oban.

Very rare tickets include those from

small and obscure halts such as Wingfield Villas Halt (closed 1921) to Plymouth, fare 1d in 1915, Gadlys Bridge Halt to Nantmelyn (an unadvertised halt), Pembroke to Golden Hill Halt (closed 1940), or Laira Halt (closed 1930) to Plymouth. Tickets from stations which closed seventy or more years ago are obviously in short supply, such as Chard Town (closed in 1917) to Axminster or NER Stepney to Sculcoates (closed 1912), while a ticket from the Wick & Lybster Light Railway (closed 1944) is an obvious desirable item. Specialist ticket collectors are interested in number sequences. For example, privilege singles from Thurso to Georgemas Junction were rarely issued, so between 1960 and 1984 the running number only moved from 1,072 to 2,220.

In conclusion to this survey of some of the types of railway documents we include a reward notice from the Dundee & Arbroath Joint Railway in 1884, showing that dangerous vandalism is not a modern creation. This notice was recovered from the middle of a sack full of mouldering goods invoices in a ruined goods depot on that line in the early 1970s. It is a prime example of how the willingness to poke around rotting and rat infested paperwork has saved for posterity the sole example of an intriguing document.

10
How and Where to Collect Railwayana

If buying from antique shops, so-called junk shops, general fairs or auctions or from that wonderful source the general public, observe one rule: a fair price is what is agreed at one time between two parties and no other criteria is needed. This is not unfair or sharp practice. If you happen to be offered LNER works-plate No 1818 of 1935 and you happen to know its origin and the owner does not, then a certain price will result. If the owner does know, then the price will be vastly greater. A second-hand shop owner may be very happy to sell you a railway matchbox for 50p and if so, pay it and go. If they contact you later and call you a swindler as they have just found that an identical one fetched £30 in a specialist auction, mention that they were happy with the deal at the time. Specialist knowledge is itself a valuable quality. So if you *can* obtain from any of the above sources, do so.

The 'general public' especially is where a great reservoir of our railwayana is still buried. Antique shops and junk shops are very difficult. From experience it has been found that only around 5-10 per cent of such places have any items of railwayana at all and even of that 5-10 per cent, the majority consists of vastly overpriced lamps, often modern BR tail lamps. However, there are bargains to be had, occasionally. Whole boxes of GWR marked china ware have quite recently been pur-chased for a song.

Most collectors will have to patronise railwayana auctions, almost wholly peopled by those 'in the know'. You will not find this cheap as most objects are sold at 'the going value'. Specialist auctions at present include:

Sheffield Auctions
Held at Myers Grove School, Sheffield three times a year. Presently the 'Mecca' of railwayana. Attendances up to 400 and over £53,000 raised at one recently held auction — a world record.
Ian Wright, Myers Grove School,
Wood Lane, Sheffield S6 5HG
☎ 0742 348805 (daytime)
☎ 0742 745085 (evening)

Premier Auctions
Regular functions currently being held at Kidlington, near Oxford, Bath, and at Leicester. By August 1988 it has become obvious that Premier are reaching the same standards of excellence as available at Sheffield.
David Jones, 8 Station Road,
Kirby Muxloe, Leicester LE9 9EJ
☎ 0533 393082

Onslow's Auctions
Their auctions are held at Baden Powell House, Queen's Gate, and Carisbrook Hall, 63 Seymour Street, London, two or three times a year. Famed mainly for posters, silverware, books and paper

items, although they have general items as well.

Patrick Bogue, Onslows Auctions,
14-16 Carroun Rd,
London SW8 1JT
☎ 01 793 0240

Wells Cundall
The oldest established railwayana auctioneers. They have two auctions per year at Malton, and others at Watford.
Harry Dimmy, Wells Cundall
15 Market Place, Malton, N. Yorks
☎ 0653 695581

Railwayana is also auctioned from time to time by Christies and Phillips. In addition, BR holds occasional auctions, usually run by auction firms, latterly at its former works like Swindon and Wolverton. There are also auction firms like South Eastern Auctions of Hastings, and others who from time to time have some railwayana items. Please note that this list makes no reference to regular past auction sites such as Bitton or Buxton which no longer function.

Another major source of railwayana is to be found in the swapmeets or collectors' fairs. These are currently located at Quorn near Loughborough, Kidlington near Oxford, Lode Heath School, Solihull, Chasewater near Walsall, Newbury (Berks) and Dinting (Greater Manchester). Dates for these are to be found in the publications *RCN* and *OTL* as shown below.

The other source of quality railwayana is through the pages of the two monthly railwayana publications — *The Railwayana Collectors' Newsletter* and *The Railwayana Journal — On the Line,* price £1.10 per issue and produced on the 2nd Monday of each month and 1st of each month at 7 Ascot Road, Moseley, Birmingham B13 9EN. *RCN* has been established for 20 years (1968-88) and is the prime advertising medium of the railwayana movement. *The Railwayana Journal — On The Line* is the flagship of the movement and is a journal in the true sense, ·recording special railwayana items as they are found. It contains regular specialist articles on all classes of railwayana and provides a constant discussion forum, with a valuable service in exposing replicas and forgeries as they are attempted. These publications are also on sale at Collectors' Corner, Euston.

Collectors' Corner is another valuable source, being run by BR themselves at Coburg Street, 5 minutes' walk from Euston Station.

Data on the subject can also be obtained from the regular articles written by the present author which appear in *Railway World* every two months, under the title 'The Railwayana Scene'.

Railwayana Museums

Moseley Railwayana Museum *
7 Ascot Road
Moseley
Birmingham
B13 9EN
☎ (021) 449 9707
Visits by arrangement and as announced in *Railway World* and the *Railwayana Press*.
Proprietors, M. J. & J. M. Mander.

Harpenden Railway Museum *
235 Luton Road
Harpenden
Hertfordshire
AL5 3DE
☎ (05827) 3524
Open: over spring and late Summer Bank Holiday weekends.
Proprietors, G. & S. Woodward.

Fawley Railway Museum
This is a private collection. Visitors by invitation only.

Warwick Railway Museum *
17 Green Lane
Warwick
GU 34 5BP
☎ (0926) 496 210
Visits by appointment.
Open: one day per year usually in May or June.
Proprietor, Alwyn Sparrow.

Winchcombe Railway Museum
23 Gloucester Steet
Winchcombe
Gloucester
☎ (0242) 602 257
Open: daily throughout the year.
Proprietor, T. Petcley.

Didcot Small Relics Museum
Didcot Steam Centre
Didcot
Oxon

National Railway Museum
Leeman Road
York
Y02 4XJ
Open: weekdays 10am-6pm, Sundays 11am-6pm.
Closed 24, 25, 26 December.

Bressingham Steam Museum
Bressingham
Diss
Norfolk
IP22 2AB
☎ (0379) 88 386
There is an important Railwayana Collection in the Gallery.

Please note that we list above only those Railwayana Museums named in the text; these represent only a fraction of all the great private collections. The ones starred are adjuncts to private houses and are thus open at limited times only. For detailed opening times please see 'On The Line' and 'The Railwayana Collectors Newsletter'.

Glossary of Companies and Jointly Owned Stations

Problems of Nomenclature

a The list is basically one of abbreviations used in this book. It is *not* a complete index of all companies who produced railwayana. The size of this book precludes such a vast aim. Omission from the list does not mean that the author is unaware of the railway! Some companies in the list are not actually named in the book.

b The list is not in any sense an index of railway companies, for which readers should consult Tim Petchey's excellent work (see Bibliography).

c In the names represented by the initials, the author has tried to use the titles most often found on railwayana items. The problem is that in the case of joint lines, the companies themselves usually never seem to have decided what to call themselves! Examples of this are given below − GWR & LNWR initials were often reversed, as were GC & MJ.

Here are some instances of the problems of nomenclature:

FR	Trespass plates marked both 'Railway' and 'Railways'
GC & MJ	'Joint Line' used on Midland pattern trespass plates.
GN & GC Joint	Trespass plates marked both 'Railway' and 'Railways', as well as West Riding & Grimsby 'Railway'; wagon labels marked West Riding Joint Committee!
GWR& GCR Joint	Plates marked 'Joint Committee' as well as 'Joint Railways'.
LNWR & FR	Cast-iron plates marked both 'Railway' and 'Railways'. Some marked 'Joint', some not. Boundary post marked 'LNW & FRY'.
LNWR & GWR Joint	Plates marked 'Railway', 'Railways', 'Joint Railway' and 'Joint Lines'.
Mid & NER	No mention of Joint in trespass plate
SDJL	Trespass plate marked 'Joint Line'. Beware of trains plate marked 'S & DJR'
SMR	Sheffield & Midland 'Railways' on trespass plate.
SURCC	Most common bridge notice marked 'Railway'. All others marked 'Railways'.
SYJL	Cast-iron plates marked 'Joint Railway', 'Joint Line', 'Joint Line Committee' and 'SYJR'.

An important point is that joint railways often reversed the order of companies on various items.

Glossary

A & NJR	Ashby & Nuneaton Joint Railway (LNW & Midland)
AJR	Axholme Joint Railway (LYR & NE)
ANSWDRC	Alexandra (Newport & South Wales) Docks & Railway Co
B & LJR	Bourne & Lynn Joint Railway
BCR	Bishop's Castle Railway
BDR	Barry Dock & Railways
BER	Bristol & Exeter Railway
BGR	Birmingham & Gloucester
Birkenhead Joint	GWR & LNWR Joint (later GWR & LMSR Joint)
BM & LNWJ	Brecon & Merthyr & LNW Joint
BMR	Brecon & Merthyr Railway
BER	Bristol & Exeter Railway

BJS	Bristol Joint Station (owned and worked by GWR & LMS)		North Western Joint Railway
		GC & MJ	Great Central & Midland Joint Line
BR	British Railways		
BTC	British Transport Commission	GCR	Great Central Railway
BRB	British Railways Board	GER	Great Eastern Railway
BP & GVR	Burry Port & Gwendraeth Valley Railway	GER & Mid	Great Eastern and Midland Railway
BWHA	Bideford, Westward Ho! & Appledore Railway	GJR	Grand Junction Railway
		GKER	Garstang & Knott End Railway
BWR	Bodmin & Wadebridge Railway	GLR	Garston & Liverpool Railway
C & OJ	Croydon & Oxted Joint Railway (owned by LBSCR & SECR)	GN & GC	Great Northern & Great Central Joint Railways
Cal R	Caledonian Railway	GN & GEJ	Great Northern & Great Eastern Joint Railway
Cam R	Cambrian Railways		
Cardiff R	Cardiff Railway	GN & LNWR	Great Northern & London & North Western Joint Lines
CCR	Chester & Crewe Railway		
CCSC	Carlisle Citadel Station Committee	GN & LYJ	Great Northern & Lancashire & Yorkshire Joint Railways
CER	Central Electric Railway	GNR	Great Northern Railway
CFDR	Central Forest of Dean Railway	GNSR	Great North of Scotland Railway
CGUR	City of Glasgow Union Railway	GSWR	Glasgow & South Western Railway
CK & PR	Cockermouth Keswick & Penrith Railway		
		GVT	Glyn Valley Tramway
CLC	Cheshire Lines Committee (owned by GC, GN & Midland)	GVR	Gwendraeth Valley Railway
		GWR& GCR	Great Western & Great Central Joint Committee
Corris R	Corris Railway		
CVR	Colne Valley Railway	GW & LNE J	Great Western & London & North Eastern Joint Railway
CWJR	Cleator & Workington Junction Railway		
		GW & LSWR	Great Western & London & South Western Joint Railway
D & AJR	Dundee & Arbroath Joint Railway (owned by NBR & Cal)	GW & Met	Great Western & Metropolitan Joint Committee
DVR	Dearne Valley Railway		
DVLR	Derwent Valley Light Railway	GW & RR	Great Western & Rhymney Joint Railway
ECJS	East Coast Joint Stock		
EGR	Edinburgh & Glasgow Railway	GWR	Great Western Railway
E Lincs R	East Lincolnshire Railway	GWR & LMS	Great Western Railway & London Midland & Scottish Railway (several lines operated jointly)
ELR	East London Railway		
EMR	Eastern & Midlands Railway		
EWJR	East & West Junction Railway		
EWYUR	East & West Yorkshire Union Railway	GWR & Mid J	Great Western & Midland Railways
F & MJR	Furness & Midland Joint Railway	H & O	Halifax & Ovenden Joint (GN & LYR)
FDR	Forest of Dean Railway	HB & GCJ	Hull & Barnsley & Great Central Joint Committee
FP & WRJR	Fleetwood Preston & West Riding Junction Railway		
		HBGC & MJC	Hull & Barnsley, Great Central & Midland Joint Committee
FR	Festiniog Railway		
FR	Furness Railway(s)	HBR	Hoylake & Birkenhead Railway
FRRH	Fishguard & Rosslare Railways & Harbours	HBR	Hull & Barnsley Railway
		HCR	Hammersmith & City Railway (owned by Met & GWR)
GB & KJR	Glasgow, Barrhead & Kilmarnock Joint Railway (owned by GSWR & Cal)		
		HHL	Halifax High Level (owned by GN & LYR)
GC & LNWJ	Great Central & London &	HR	Highland Railway

IMR	Isle of Man Railway	M & SWJR	Midland & South Western
IWCR	Isle of Wight Central Railway		Junction Railway
IWR	Isle of Wight Railway	Macc Comm.	Macclesfield Committee
KER	Kington & Eardisley Railway		(renamed from Macclesfield
KESR	Kent & East Sussex Railway		Bollington & Marple
KWR	Kendal & Windermere Railway		Railway)
LBR	Leicester & Birmingham	MCR	Maryport & Carlisle Railway
	Railway	MCR	Midland Counties Railway
LBR	London & Birmingham Railway	Met & GCJC	Metropolitan & Great Central
LBSCR	London Brighton & South Coast		Joint Committee
	Railway	Met & LNE	Metropolitan and London
LCDR	London Chatham & Dover		& North Eastern Joint
	Railway	Met.R	Metropolitan Railway
LCR	Lancaster & Carlisle Railway	MGWR	Midland Great Western Railway
LCR	Liskeard & Caradon Railway		(Ireland)
LDECR	Lancashire Derbyshire & East	Mid & LNWR	Midland and London & North
	Coast Railway		Western Railway Joint Lines
LEGR	Lewes & East Grinstead Railway	Mid & NER	Midland & North Eastern
LHL	Leeds High Level		Railway Co
LKR	Leominster & Kington Railway	Mid R	Midland Railway
LLR	Liskeard & Looe Railway	MJC	Methley Joint Committee
LMS & LNER	London Midland & Scottish and		(owned by LYR, NER & GNR)
	London & North Eastern Joint	MMR	Manchester & Milford Railway
	Railway	Monk R	Monkland Railways
LMSR (NCC)	London Midland & Scottish	MR	Mersey Railway
	Northern Counties Committee	MRC Co	Monmouth Railway & Canal Co
LMS (or LMSR)	London Midland & Scottish	MSCR	Manchester Ship Canal
	Railway		Railways
LNER	London & North Eastern	MSJAR	Manchester South Junction &
	Railway		Altrincham Railway (owned by
LNWR	London & North Western		GC & LNWR)
	Railway	MSLR	Manchester, Sheffield &
LNWR & Cal	London & North Western &		Lincolnshire Railway
	Caledonian Joint	MSLR	Mid Suffolk Light Railway
LNWR & FR	London & North Western and	MWR	Mid Wales Railway
	Furness Railway Joint Lines	N & BR	Neath & Brecon Railway
LNWR & GWR	London & North Western &	NBJR	Northampton & Banbury
	Great Western Joint Railway		Junction Railway
LNWR & LYR	London & North Western and	NBR	North British Railway
	Lancashire & Yorkshire Joint	NCR	Newcastle & Carlisle Railway
	Lines	NCR	Northern Counties Railway
LNWR & NER	London & North Western and	NDCJLR	North Devon & Cornwall
	North Eastern Railway Joint		Junction Light Railway
LSWR	London & South Western	NER	North Eastern Railway
	Railway	NLLR	North Lindsey Light Railway
LTSR	London Tilbury & Southend	NLR	North London Railway
	Railway	NNSTR	Newcastle North Shields &
LUR	Lancashire Union Railway		Tynemouth Railway
	(owned by LNWR & LYR)	NPF	North Pembroke & Fishguard
LYR & GNR	Lancashire & Yorkshire & Great		Railway
	Northern Railway Cos	NSJC	Norfolk & Suffolk Joint
LYR	Lancashire & Yorkshire Railway		Committee (owned by GER and
M & GNJR	Midland & Great Northern Joint		M & GNR)
	Railway	NSR	North Staffordshire Railway

NUJ	North Union Joint Railway (owned by LNWR & LYR)	SR	Southern Railway
		SSR	Sittingbourne & Sheerness Railway
NWNGR	North Wales Narrow Gauge Railway	SSR	South Staffordshire Railway
OAGBR	Oldham, Ashton & Guide Bridge Railway (owned by GC & LNWJ)	ST	Selsey Tramways
		St HCR Co	St Helens Canal & Railway Co
OWWR	Oxford Worcester & Wolverhampton Railway	SUR	Stafford & Uttoxeter Railway
		SURCC	Shropshire Union Railways & Canal Co
P & LJR	Preston & Longbridge Joint Railway (owned by LNWR & LYR)	SWMR	South Wales Minerals Railway
		SYJL	South Yorkshire Joint Line Committee (owned by GCR, GNR, LYR, Mid & NER)
P & WJR	Portpatrick & Wigtown Joint Railway (owned by Cal, GSWR, Mid & LNWR)	TBJ	Taff Bargoed Joint Railway (owned by GWR & Rhymney)
PBHR	Paisley Barrhead & Hurlet Railway	THJR	Tottenham & Hampstead Junction Railway (owned by GER & Mid)
PCNR	Pontypridd Caerphilly & Newport Railway		
PDSWJR	Plymouth Devonport & South Western Junction Railway	TRE	The Railway Executive
		TVR	Taff Vale Railway
PJ	Penrith Joint Station	TWT	Thetford & Watton Tramway
PR	Peebles Railway	VOTR	Vale of Towy Railway (owned by LNWR & GWR Joint)
PTRD Co	Port Talbot Railway & Docks Co		
PWR	Preston & Wyre Railway (owned by LNWR & LYR)	VRR	Vale of Rheidol Railway
		W & PJ	Weymouth & Portland Joint Railway (owned by GW & LSWR)
R & LNW	Rhymney & LNW Joint		
RR	Rhymney Railway	WCJS	West Coast Joint Stock
RSBR	Rhondda & Swansea Bay Railway	WCP	Weston, Clevedon & Portishead Railway
S & WJR	Severn & Wye Joint Railway (owned by GWR & LMS)	WCR	West Cornwall Railway
		WJC	Watford Joint Committee
SDJC	Somerset & Dorset Joint Line Committee	WJPS	Wakefield Joint Passenger Station
SDR	South Devon Railway	WLE	West London Extension Railway
SDR	Stockton & Darlington Railway	WLJ	West London Joint (owned by LNWR & GWR)
SECR	South Eastern & Chatham Management Committee		
SER	South Eastern Railway	WLR	West Lancashire Railway
SHDR	Seacombe Hoylake & Deeside Railway	WMCQR	Wrexham Mold & Connah's Quay Railway
SHR	Shrewsbury & Hereford Railway	WMR	West Midland Railway
SJS	Stalybridge Joint Station	WR	Wirral Railway
SMJC	Sheffield & Midland Joint Committee	WRJC	West Riding Joint Committee (owned by GN & GC)
SMJR	Stratford-upon-Avon and Midland Junction Railway	WSMR	West Somerset Minerals Railway
		WT	Wantage Tramway
SMR	Shropshire & Montgomery	WUT	Wisbech & Upwell Tramway
SR & LMS	Southern Railway and London Midland & Scottish Joint Railway	WVR	Wye Valley Railway
		YNR	York & Newcastle Railway

Acknowledgements

I must record my grateful thanks to the following for their help and encouragement so willingly given towards the writing of this book. Many of them will recognise items in their collection featured in the author's photographs. To anyone whose name is unwittingly omitted may we emphasize that the omission is entirely unintentional.

Chris Atkin for the inspiration behind his collection; Richard Barton (SECR); David Bee for his railwayana poems; R. K. Bird for his constant encouragement; Dr Gordon Blears (LNER); John Bourhill for his generous and repeated help in LMS matters; Mike Brooks; Keith Buckle for his time and patience explaining locomotive worksplates; Frank Burridge of the Big Four Railway Museum; Roy Burrows (Midland Railway); Paul Carter for information on totems; Andy Cutcliffe (wagon plates); Michael Dunn and his railway office, one of the founders of Railwayana Preservation; Tony Edsor (GER); Ray Franks for the unstinting trust in allowing long term borrowing of share certificates and GWR circulars; Stuart Furniss, the inspirer of the author's vision of an iron-scape; Brian Gell for his classification of tokens, staffs and keys; Dr David Glynn for his additions and corrections to the chapter on Signalling; Julian Hanwell for help on Silverware and Cornish Railways; Gerald Hartley for his advice on Crests; David Hayball (police truncheons); David Hughes for his invaluable knowledge on finials and inkwells; Peter Jordan for advice on block instruments; Trevor Kay (Yorkshire and GCR Railwayana); Marc Lund (railwayana poetry and locomotive data); Hon W. McAlpine (Fawley Railway Museum); Colin Moore - the originator of railwayana cartoons; Rodney Marshall, an ever ready contributor to our railwayana field; Tim Petchey (curator of Winchcombe Railway Museum), the founder of organised Railwayana Preservation; National Railway Museum, York, for facilities for photographs of exhibits; Peter Rodgers for his crucial encouragement and advice at critical moments and especially for tolerating our two unsuccessful attempts to photograph his lamps and his eventual recourse to a professional photographer, and for his editing of the section on lamps; Pete Sargieson, totems; Frank Soule for help on whistles; Allwyn Sparrow (Warwick Railwayana Museum); Graham Timson for his amazing perseverance and example to the author in metal-detecting, deep digging and general historical recovery methods; Bob Withers; Ian Wright of Sheffield Auctions, my constant confidante and finally, without the toleration of my helper, confidante, typist and wife Margaret, this book would not have been written.

Bibliography

Below is a selected bibliography of the main books and booklets previously published on railwayana. Please note: books largely dealing with company histories, locomotives, carriages, wagons where these touch only incidentally with what the present work classes as railwayana, have been omitted.

A Bibliography of British Railway History, George Ottley and others. (HMSO [Science Museum and National Railway Museum] 1st Ed 1965, 2nd Ed 1985). Commonly referred to as 'Ottley'.

A List of Railway Undertakings in England, Scotland and Wales, Tim Petchey (Winchcombe Railway Museum 1987)

A Pictorial Record of Great Western Signalling, A. Vaughan (OPC 1973)

A Pictorial Record of LNWR Signalling, Richard D. Foster (OPC 1982)

A Pictorial Record of Southern Signals, G. Pryer (OPC 1977)

Collecting Railway Antiques, Cyril Bracegirdle, Patrick Stephen 1988

Complete British Railways Maps and Gazetteer 1830-1981, C.J. Wignall (OPC 1983)

Known Postcards, Ian Wright, Brian Hilton, John Alsop. Privately published.

Go Great Western. A History of GWR Publicity, R.B. Wilson (1st Ed 1970, 2nd Ed 1987 David & Charles)

GWR Company Servants, Janet K.L. Russell (Wild Swan 1983)

Great Western Miscellany Vol 1, J.H. Russell (OPC 1978)

Great Western Miscellany Vol II, J.H. Russell (OPC 1979)

Happy Holidays. The Golden Age of Railway Posters, Michael Palin. Pavilion Books 1987.

Highland Miscellany, Peter Tatlow (OPC 1985)

Lancashire & Yorkshire Railway Miscellany, Noel Coates (OPC 1983)

LMS Miscellany Vol 1, H.N. Twells (OPC 1982)

LMS Miscellany Vol 2, H.N. Twells (OPC 1984)

LMS Miscellany Vol 3, H.N. Twells (OPC 1986)

LNWR Liveries, E. Talbot, P. Millard, G. Dow, P. Davis (Historical Model Railway Society 1985)

LNWR Miscellany, E. Talbot (OPC 1978)

LNWR Miscellany Vol 2, E. Talbot (OPC 1980)

Nameplates of the Big Four Including British Railways, F. Burridge (OPC 1st Ed 1975, 2nd Ed 1985)

Nameplates on Display, Ian Wright (Pennine Publications 1986)

Railway Antiques, James Mackay (Ward Lock 1978)

Railway Picture Postcards, Maurice Bray (Moorland Publishing 1986)

Rail Atlas of Britain, S. Baker (OPC 1977)

Railway and Other Rare Insulators, W. Keith Neal (Signal Box Press 1987)

Railway Buttons, Badges and Uniforms, David J. Froggatt (Ian Allan 1986)

Railway Horse Brasses, Ran Hawthorne (National Horse Brass Society 1987)

Railway Junction Diagrams, 1915 re-print (David & Charles 1969)

Railway Relics, Bryan Morgan (Ian Allan 1969)

Railway Relics & Regalia, P.B. Whitehouse (Country Life 1975)

Railway Tickets, Timetables & Handbills, Maurice Bray (Moorland Publishing, 1986)

Sectional Maps of the British Railways at 31.12.47 (Ian Allan)

The Golden Age of the Railway Poster, J.T. Shackleton (New English Library 1975)

The Official Railway Postcard Book, John Alsop (John Alsop 1987)

The Railwayana Journal — On The Line, monthly periodical July 1985 onwards, Moseley Railwayana Museum, 7 Ascot Road, Moseley, Birmingham. B13 9EN

The Railway Heritage of Britain, G. Biddle & O.S. Nock (Michael Joseph 1983)

The Signal Box, Signalling Study Group (OPC 1986)

Searching for Railway Telegraph Insulators, W. Keith Neal (Signal Box Press 1982)

Index

A

Air raid notices 143
Ambulance badges 140-1
Ambulance equipment 144-6
Andrews Allan & Co. 70
Andrews Barr & Co. 70
Annett's Keys 93
Antimacassars 63
Appleby Frodingham 82
Appleton Patent Lamps 102
Armbands 138-9
Armstrong T. Bros. 15
Armstrong-Whitworth 68
Ashtrays 50-54, 165
Asparagus grill 63
Auctions 180-1
Avonside 68, 69
Axlebox covers 86

B

Badges 139-41
Bagnalls 68
Baker, J & Co. 82
Ball, S & Co. 15
Bannisters & Co. 82
Barclays, Andrew 68
Barclay & Co. 70
Barr Morrison & Co. 70
Baynton Lamps 100
Beardsmore 69
Bedrooms, Hotel 53
Beer bottles 54-8
Benches 12
Benson J. W. 17
Best Kept Stations 174
Beyer Peacock 68
Birkenshaws & Co. 82
Birmingham Wagon Co. 82
Biscuit barrel 61
Black Hawthorn & Co. 72
Black Leaf China (GWR) 7
Bladon Lamps 100

Blake Boiler Co. 82
Blaker, R. 47
Blankets 146
Blears, G. 28, 84
Block Instruments 90-2
Bolton Railway Wagon & Iron Works 82
Booking Offices 13
Bookmarks 165
Boundary Markers 119-22
Brandy Glass 56
Brass collars 94
Bray, M. 158, 178
Bressingham Small Relics Museum 57
Bridge Numbers 123
Bridge Restrictions 117, 122-4
Bristol & S. Wales R. Wagon Co. Ltd. 82
British Locomotive Catalogue B. Baxter 73
British Steam Locomotive Builders J. W. Lowe 73
British Railway Traffic & Electric Co. 82
British Wagon Co. 82
Brown Marshall & Co. 82
Brushes 13
Buckets 130, 135
Buckle K. 69
Buffer Stop Lamps 111
Buffet cars 62
Builders' Plates 68-73
Bullseye Lamps 110
Bulpitt Lamps 100
Burridge, F. 74
Butter dish 51
Butter knife 63
Butterley & Co. 81
Buttons 135-8

C

Cabsides 73-4
Cake slice 63

Cammell Laird 82
Candlestick holder 63
Canvas aprons 131
Caps 132
Cap badges 133
Carafes 56
Carbide lamps 110
Carpets 63, 80
Carriage boards 79-80
Carriage lamps 81
Carriage prints 79
Carriage notices 79
Cast iron notices 95, 117-30
Cattell, G. Sutton Coldfield 7
Central Wagon Co. 82
Chamberpots 48, 51, 53, 74
Chinaware 48-54
Choirs 140
Chorley Wagon Co. 82
Christies 71
Clapham Transport Museum 7
Clayton Wagons Co. 82
Clocks 15-16
Clogs 131
Coal Buckets 13
Coats of arms 18, 50, 79
Coffee cups, saucers 50
Coffee pots 60-1
Collectors Corner 7, 58, 181
Condiment trays 50, 52
Convalescent homes 141
Coronation Ware 60
Copper ware 64-5
Crane notices 25
Cream tots 51
Crests 21
Crested notepaper 150-1
Crossing Gate Lamps 111
Cruets 57
Cups and saucers 49-54
Cutlery 62-4
Cutcliffe, A. 84

Cyma 17

D

Darlington Wagon & Engine Co. 82
Davis, W. H. Langwith 82
Decanters 56
Demurrage 30
Derbyshire Wagon Co. 82
Detonator cans 94
De Winton 68
Diamond bridge notices 122-3
Dick Kerr & Co. 70
Didcot Small Relics Museum 28
Dining cars, rooms, clubs 46-7, 53
Dinner plates 49, 50, 51
Door handles 78
Draednought 67
Drinking glasses 54
Dübs 68
Dutton's 88

E

Eagle Pencil Co. 44
Eccles, G. & Son 15
Edwards & Son 15
Eggs 167
Egg cups 167
Electric flash motif 62
Elkington 65
Enamel notices 95, 128-9
English Electric Co. 73
Engraved worksplated 69
Entrée dish 64
Etched glass 54
Evans & O'Donnell 88

F

Fenders 12
Finials 89
Fire buckets 23-4

Fire fighting items 143-4
Firemen 132
Fireplaces 12
Firepoints 10, 24
First aid boxes, etc. 94, 145-6
Fish knife, fork 64
Fishslice 64
Flags 94
Fletchen's Instruments 90
Fletcher Jennings 68
Flower holder 64
Fog machines 97
Footpath signs 9
Footwarmer 80
Forks 48, 63
Forms 152
Fowlers 68
Froggatt, D. J. 131
Funnels 116

G
Gate notices 118-9
Gell, Brian 93
General Electric Co. Ltd. 73
General Strike medals 141
General Wagon Repairs Co. 83
Gittus, W. M. Wagon Co. 82
Glass 167
Glasscloths 66
Glassware 54-8
Goods labels 169
Goods memos 33-6
Goods Transport 23-45
Goods warehouses 23
Gradient Posts 124-5
Grant Ritchie 70
Grapefruit dish 64
Grape scissors 64
Gravy boats 50, 64
Grazebrook, M. & W. 82
Great Silver Tomb 58-9
Griffith's Lamps 100
Guard's jacket 133
Guillard (Paris) 65

H
Hall Lewis & Co. 82
Hampers 57
Ham stand 64
Hanwell J. 58
Hardware 130
Harris & Camm Ltd. 82
Hat bands 135
Hawkseyes 19
Hawthorne R. 28
Hawthorne Leslie 68
Headboards 77-8

Hendry Lamp Co. 100
Heraldic Devices 17
Hetherington Lamps 100
Hock glass 57
Holcroft 88
Horlicks mixer 64
Horse railwayana 27-9
Horse box plates 77
Hot water bottles 81
Hotels 46
Hot water jug 51, 64
Hudswell Clarke 68
Hughes, D. 89
Hunslet 68
Hunter, Thos. 82
Hurst Nelson & Co. 82
Hydrants 24

I
Ian Allan Regional Gazetteer 117
Ice bucket 64
Icecream dish 64
Inkwells 57-8
Inspection covers 25
Invoices 32
Irons 13
Ivory passes 175

J
Jam dish 57
Jam holder 62
Jew Lamp 100
Jigsaws 166
Joyce's of Whitchurch 15

K
Kay's of Paris 15
Kerr Stuart 68
Kesick, Keswick ware 49
Kettle pattern inkwells 58
Keys 79
Kilmarnock Engineering Co. 70
Kitson 68
Knives 63

L
Lamps 99-116
Lamp names 19
Lamp rooms 115
Lamp standards 113
Lamp yokes 115
Lancashire Watch Co. 17
Lancaster Wagon Co. 82
Landmine pattern inkwells 58
Leather passes 175
Letters 147-52
Levers 94

Levick Lamps 100
Light bulbs, holders 80
Lincoln Wagon & Engine Co. 83
Linley Lamps 100
Lobster pick 64
London Lamp Manu. Co. 100
Lozenge patterns 48
Lucas Lamps 100
Luggage rack supports 80
Luggage stickers 163

M
Maclellan Lamp Co. 100
McCulloch Sons & Kennedy 70
McKenzie Holland 88
Macintoshes 132
Manholes 10
Manning Wardle 68
Matchbox holder, striker, boxes 64, 165
Meat dish 64
Medals 64
Medallions 139
Memoranda 147-52
Menus 63-6, 174
Messenger Lamps 100
Metro Cammel 83
Midland R'way Carr. & Wagon Co. 83
Mileposts 124-5
Milk jugs 50
Minton 49
Mirror 54-8
Monograms 11, 113
Moreton & Co. 83
Moseley Railwayana Museum 13
Moy, Thomas & Co. 83
Muffin dish 62
Murray Lamp Co. 100
Mustard pots and spoons 57, 64

N
Nameplates 74-6
Napkins 63
Neilson, Neilson Reid 68
Newspaper Stamps 30
No Smoking Signs 26
North British Loco. Ltd. 68, 71-3
North Central Wagon Co. 83
Number takers 25
Nutcracker 64

O
Oilskins 131
Omega 17

Onslow's Auctions 181
On The Line (The Railwayana Journal) 7
Outside porter 139
Overcoats 132
Overstamps 35
Oyster fork 64

P
Padlocks 130
Paper History 31-45
Parcel vans 27
Parcel Stamps 29-30
Paraffin pourers 86
Passes 174-9
Pavement markers 121
Pay checks 142-3
Peckett 68
Pencils 44
Pens, pen nibs 44-5
Pepper pots 57
Petchey, T. 144
Pewterware 58
Pickering & Co. 83
Pickle fork 64
Platform tickets 176-8
Platform ticket machines 22
Platform lamps 112-4
Police items 141-2
Polkey Lamps 100
Poole Lamps 100
Pooley's 22
Porcelain 58
Porte-Cochère 18
Posters 159-63
Poster boards 14
Potato labels 40
Powell Dyffryn 84
Preece Instrument 90
Premier Auctions 7, 181
Premier Lamps 100
Principality Wagon Co. 83
Private road signs 9
Prize length certificates 174
Procor Ltd. 84
Publicity 163-7
Punchbowl and ladle 63

R
Race items 159
Railway Clearing House 83
Railwayana Collectors' Newsletter 7
Railway Relics & Regalia 69
Railway Service badges 141
Railway Signal Co. 87, 90

Reform Lamp Co. 100
Refreshment rooms 46
Repeaters 90-3
Rifle clubs 140
Rippingilles Lamps 100
Risdales Lamps 100
Robb Moore & Neil
    Lamps 100
Roberts, Charles & Co.
    83
Rob. Stephenson & Co.
    68
Rogers, Pete 99-116
Roundel pattern 49
Roundel signs 20
Route Labels 167-70
Rowney, G. & Sons 44
Rugs 80
Rulebooks 133, 171
Running-in boards 19
Russel, J. K. L. 27, 135

S
St Pancras vaults 58
St Rollox Works 71
Sacks 30, 151
Sack trucks 12
Sailors' hats 133
Saltley Oilbath &
    Axlebox Co. 86
Salt pots 57
Salvers 64
Samson Lamps 100
Scissors 145
Scroll pattern 48
Seahorse motif 53
Seatbacks 12
Seth Thomas 17
Settle Spakman & Co.
    83
Shares 152-7
Sharman, M. 99
Sharp Stewart 68, 72
Shedplates 76
Shelf plates 94
Sheffield Auctions 7
Sherry glasses 56-8
Ships 46
Shirras & Co. 99
Shovels 13
Shunt with care 42
Signal diagrams 95
Signal lamps 111-2
Signalbox lamps 114

Signalbox names 96
Signalling 87-98
Signal pulleys 96
Silverware 58-64
Smith, John. Derby 15
Smith & Chamberlain
    Lamps 100
Smokeboxes 74
Soap dish 53
Soule, F. 76-7
Soup plates 51
Soup spoon 64
Soup tureen 62
Spagnoletti & Co. 90
Spandrels 17
Spence, J. 134
Spirit measure 64
Spirit stove 60
Spoons 63
Staffs 93
Staff associations 141
Standard Wagon Co. 83
Stanton Iron Works 83
Station furntiure 11
Station Hotels and
    employees 11
Station names 19
Station wagon 40
Steamers 49
Stephenson & Hawthorn
    68
Stevens Signal Co. 88
Stockall Marples 15
Stop valves 10
Stoves 13, 130
Stretches 145
Sufferance Roads 147
Sugar bowls 51, 53
Sugar caster 64
Sugar tongs 64
Sugg Lamps 100, 114
Sundae dish 62
Sunshine script 26
Sweet bowl 64
Swapmeets 182
Sykes Signal Co. 90

T
Tablecloth 63
Tablelamps 114
Tablets 90-5
Tablet catchers 96
Tableware 46-67
Talbot, E. 27

Tankards 62
Targets 20
Tarpaulins 30
Teacups, pots 48, 61
Tearooms 46
Tea urns 63
Telephones 94
Temperance societies
    55, 141
Tender plates 76
Thornton 17
Thwaite & Read 15
Tickets 174-9
Ticket notices 14
Timetables, covers 15,
    165
Tinplate 164
Tin trunks 164
Tips, railway 55
Toe plates 96
Toilet roll holders, paper
    67, 81
Toothbrush holder 53
TOPS 30
Totems 19
Towels 81
Track circuit diagrams
    94
Trackside signs 117-130
Train describers 93-5
Train staff 93-5
Transhipment 32
'Transitional' railwayana
    26, 30, 42
Trays 63
Tresspass signs 128
Trophies 64
Truncheons 141
Tureens 48, 60
Turner, G. T. R. & Co.
    83
Twells, H. N. 12
Tyers & Co. 90

U
Undersheet label 40
Uniforms 131-5
Urgent labels 44
Urinals 22

V
Vegetable tureens 51
Venus Pencil Co. 44

Veritas Lamp Co. 100
Viaduct numbers 123
Vulcan 68

W
Wagon labels 31-44
Wagon plates 31, 81-86
Waiting Rooms 13
Walkers (Signalling) 91
Walkers, John. (Clocks)
    15
Warehouses 24
Warwick Railway
    Museum 94, 97
Watches 17
Water bowl 52
Water jugs 146
Watford Joint Station 10
Waybills 32-45
Webb & Thompson 93
Weighbridges 24
Weighing machines 22
Wells Cundall Auctions
    182
Westinghouse Brake &
    Signal Co. 88
Wheelbarrows 12
Wheelchairs 145
Whisky flasks 57
Whisky tots 57
Whistles 76-7
Whistle signs 129
Wigan Coal & Iron Co.
    72
Wigan Wagon Co. 83
Winchcombe Railway
    Museum 13, 20
Window straps 79
Wine carafes, glasses
    56-8
Wine holders 63
Wine bottle 63
Winterholder &
    Hofmeyer 15
Wooden nameboards 19
Wright, I. 74, 166
Wyvern 18

Y
Yorkshire Engine Co. 68
Yorkshire Railway
    Waggon Co. Ltd. 83